Safari Guides

Galápagos

Julian Fitter, Daniel Fitter & David Hosking
Line illustrations by Martin B. Withers

HarperCollins*Publishers*

HarperCollins*Publishers*
77–85 Fulham Palace Road
London
W6 8JB

The HarperCollins Website address is:

www.**fire**and**water**.com

Collins is a registered trademark of HarperCollins*Publishers* Ltd.

First published 2000

10 9 8 7 6 5 4 3 2 1

05 04 03 02 01 00

ISBN 0 00 220137 2

Photographs supplied by FLPA; photographs by Daniel Fitter, David
Hosking and Julian Fitter apart from the following: p.73 tr Dembinsky,
p.119 tl, br Dr Lazaro Roque-Albelo; p.127 ucl, lcr Dr Leon Baert
Line illustrations by Martin B. Withers
Maps and diagrams by Carte Blanche

Dedication
To Mary and the people of the Galápagos

Edited and designed by D & N Publishing, Berkshire
Colour reproduction by Colourscan, Singapore
Printed and bound by Rotolito Lombarda SpA, Milan, Italy

CONTENTS

FOREWORD

On 16th September 1835 Charles Darwin first set foot in the Galápagos at the western end of San Cristóbal which was then called Chatham Island. By a happy coincidence, his landing place at Cerro Tijeretas has now become a visitor site of the Galápagos National Park, close to Puerto Baquerizo Moreno on Isla San Cristóbal. He described the island somewhat unflatteringly as 'black lava, *completely* covered by small leafless brushwood and low trees. The fragments of lava where most porous are reddish and like cinders; the stunted trees show little signs of life. The black rocks heated by the rays of the vertical sun like a stove, give to the air a close and sultry feeling. The plants also smell unpleasantly. The country was compared to what we might imagine the cultivated parts of the Infernal regions to be.'

The *Beagle* moved next day to Stephen's Bay, close to the present Puerto Grande, which to Darwin's delight 'swarmed with animals; fish, shark and turtles were popping their heads up in all parts ... The black lava rocks on the beach are frequented by large (2–3 ft) most disgusting clumsy lizards. They are as black as the porous rocks over which they crawl and seek their prey from the sea. Somebody calls them "imps of darkness". They assuredly well become the land they inhabit ... The birds are strangers to man and think him innocent as their countrymen the huge tortoises.'

The scene has changed in some respects today, for thanks to predation by feral cats, dogs and rats introduced by man, marine iguanas have almost vanished from the shores of Isla San Cristóbal, though in other islands they are still plentiful. The huge tortoises too have been drastically reduced in numbers, partly because for many years they served as an apparently inexhaustible source of food for the whalers in the Pacific – the *Beagle* herself shipped 30 for eating when she departed – and partly because generations of goats competed with them far too effectively for the available plants. Only the birds remain as unafraid of man as they were when Darwin pushed a hawk off a branch with his gun. Las Islas Encatadas, as they were termed by early voyagers, fully retain their enchantment.

Richard Keynes

THE AUTHORS

Julian Fitter

Julian Fitter arrived in Galápagos in May 1964 on the Charles Darwin Foundation's first support vessel, *Beagle*. It had not been his intention to stay there, but falling in love changed all that, and after a brief spell in Quito, Ecuador, teaching at the Central University, he returned to Galápagos with his wife, Mary Angermeyer. Julian spent the next fourteen years travelling the islands and building the first yacht charter business in Galápagos. He returned to England in 1979 and became involved in attempting to develop tourism in the Falkland Islands. Being ahead of his time, he turned to a more mundane means of earning a living, as a financial adviser. Julian maintained his links with Galápagos and in 1995 was instrumental in establishing the Galápagos Conservation Trust in the UK. He served as its first Chairman and is now a Vice-President. He also helped establish Falklands Conservation and was its first secretary and is now a trustee of that organisation. Julian has a strong and committed interest in the conservation of the natural environment and of the need to include the local population in a sustainable use of resources to that end.

Daniel Fitter

Daniel was born and raised on the Galápagos islands, From a very young age he travelled around the islands on one of his father Julian's charter yachts. This helped him to develop a keen interest in their natural and human history.

After a couple of periods spent in England, where he completed his education, Galápagos lured him back and has been his home again since 1995.

He currently guides and leads nature oriented tours around the islands and in mainland Ecuador. A keen birdwatcher, historian and photographer he possesses one of the largest photo-libraries on Galápagos subjects.

David Hosking

David Hosking first visited Galápagos in 1970 with his late father Eric Hosking, and as a direct result of this visit decided to follow in his father's footsteps and pursue a career in wildlife photography. David is a Fellow of the Royal Photographic Society and sits on the Associateship and Fellowship Assessment Panel. His reputation as a master photographer has been enhanced by the publication of his work in a wide range of magazines and books, including two other Safari Guides on the birds and mammals of East Africa. With his wife Jean he is deeply involved in the administration of the Frank Lane Picture Agency (FLPA), one of the oldest picture libraries specialising in natural history photographs. David is a frequent visitor to Galápagos with Hosking Tours Ltd, a company specialising in nature photographic holidays, which he runs with his business partner Martin Withers.

ACKNOWLEDGEMENTS

It will come as no surprise to learn that a book such as this needs a lot of help to compile. As naturalists, we have a good understanding, but often not the specific knowledge or information. Additionally, the accepted identification of many species changes as our knowledge of the biology of the islands increases. This is particularly true with plants whose generic and specific names change with disturbing frequency. The generic name of the lava lizards changed recently and all the snakes were reclassified in 1997. There is even disagreement about the nomenclature of the tortoises! So expect changes in the future.

A big thank you must go to the various scientists, all associated with the Charles Darwin Research Station (CDRS), who willingly responded to my queries, helped with identification of species, and corrected sections of text relating to their field. In particular we would like to thank Dr Alan Tye, Dr Rodrigo Bustamante, Dr Lazaro Roque-Albelo, Dr Marco Altamirano B, Dr Hernan Vargas, Dr Charlotte Causton and Dr Ivan Aldace, all resident scientists at CDRS. Dr Howard Snell and Dr Heidi Snell also deserve a special mention. In Canada, Dr Stewart Peck and Dr Bernard Landry, and in Belgium Dr Leon Baert, helped immeasurably with the invertebrate section. Dr Patty Parker was a mine of information on the Galápagos Hawk. Christian Caceres from the Galápagos National Park Service gave invaluable help and it goes without saying that we would like to thank Dr Eliecer Cruz the Director of the Galápagos National Park Service and Dr Robert Bensted-Smith, Director of the CDRS for their help and co-operation and for agreeing to contribute a preface to this book.

Thanks also to Godfrey Merlen and David Day, two scientists who have lived many years in Galápagos and have come to know and love them with an intimacy that is hard to appreciate. Their help with the cetaceans in particular is much appreciated. Gayle Davies, the CDRS Librarian, was the patient recipient of many emails, to all of which she replied to quickly and helpfully.

We also owe a debt of gratitude to Conley McCullen, author of the *Flowering Plants of Galápagos*, published in the nick of time to enable us to identify the large pile of plant slides that had question marks against them! The other text that was invaluable in putting together this guide was Michael Jackson's *Galápagos: A Natural History*, which is the accepted general reference work on the islands wildlife.

In the production of the text, we owe a considerable debt to Richard Fitter and to Jane Riddell who went through most of it with helpful suggestions, corrections, queries and above all patience. Tina Fitter was a vital contributor in Galápagos. Thanks to Jean Hosking and the staff at FLPA for their help with picture research and collation. Graham Armitage at Jenoptik UK is thanked for the loan of Sigma Lenses. Our thanks also go to the production team, without whom the mass of information would never have become a book. Katie Piper at HarperCollins and David Price-Goodfellow from D & N Publishing were particularly patient and helpful.

CONSERVATION PLEA

Biol. Eliecer Cruz
DIRECTOR
Galápagos National Park Service

Dr Robert Bensted-Smith
DIRECTOR
Charles Darwin Research Station,
Galápagos

The visitor to Galápagos does not need a field guide to identify such unmistakable creatures as the Marine Iguana or the Flightless Cormorant! But the islands are home to many more unique but less prominent species of reptiles, birds, plants and insects. Furthermore, it is the subtle differences between species that reveal the secrets of evolution, the most famous case being the finch species that inspired Charles Darwin. This guide is an excellent companion for the visitor who wants to go a step beyond the superficial look and observe more closely the nature of the archipelago. And Galápagos is the perfect place for such observation, for here the wildlife nonchalantly permits our scrutiny; we can enjoy closeness to wildlife here, as nowhere else.

These characteristics, and the fact that the Galápagos Islands, unlike the rest of the world's archipelagos, still has 95 per cent of its original pre-man quota of species, make this a truly special place, which has been recognised as a National Park, Marine Reserve, Whale Sanctuary, Man and Biosphere Reserve and World Heritage Site. But the isolation that engendered the unique flora and fauna of Galápagos has long since ended and the islands now face the threat of invasive alien species, from the notorious goats and pigs to insidious enemies such as insects, weedy plants and diseases. The worldwide problem of over exploitation of the marine ecosystem has also reached Galápagos. These threats must be kept at bay. The preservation of Galápagos is the shared mission of the Galápagos National Park Service and the Charles Darwin Foundation for the Galápagos Islands. The Park Service is the government agency charged with managing the Park and the Marine Reserve. Its partner, the Charles Darwin Foundation, is an independent international organisation, providing scientific research, training, education and advisory services.

Our two organisations are dedicated to the conservation of Galápagos, but we need the commitment and co-operation of others. We need the active participation of the local island community to help tackle the root causes of the threats to biodiversity, and we need the co-operation of all who are lucky enough to visit the Galápagos Islands. We hope that, if you care enough about Galápagos to identify and observe its plant and animal life, you will also care enough to help the conservation effort by becoming a *Friend of Galápagos*. To find out more about conservation of the islands and about the worldwide Friends of Galápagos movement, please visit our websites on *www.galapagos.org* or send an e-mail to *cdrs@fcdarwin.org.ec*.

Welcome to the wonders of Galápagos!

INTRODUCTION

Had I known at the start how much work would be needed to put togeth-er a guide of this nature, I might not have started out on the journey. I am glad however that I did start even though it has been far more time con-suming than I had thought possible. It has also been immensely reward-ing. I spent fifteen years with Galápagos as my home. I thought I knew them pretty well, but in writing and researching this book I have found out how little I really knew and how much we still have to learn about the biology of the Galápagos ecosystem.

I arrived in Galápagos 129 years after Charles Darwin. I came by sea, on a small sailing vessel with the same name, *Beagle,* and our landfall, San Cristóbal, was the same. Thereafter our experiences were very dif-ferent, but what is amazing about Galápagos, what impressed Charles Darwin, is still there to amaze and impress the visitor of the twenty-first Century. While much has changed, much was the same for me in 1964 as it was for Darwin in 1835 and is the same for the visitor today. But it is only the same because of a lot of hard work and effort by the people of Galápagos, the Ecuadorian authorities, the National Park Service and the Charles Darwin Foundation, and many more.

As we seek to preserve the unique Galápagos ecosystem, we are faced with two main problems. On the one hand there is the very serious threat posed by invasive or introduced species. Most obvious of these are the feral goats that have recently devastated Volcan Alcedo on Isabela. Less obvious are the fire ants *Wasmannia auropunctata* and *Solenopsis gem-inata,* and an untold number of other invasive invertebrate and plant species which threaten to destroy this fragile ecosystem. On the other hand, there is the human population of the islands, which while being 'invasive' has every right to be there.

Today the population of Galápagos is approaching 20,000. It is grow-ing fast and, even if immigration to the islands is successfully controlled, it is likely to continue to grow fast. With only a 5 per cent annual increase, the population in 2020 will be in excess of 50,000. If anyone

thinks that the Galápagos has a population problem now, then it is time to start thinking long and hard about how to deal with such an increase, especially as 5 per cent is a very conservative estimate.

There is currently a programme underway for the eradication of invasive species in the islands, starting with the feral goats on northern Isabela. The cost of this programme will run into tens of millions of dollars and will last until 2010 and beyond. This is only one species, and initially only on one island. The task is huge. Nevertheless we must start a serious programme of control and eradication of invasive species and stop the importation of new alien species.

The key to the future of the Galápagos, both as a natural laboratory for the study of evolution and as the world's most amazing zoo, is how we deal with these two 'problems'. Clearly the only answer to invasive species is their control or preferably eradication. Population growth, however, is far more difficult. If we put our heads in the sand and ignore it, then it will surely make the conservation of the ecosystem academic. If however we stop seeing the people as the problem, and look on them as the solution, then we have a chance of succeeding. If we can help the people of Galápagos to appreciate fully the importance of conservation, of not importing alien species, of looking after the environment, then we will have a chance to save this remarkable group of islands that has had so great an impact on the history of human thought.

To do this will require a radical reappraisal of the economic use of the resources of Galápagos. This does not mean selling tortoise or iguana steaks. But it does mean making best use of the existing and clearly identifiable renewable resources, agriculture, fisheries and tourism. It also means finding new resources that can exploited without harming the environment or jeopardising the isolation of the islands that has made them so very special.

You may ask what such an 'appeal' is doing by the introduction of a guide to the animals and plants of the Galápagos. Quite simply this: it is only by understanding that you can come to have a full appreciation of the importance and value of the Galápagos. I hope that by using this guide to help identify the plants and animals of Galápagos you will come to appreciate ever more deeply the amazing nature of the biology of the islands, their significance and the importance of preserving them.

One of the attractions of the Galápagos for the novice is that there are relatively few species. This makes identification a great deal easier. Iguanas are very straightforward to spot: the black ones are marine, the yellow ones land! Lava lizards and tortoises vary according to the island they are on, as do Scalesia and Cacti. Darwin's finches are probably the trickiest, especially as they vary so much and even cross-breed at times.

So this book is not just about identification. It is about the animals and plants themselves and why they are interesting or important. Take a closer look at your surroundings, understand it a little better, look after it a lot better and your children and grandchildren will be able to visit these wonderful islands and see and appreciate what you have seen. You will then see what I first saw in 1964 and what Charles Darwin saw back in 1835.

Julian Fitter
Shroton, April 2000

GALÁPAGOS ISLANDS
(Ecuador)

roads
✈ airports
113 height in metres
(3700) height in feet
Floreana location name

0   34 Km

PACIFIC OCEAN

Equator

I. Darwin
I. Wolf

· Roca Redonda

C. Berkeley
Volcán Ecuador ▲ 1707 (5600)
Pta. Vincente Roca
Pta. Espinosa
C. Douglas
Volcán La Cumbre ▲ 1494 (4900)
I. Fernandina
Pta. Mangle
C. Hammond
Bahía Elizabeth

Pta. Albemarle
Volcán Wolf ▲ 1707 (5600)
James Bay
Volcán Darwin ▲ 1326 (4350)
Volcán Alcedo ▲ 1125 (3700)
Isla Isabela
Pta. Moreno
Volcán Sierra Negra
Volcán Chico 1491 (4890)
Santo Tomás
Cerro Azul ▲ 1689 (5540)
Puerto Villamil ✈
C. Rosa
Pta. Cristóbal
Pta. Essex

I. Marchena ▲ 343 (1125)
I. Pinta ▲ 777 (2550)

I. Genovesa

I. Santiago ▲ 907 (2974)
I. Bartolomé
I. Sombrero Chino
I. Rábida
I. Pinzón
I. Los Hermanos
I. Tortuga

I. Seymour
I. Baltra ✈
▲ 863 (2830)
Santa Rosa
Bellavista
Santa Cruz
Puerto Ayora
I. Daphne Mayor
I. Santa Fé

I. San Cristóbal
Pta. Pitt
717 (2350)
El Progreso
Baquerizo Moreno
Kicker Rock

I. Española
Pta. Suárez
R. Gardner

Post Office Bay
I. Enderby
I. Champion
Puerto Velasco Ibarra
I. Gardner

90°
92°
0° 30'

Island Names and Origins

Most of the islands in Galápagos have more than one name. Santa Cruz has had up to 13 different names over the years. In 1892, on the quarcentenary of Columbus' voyage, the Ecuadorian government renamed the islands El Archipelago de Colon and gave all the islands official names. With two exceptions, these are the names in common usage today. The exceptions are Santiago whose official name is San Salvador and Floreana which has the official name of Santa Maria.

COMMON NAME	ENGLISH NAME	DERIVATION	ENGLISH DERIVATION
Pinta	Abingdon	One of Columbus' ships	The Earl of Abingdon
Isabela	Albemarle	Isabela of Castille	The Duke of Albemarle
Baltra	South Seymour		
Santa Fé	Barrington	Holy Faith	Admiral Samuel Barrington, RN
Beagle	Beagle	HMS Beagle	
Marchena	Bindloe	Fray Antonio Marchena	Captain John Bindloe
Tortuga	Brattle	Spanish for turtle	Nicholas Brattle
Bartolomé	Bartholomew	Lt David Bartholomew, RN	
Caldwell	Caldwell	Admiral Caldwell, RN	
Champion	Champion	Andrew Champion, whaler	
Floreana	Charles	King Charles II	
San Cristóbal	Chatham	Christopher Columbus	William Pitt, First Earl of Chatham
Cowley	Cowley	Ambrose Cowley, buccaneer	
Crossman	Crossman	Richard Crossman	
Darwin	Culpepper	Charles Darwin	Lord Culpepper
Daphne	Daphne	HMS Daphne	
Pinzón	Duncan	The brothers Pinzón	Admiral Viscount Duncan, RN
Eden	Eden		
Enderby	Enderby	Samuel Enderby, whaler	
Gardner	Gardner	Lord Gardner	
Guy Fawkes	Guy Fawkes	Guy Fawkes, the English conspirator	
Española	Hood	España – Spain	Admiral Viscount Samuel Hood, RN
Santa Cruz	Indefatigable	Holy Cross	HMS Indefatigable
Santiago	James	Spanish for James	King James II
Rábida	Jervis	Convent of La Rábida	Admiral John Jervis
Sin Nombre	Nameless		
Fernandina	Narborough	Admiral Sir John Narborough	
Onslow	Onslow		
Plaza	Plaza		
Seymour	North Seymour		
Genovesa	Tower	Genoa, birthplace of Columbus	
Watson	Watson		
Wolf	Wenman	Lord Wenman	

Sources: Slevin, J. R. The Galápagos Islands. A History of their Exploration. (1959)

NATIONAL PARK RULES

The Galápagos Islands are one of the few places in the world that remain relatively untouched by human exploitation. The preservation of the environment is everybody's responsibility. You can help, by following some simple rules which will help to maintain the archipelago's fragile ecosystem intact. The future depends on you.

1. Be careful not to transport any live material to the islands, or from island to island (insects, seeds, soil). You are not allowed to bring pets to the islands.

2. No plants, rocks, animals or their remains, such as bones, pieces of wood, corals, shells, or other natural objects should be removed or disturbed. You may damage the islands ecological conditions.

3. Animals should not be touched or handled. A sea lion pup will be abandoned by its mother, for example, if she smells the scent of a human on her young. The same applies to chicks of birds.

4. Animals may not be fed. It may alter their life cycle, their social structure and affect their reproduction.

5. Do not disturb or pursue any animal from its resting or nesting spot. This is especially true for birds such as boobies, cormorants, gulls and frigates. The nests should be approached carefully, keeping a distance of at least 1 to 2 metres. If disturbed, the bird will flee and abandon its egg or chick, which could be predated or die under the strong sun within 30 minutes.

6. All groups that visit the National Park must be accompanied by a qualified guide approved by the National Park. The visitor must follow the trails, marked with small black-and-white posts, and never leave it. If you do so, you may destroy nests without being conscious of it (marine iguanas nest in the sand).

7. Follow the guide; stay with him/her for information and advice. He or she is responsible for you. If the guide behaves badly or does not follow the rules himself, report him or her to the National Park.

8. Litter of all types must be kept off the islands. Disposal at sea must be limited to certain types of garbage, only to be thrown overboard in selected areas. Keep all rubbish: film wrappers, cigarette butts, chewing gum, tin cans, bottles, etc. in a bag or pocket, to be disposed of on your boat. Do not throw anything on the islands or overboard. It could end up at the coast or the beach, or eaten by sea turtles or sea lions. A sea lion may play with a tin can found on the bottom and cut its sensitive muzzle. Sea turtles may die from swallowing a plastic bag.

9. Do not paint names or graffiti on rocks. It is against the law, and you will be fined for it.

10. Do not buy souvenirs or objects made from plants or animals of the islands (with the exception of articles made from wood). Among such articles are turtle shells, sea lion teeth, black coral. This is the best way to discourage such a trade.

11. To camp, you need a permit from the National Park Service (Santa Cruz, San Cristóbal, Isabéla). Do not make fires, but use a gas stove instead.

12. Do not hesitate to show your conservationist attitude. Explain these rules to others, and help to enforce them.

The Galápagos National Park thanks you for respecting these rules. Think about others who come after you; they'll be grateful to you for your conservationist attitude.

A TRAVELLERS' GUIDE TO SAFARI PHOTOGRAPHY

Before your Departure

It is always unwise to commence a holiday with new untested equipment. Always put at least one roll of film through a new camera and carry out a full test on any newly purchased lenses. Before departure, make yourself familiar with all the commonly used camera and lens functions.

Do not forget to check that your equipment is insured and that the policy covers travel in South America. Keep a check list of camera and lens numbers. This will be useful if you do have to make an insurance claim and as a record of what equipment you have taken with you. Should equipment be stolen, report it to the police and obtain a statement confirming that you have reported the theft, as some insurance companies will be reluctant to settle any claim without such confirmation.

Apart from checking existing equipment before your departure, it's a good idea to check and clean all equipment at the end of each day. The salt atmosphere present in the Galápagos will damage cameras and lenses if not carefully cleaned. Remember that a single sand grain, on the film pressure plate, can badly scratch a complete roll of film. A rubber blower brush is ideal for keeping the inside of your camera clean, while lens elements and filters are best cleaned with specially purchased cleaning

Salt spray in Galápagos is a big problem and cleaning equipment, including tripods, is very important!

Deciding on a good SLR or compact camera can be difficult, so take both.

fluid and tissues, alcohol or even fresh water could be used as a last resort. The outer casings of both cameras and lenses can be cleaned using an ordinary paintbrush. A supply of different size plastic bags would be handy for protecting both equipment and camera bags from the potentially damaging effects of wet landings. A shower cap, like those supplied by hotels, offers effective protection from light salt spray.

What to Take

Cameras

Galápagos is one of the very best places in the world to photograph not only wildlife but also plants, landscapes and lava patterns. For many people this could well be a once in a lifetime visit, so it's worth making the effort to obtain as good a photographic record as possible. The choice of cameras available today is vast. For really successful results a top of the range 35 mm Single Lens Reflex (SLR) camera with interchangeable lenses would be ideal. Most will also offer an autofocus facility, which is a great asset, saving valuable seconds and helping to secure pictures that may have been missed with manual focus equipment. Remember that the Galápagos is a very demanding environment, consisting for the most part of volcanic rock and seawater. This is therefore most unforgiving terrain should equipment be dropped. As a safeguard, it is worth considering taking two identical SLRs. If you are interested in underwater photography, it is possible to get underwater housings for some models, or if you are really keen, there are some dedicated underwater SLR cameras available. Because of the tameness of the wildlife, the use of medium format equipment is well worth considering. These cameras use 120 and 220 film and produce either slides or negatives two to three times bigger than 35 mm.

Compact cameras have either a fixed or a zoom lens, are quick and easy to use and ideal for those visitors wanting just a photographic record. It is also possible to get underwater compacts and this is a cheap way of getting into underwater photography. As most of these underwater compacts are not pressurised, they are only operational to depths of just over 1 m.

Most digital cameras are similar to compact cameras in size and operation but have the added advantage of instant replay, either through a small built-in monitor or computer link. Images are recorded on an internal memory, flash card or floppy disc, so pictures can be quickly sorted, saved or deleted, to make space for more photography. An increasing number of digital video records have a stills option and these have the added advantage of being able to record hours of action.

Camera Accessories: A cable release is an excellent way of reducing camera shake and your camera should accept either an electronic or mechanical type. A wide camera strap with some degree of elasticity will help distribute camera and lens weight. A small hot-shoe spirit level for checking horizons can be a great aid to landscape work. Don't forget to take lots of spare camera batteries, but please do not dump the old ones in Galápagos, take them home to protect the environment.

Lenses: If you have chosen the SLR option you will need to think about what interchangeable lenses to take with you. Most of the wildlife in Galápagos is very tame, so you don't have to consider very long focal length lenses. The manufacturer of your camera will have an excellent range of

A medium zoom 70–200 mm is the most useful.

Close-up and macro lenses help view Galápagos wildlife in a different way. This is a Sally Lightfoot Crab.

16

Swallow-tailed Gull taken with 15-mm lens gives an unusual perspective.

lenses from which to choose. In addition, independent lenses makers will be able to offer competitive prices and some different lens combinations. A medium zoom, something between 70 and 300 mm and a short zoom 28 to 135 mm will cover most photo opportunities. For the more adventurous it would be worth looking at lenses that are wider than 28 mm, some very dramatic pictures can be taken with a 15 mm lens. A macro lens would be very useful for insects, plants and pattern photography. One camera manufacturer even offers image-stabiliser lenses. These use a vibration gyro which detects shaking and then counterbalances the movement with a magnet and coil-driven optical-compensation system. These particular lenses are very useful for handholding situations such as from a boat. Almost all new lenses will have autofocus and this will offer you three options. Firstly, by switching it off, you can manually focus. Secondly, using single shot autofocus, the camera will lock onto whatever you are pointing at, but will need activating again if the subject moves. Thirdly, servofocus can be selected where the autofocus is constantly updating the focus point; this is ideal for moving subjects.

Lens Accessories: Tele-converters increase the lenses' magnification by a factor of either 1.4 × or 2 × and some zoom lenses are designed specifically to work with them. Extension tubes and close-up filter attachments are another way of increasing magnification. A UV or skylight filter on each lens offers extra protection from accidental damage to the front lens element. A polarising filter is well worth taking. It will help control reflections and increases colour saturation.

Film: Whether you require negatives for prints or transparencies for projection, there is a vast array of different films from which to choose. Film speed or sensitivity to light is gauged by an ISO rating. The higher the ISO, the more sensitive to light the film will be. As light levels in Galápagos are, in general, very good, it should be possible to take advantage of the finer quality of the lower ISO films. Films with ratings of 50 ISO to 100 ISO for transparencies and 100 ISO to 200 ISO for negatives should prove ideal. The quantity of film you require may be difficult to calculate. Try and work out a daily requirement and then double it!

Remember, it's better to have too much and bring some home, than to run out. While it might be possible to buy more at Puerto Ayora, it could be out of stock when you need it, or you could be at the other end of the archipelago when you run out.

X-ray security checks at airports are standard procedure; while those used for hand-luggage checks should not cause any problems, luggage destined for aeroplane holds is often checked with more powerful X-rays. This will cause some fogging. So always take your film as hand luggage. A useful way to carry film is to utilise old slide boxes, these take four rolls of 35 mm film and offer protection from impact and dust. Their transparent lids facilitate quick security checks and they stack more easily in a camera bag. This will also save dumping film packaging in Galápagos where waste is a big environmental problem.

If you are using a digital camera, make sure you have a supply of flash cards. Anyone using video should make sure they have plenty of blank tapes.

A rucksack-style camera bag is the most comfortable way of carrying equipment.

Whatever camera bag you have, the mockingbirds will be interested.

Other Accessories: An *electronic flashgun* is well worth its place in your camera bag, as a 'fill in' to soften harsh shadows during the daytime and to light any close-up macrophotography. Remember that some animals get stressed when repeatedly flashed, so be considerate in its use.

There are a large number of *camera bags* available and purchasing one is a matter of personal choice. However, it is worth considering one that doubles as a rucksack, which is a much more comfortable way of carrying equipment over rough ground. Some camera bags of this type also have a built-in waterproof cape, which is useful extra protection for wet landings. In selecting a suitable bag, resist the temptation to purchase one that is too big – you will only feel obliged to fill it! Airlines are generally reducing hand-luggage allowances so make sure that your bag size

A tripod is the best way of reducing camera shake.

comes within recommended limits. A *photographic waistcoat* is a handy garment for keeping films, filters, cable releases, etc. readily to hand.

The commonest cause of picture failure is lack of definition as a result of camera shake. The most effective way of overcoming this is by using a good *tripod*. There are many light, yet sturdy, models on the market, which will fit comfortably into the average suitcase. In the salty and sandy environment of Galápagos, any tripod is going to need extra care and maintenance. Keeping moving parts well oiled and wiping down the tripod each night will help to keep corrosion at bay. *Monopods* are also a good means of steadying the camera, but they do require a little practice. *Rifle stocks* and *pistol grips* are another form of support and allow freedom of movement when attempting to photograph moving subjects.

Photographic Techniques

Lighting

The Galápagos Islands are on the equator where the sun will rise quickly to a point directly overhead. This top lighting effect is not ideal for photographing wildlife or landscapes; low side lighting is better for showing detail in wildlife subjects and creates more interesting shadows in landscapes. So it's important to get ashore at sunrise and again in the later afternoon. While most wildlife photographs are taken with the sunlight behind the photographer thereby fully lighting the subject, it should be remembered that some spectacular images can be taken using side or back lighting, particularly using the warm glow created at sunrise and sunset.

Exposure

Correct exposure is the key to successful photography and modern cameras, with their built-in metering systems, go a long way to reducing the possibility of incorrect exposure. However, there are situations in Galápagos where even the most complex metering system is going to struggle. A good example would be a white bird like a Masked Booby on very dark volcanic rock. The meter is likely to try and expose correctly for the

While autofocus is a great help for photographing birds in flight, don't forget to use a faster shutter speed.

rock, which will overexpose the bird. This is where a good understanding of your camera comes into play. Most SLR cameras will have a +/- (over-/underexposure) override and, in the situation outlined above, you will need to under expose by about one to two stops to ensure correct exposure of the booby. The same effect can be obtained by doubling the (ISO) film speed, i.e. 100 to 200 ISO, but remember to change these settings back before moving on.

In any situation where you are not sure about the exposure you can always bracket. For example, if your metering reading is 1/60th at f8, take one picture at this setting, then two further exposures at 1/60th at f11 and 1/60th at f5.6. To do this you may have to switch the camera to manual mode or use the +/- override.

Depth of Field

When the camera lens is focused to give a sharp image of a particular subject, other objects, closer or further away, do not appear equally as sharp. They can be made sharp by 'stopping down' using a smaller 'f stop'. The higher the 'f stop' number, the more depth of field is available. It should be remembered that as you stop down, your shutter speed will get slower and subject movement will become more of a problem. 'Stopping down' is important when photographing plants, insects and other small subjects, as it reduces out-of-focus distractions. The opposite procedure can be used to help isolate your main centre of interest by making background or foreground distractions go out of focus.

Don't forget that you can check the depth of field created by any given 'f stop', by using the depth-of-field button on your camera. This button allows you to preview the finished image though the viewfinder and to make adjustments to your own satisfaction prior to making any exposure.

Shutter Speed

Different shutter speeds produce varying effects with regard to subject blur and camera shake. Fast shutter speeds are desirable for stopping movement, such as flying birds and eliminating camera shake. It is worth remembering that in some situations, movement of the subject during exposure can often result in a pleasing pictorial image.

Composition

The automation of modern cameras has precluded most of the technical pitfalls of photography. Composition is the tool by which we can express our artistic thoughts and so demands an active input. It is therefore in your own interest to be fully conversant with the factors relating to good composition.

Many newcomers to photography tend to produce all their images in a horizontal format, partly because of the layout of modern cameras which lend themselves to this shape. Remember they work equally well when turned through 90° to a vertical format.

Changing your viewpoint can totally alter your image. We get used to seeing everything from a standing position. By kneeling or even lying

Don't forget to use your camera vertically as well as horizontally.

(Below) *Changing viewpoint, even with a compact camera, can make really interesting pictures.*

down, you are going to show an unfamiliar angle, which will often produce a more unusual result. A wide-angle lens used in this way can create some very interesting effects.

Think about where you are going to place the main point of interest in your image. Avoid placing your subject in the centre of the frame. If it's an animal, it needs room to move or to look into the picture space. A flying bird should be flying into the picture rather than out of it. Always attempt to get a 'highlight' in the eye, as this gives life to the subject. Do pay attention to the horizon line, particularly in landscapes and avoid splitting your picture in half. Think in 'thirds'. Zoom lenses have become a great asset by allowing control over subject size and perspective, without moving the camera position.

By utilising a range of lenses it is often possible to secure an interesting sequence of images of an animal: the longest lenses for a close up of the head, through to a wide angle showing the unique Galápagos landscape.

Notes: The identification of Galápagos species often depends upon which island the subject was photographed. Either date and/or number each film, using an indelible felt-tip pen. Then, by keeping detailed notes of what you saw and which island you were on each day, you will then be able to sort out and identify species much more easily.

Code of Conduct

It should always be remembered that the welfare of the subject is more important than the photograph:

Do not go too close.
Do not leave the trail.
Do not use flash if it might disturb the subject.
Do not make lots of noise.
Do not discard any form of litter.
Do not smoke on the islands.
Take only pictures, leave only memories!

KEY TO SPECIES' STATUS

(*e*)   Endemic – found only in Galápagos.

(*es*)   Endemic subspecies – found only in Galápagos, but other closely related members of the species found elsewhere.

(*n*)   Native – found in Galápagos and elsewhere, but arrived in Galápagos by natural means (plants and invertebrates).

(*r*)   Resident – equivalent to Native; breeds in the islands (birds).

(*pr*)   Possible resident – seen throughout the year, but has not yet been recorded as breeding.

(*i*)   Introduced – brought to Galápagos by man, either deliberately or inadvertently.

(*ip*)   Introduced pest – introduced species that is a serious threat to the Galápagos ecosystem.

(*m*)   Migrant – regular visitor, normally in the northern winter.

(*ro*)   Regularly observed (cetaceans and turtles).

(*oo*)   Occasionally observed (cetaceans and turtles).

BIRDS

Yellow Warbler sitting on a nest.

One of the most attractive features of birdwatching in the Galápagos is that you can identify most species without being an expert. In the first place there are only about 60 resident species and 13 of these are the finches! These constitute 50 per cent of all the resident land species and several can be identified according to island location and vegetation zone. Some species, like the penguin and Flightless Cormorant, virtually identify themselves. So while you will be able to identify most species quite easily by location, there are others, including some finches, where you need a good view and a good guide to help in the identification.

The relative paucity of species is actually one of the beauties of the birds of Galápagos. The finches and mockingbirds are excellent examples of adaptive radiation, where a species has evolved characteristically on an isolated island. This is not surprising in the case of reptiles and mammals that cannot fly but is quite surprising with birds that could, in theory, move from island to island relatively easily. You should not look on adaptive radiation, or the evolution of new species on particular islands as a thing of the past. It is almost certainly continuing even now, but so slowly that it may be hundreds of years before any visible differences are evident.

It is also worth noting that the number of resident species of bird is growing. At least five species have become resident in the last fifty years, Common Egret, Cattle Egret, Paint-billed Crake, Common Gallinule and Smooth-billed Ani. The last of these was almost certainly introduced by man, but the others appear to have arrived independently and thrived in a habitat conducive to development. None of these arrivals has been reported as having any negative impact on other species already in residence, but it is too early to be sure of this.

In addition to the resident species, there are a number of regular visitors. These are mainly migratory waders from North America. They are therefore generally to be seen in their winter plumage and so can be quite difficult to identify. However, some can be found in the islands all year round and it is possible that these may eventually become resident and breed.

We know of no endemic bird species that has become extinct. However, there are several species that are vulnerable owing to their very restricted breeding range and habitat. Chief among these is the Mangrove Finch that is found in only a few patches of mangrove on Isabela. The total population is thought to number only in the low tens of pairs. The Charles Island Mockingbird also has a very restricted range but is not under threat, but with only 150 or so individuals, it is vulnerable. Several other species, such as the Flightless Cormorant and the Galápagos Rail or Crake, are vulnerable to habitat change or the introduction of new predators. Complacency is a real danger and many species must be viewed as vulnerable. Apart from the finches and the boobies, relatively little work has been done on Galápagos bird species. It is only when armed with accurate information and a full understanding of the species that we can feel completely confident of their future.

SEA BIRDS

(e) Galápagos Penguin *Sphensicus mendiculus*

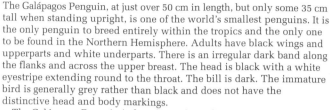

The Galápagos Penguin, at just over 50 cm in length, but only some 35 cm tall when standing upright, is one of the world's smallest penguins. It is the only penguin to breed entirely within the tropics and the only one to be found in the Northern Hemisphere. Adults have black wings and upperparts and white underparts. There is an irregular dark band along the flanks and across the upper breast. The head is black with a white eyestripe extending round to the throat. The bill is dark. The immature bird is generally grey rather than black and does not have the distinctive head and body markings.

The Galápagos Penguin is found mainly in the western islands where the water is cooler but has appeared recently to be widening its range and is regularly seen around the eastern end of Santiago, Floreana, and western Santa Cruz. It is not known whether it breeds in these areas or only on Fernandina and Isabela. The total population is thought to number around 1,000–1,300 pairs.

Galápagos Penguins may breed at any time of the year that the food supply is adequate. This generally means when the water temperature is below 23°C. The nest is in a hole or crevice in the rocks close to the shore. The normal clutch is two eggs of which only one chick generally survives. Incubation takes around 40 days. The chick is then looked after by the parents for a further 60 days before it is able to fend for itself. However, it may well stay in a small group with its parents for appreciably longer.

Its call is a soft, donkey-like bray similar to its cousin, the Jackass or Magellanic Penguin (*Sphensicus magellanicus*).

Best viewed: Fernandina – Punta Espinosa; Isabela – Tagus Cove, Bahia Elizabeth, Punta Albermarle; Santiago – Bahia Sullivan; Bartolomé; Sombrero Chino.

(e) Waved Albatross *Diomedea irrorata*

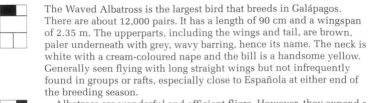

The Waved Albatross is the largest bird that breeds in Galápagos. There are about 12,000 pairs. It has a length of 90 cm and a wingspan of 2.35 m. The upperparts, including the wings and tail, are brown, paler underneath with grey, wavy barring, hence its name. The neck is white with a cream-coloured nape and the bill is a handsome yellow. Generally seen flying with long straight wings but not infrequently found in groups or rafts, especially close to Española at either end of the breeding season.

Albatross are wonderful and efficient fliers. However, they expend a great deal of energy to become airborne. When at sea they make use of their webbed feet, the wind and the waves. On land, where becoming airborne is even more difficult, they need a cliff which they can 'jump' off and an onshore wind. This is especially so for a young bird that has just fledged.

The Waved Albatross feeds on small fish and squid, normally well out to sea, especially to the south of the islands. It is not generally present on the islands from mid-January to mid-March, the period of least wind and warmest water.

The Waved Albatross breeds only on the southern island of Española close to the cliff which runs the whole length of the south coast of the islands. The single egg is laid on bare ground between mid-April and late June after an elaborate courtship ritual which includes bill circling and clacking, a formalised dance (waddle), and a cow-like 'moo' with an upraised bill. Incubation, which is shared, takes some 60 days. The young grow rapidly to become a large ungainly fluffy brown ball fed every week or two by one or other of the parents. They are fed with a predigested oil manufactured by the parent from fish and squid. Fledging takes place some 170 days after hatching. The species migrates to the coast of Ecuador and Peru before returning to the islands to breed from mid-March onwards. The young take about six years to reach maturity and pair for life.

Best viewed: Española – Punta Suarez; also at sea throughout the archipelago.

ⓔⓢ Dark-rumped Petrel *Pterodroma phaeopygia*

Also known as the Hawaiian Petrel. A large (length 43 cm, wingspan 90 cm) graceful petrel, black upperparts, white underneath with a distinctive white forehead. Breeds in the Miconia Zone and comes to the nesting area only at night. Distinctive 'kee-kee-kee' call can be heard at night during the breeding season. Feeds mainly on small fish and squid. Breeds during the garua season; the single egg hatches after 50 days; the young then take five months to fledge and five or six years to reach sexual maturity. The species mates for life and uses the same burrows each year.
Best viewed: At sea around the islands.

ⓔⓢ Audubon's Shearwater *Puffinus lherminieri subalaris*

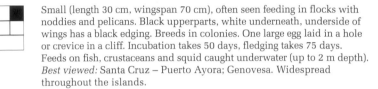

Small (length 30 cm, wingspan 70 cm), often seen feeding in flocks with noddies and pelicans. Black upperparts, white underneath, underside of wings has a black edging. Breeds in colonies. One large egg laid in a hole or crevice in a cliff. Incubation takes 50 days, fledging takes 75 days. Feeds on fish, crustaceans and squid caught underwater (up to 2 m depth).
Best viewed: Santa Cruz – Puerto Ayora; Genovesa. Widespread throughout the islands.

Storm Petrels

Small, swallow-like birds. Three species breed in Galápagos. All are 15–20 cm long with a wingspan of about 40 cm. The plumage is black with a white rump. They have pronounced tubular nostrils, characteristic of all petrels. Feed on plankton, crustaceans, fish and squid larvae.

ⓔⓢ Elliot's Storm Petrel *Oceanites gracilis galapagoensis*

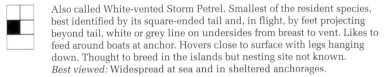

Also called White-vented Storm Petrel. Smallest of the resident species, best identified by its square-ended tail and, in flight, by feet projecting beyond tail, white or grey line on undersides from breast to vent. Likes to feed around boats at anchor. Hovers close to surface with legs hanging down. Thought to breed in the islands but nesting site not known.
Best viewed: Widespread at sea and in sheltered anchorages.

ⓔ Galápagos Storm Petrel *Oceanodroma tethys tethys*

Also known as the Wedge-rumped Storm Petrel. Look for the very large triangular white rump on this species extending almost to the end of the slightly notched tail. Easily identifiable at its nesting sites as it is the only diurnal storm petrel. Breeds between April and October. A single white egg is laid in a small burrow or cavity in the rocks. The colony on Genovesa numbers up to 200,000 pairs.
Best viewed: Genovesa – Darwin Bay; San Cristóbal – Isla Pitt.

ⓡ Madeiran Storm Petrel *Oceanodroma castro*

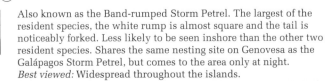

Also known as the Band-rumped Storm Petrel. The largest of the resident species, the white rump is almost square and the tail is noticeably forked. Less likely to be seen inshore than the other two resident species. Shares the same nesting site on Genovesa as the Galápagos Storm Petrel, but comes to the area only at night.
Best viewed: Widespread throughout the islands.

ⓡ Red-billed Tropicbird *Phaethon aethereus*

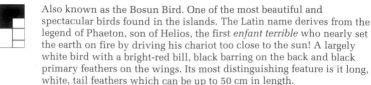

Also known as the Bosun Bird. One of the most beautiful and spectacular birds found in the islands. The Latin name derives from the legend of Phaeton, son of Helios, the first *enfant terrible* who nearly set the earth on fire by driving his chariot too close to the sun! A largely white bird with a bright-red bill, black barring on the back and black primary feathers on the wings. Its most distinguishing feature is it long, white, tail feathers which can be up to 50 cm in length.

The Red-billed Tropicbird nests on cliffs throughout the islands. On South Plaza, it has an annual cycle, but appears to breed throughout the year elsewhere. A single egg is laid in a crevice in the rocks and incubated by both parents for some 42 days. In the breeding season, it can often be seen and heard in a spectacular courtship flight, making a shrill 'kree-kree-kree'. The upper middle right photograph shows a Red-billed Tropicbird being attacked by a frigatebird.

Best viewed: Genovesa; South Plaza.

ⓔⓢ Brown Pelican *Pelecanus occidentalis urinator*

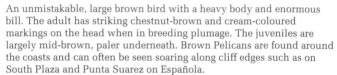

An unmistakable, large brown bird with a heavy body and enormous bill. The adult has striking chestnut-brown and cream-coloured markings on the head when in breeding plumage. The juveniles are largely mid-brown, paler underneath. Brown Pelicans are found around the coasts and can often be seen soaring along cliff edges such as on South Plaza and Punta Suarez on Española.

Fish and small crustaceans are the Brown Pelican's diet. They catch prey by what looks to be an entirely graceless (but actually very effective) plunge dive. They fill their pouch with a large amount of water and then filter out the small fish and crustaceans. Ships, fishing boats and yachts are a very ready source of food of a wider variety.

The Brown Pelican breeds in small colonies or individually in mangroves or small bushes, occasionally on rocks. Two or three large eggs are incubated by both parents for about 30 days. The young are remarkably ugly and noisy – bird lice can clearly be seen on them before they fledge!

Best viewed: Central islands. Often perch on boats waiting for tit-bits.

The Boobies

The Galápagos are the home of three species of booby, large diving seabirds with dagger-like bills in the same family as the Gannet of the Northern Hemisphere. The Blue-footed Booby (*Sula nebouxii*) is the star performer for most visitors, but the other two species, Masked Booby (*Sula dactylatra*) and Red-footed Booby (*Sula sula*) are very handsome birds and will be seen by most visitors to the islands. It is interesting to note that the three species, while breeding close to each other, do not generally fish close to each other. Blue-foots generally fish inshore, often in spectacular numbers and in conjunction with skipjack tuna, pelicans and noddies. The Masked Booby fishes further out within the islands while the Red-footed is rarely seen fishing within the islands, preferring to fish far out at sea. The name 'booby' derives from the Spanish word *bobo* meaning a fool or clown.

(es) Blue-footed Booby *Sula nebouxii excisa*

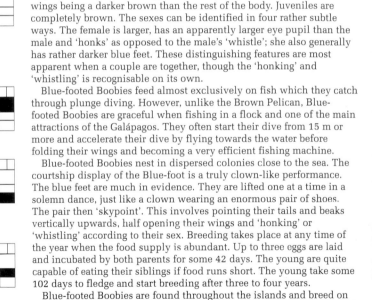

As its name suggests, the chief identifying feature of this booby is the bright blue feet. The plumage is brown above, white below, with the wings being a darker brown than the rest of the body. Juveniles are completely brown. The sexes can be identified in four rather subtle ways. The female is larger, has an apparently larger eye pupil than the male and 'honks' as opposed to the male's 'whistle'; she also generally has rather darker blue feet. These distinguishing features are most apparent when a couple are together, though the 'honking' and 'whistling' is recognisable on its own.

Blue-footed Boobies feed almost exclusively on fish which they catch through plunge diving. However, unlike the Brown Pelican, Blue-footed Boobies are graceful when fishing in a flock and one of the main attractions of the Galápagos. They often start their dive from 15 m or more and accelerate their dive by flying towards the water before folding their wings and becoming a very efficient fishing machine.

Blue-footed Boobies nest in dispersed colonies close to the sea. The courtship display of the Blue-foot is a truly clown-like performance. The blue feet are much in evidence. They are lifted one at a time in a solemn dance, just like a clown wearing an enormous pair of shoes. The pair then 'skypoint'. This involves pointing their tails and beaks vertically upwards, half opening their wings and 'honking' or 'whistling' according to their sex. Breeding takes place at any time of the year when the food supply is abundant. Up to three eggs are laid and incubated by both parents for some 42 days. The young are quite capable of eating their siblings if food runs short. The young take some 102 days to fledge and start breeding after three to four years.

Blue-footed Boobies are found throughout the islands and breed on all the islands south of the Equator, though on occasion they also breed on Genovesa. The Galápagos have three-quarters of the world's population of Blue-footed Boobies.

Best viewed: Coastal waters throughout the islands. Española – Punta Suarez; San Cristóbal – Punta Pitt; Daphne; North Seymour.

ⓔ Masked Booby *Sula dactylatra granti*

The largest of the three species of booby found in the islands, the Masked Booby is also arguably the handsomest. The adult is almost entirely white with a black tail and black ends to the primary feathers on the wing. The bill is yellow, rather paler in the female than in the male. The skin at the base of the bill is black, thus giving it a 'masked' appearance. The immature is largely brown on top and pale underneath

As with the other boobies, the Masked Booby feeds almost entirely on fish which it catches by plunge diving. Unlike the Blue-footed Booby which fishes close inshore, the Masked Booby fishes further offshore and so is less frequently observed fishing.

Breeding takes place on an annual cycle but not quite the same cycle on all islands. The courtship is along the same lines as the Blue-footed Booby but far less elaborate. Two eggs are laid but only one chick is reared. Laying takes place on Genovesa between August and November, while on Española, most eggs are laid between November and February.

Best viewed: At sea throughout the islands and at the breeding colonies. Española – Punta Suarez; San Cristóbal – Punta Pitt; Genovesa.

ⓔ Red-footed Booby *Sula sula websteri*

The Red-footed Booby, the smallest of the three Galápagos boobies, is semi-nocturnal and nests and perches in trees. It has two distinct plumage phases: the brown phase, which is by far the commonest in Galápagos, is almost entirely mid-brown in colour with red feet and legs and a blue-grey bill with pink facial skin. The white phase is almost entirely white apart from the tips of the primary feathers and the tail which are black. The Red-footed Booby can be differentiated from the Masked Booby in flight by its smaller size; also, it has a blue rather than yellow bill and whiter appearance. In flight, it is rather more graceful than the other two species of booby found on the islands.

Red-footed Boobies feed out in the open ocean, well away from land, often on the 'bajos' or submarine volcanoes which are found to the north and east of the archipelago. They feed exclusively on fish, sometimes catching flying fish leaping out of the water.

The breeding cycle of the Red-foot is long and can often last for 12 months or more. Courtship is akin to the Blue-footed Booby, but performed in the trees. A single egg is laid on a platform of twigs and guano and is incubated by both parents for 45 days. The chick fledges after 130 days but is still dependent upon the adults for a further 90 days. This is clearly linked to the semi-nocturnal deep-sea fishing habits of the species.

Best viewed: At sea. Genovesa; San Cristóbal – Punta Pitt; North Seymour; Wolf; Darwin.

ⓔ Flightless Cormorant *Nannopterum harrisi*

The only cormorant found in the islands, the Flightless Cormorant is a large (95 cm) dark brown-to-black bird. Aptly named owing to its complete inability to fly. Its wings are no more than vestigial appendages which appear to serve no useful purpose. Unmistakable when seen hanging its stubby wings out to dry after coming ashore. When in the water, the body is almost entirely submerged with just the snake-like head and neck visible. Adults are black above and dark brown below, but look completely black when wet. Juveniles are completely black. They have large, black-webbed feet with very short sturdy black legs. The eyes are brilliant turquoise and the bill is long and strong, with a pronounced hook at the tip. The males are noticeably larger than the females.

The flightless cormorant feeds on small fish, eels and octopus which it catches within 100 m of the shore. It dives from the surface with a jack-knife movement and uses only its large and powerful webbed feet to pursue its prey.

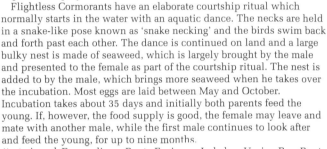

Flightless Cormorants have an elaborate courtship ritual which normally starts in the water with an aquatic dance. The necks are held in a snake-like pose known as 'snake necking' and the birds swim back and forth past each other. The dance is continued on land and a large bulky nest is made of seaweed, which is largely brought by the male and presented to the female as part of the courtship ritual. The nest is added to by the male, which brings more seaweed when he takes over the incubation. Most eggs are laid between May and October. Incubation takes about 35 days and initially both parents feed the young. If, however, the food supply is good, the female may leave and mate with another male, while the first male continues to look after and feed the young, for up to nine months.

Best viewed: Fernandina – Punta Espinosa; Isabela – Urvina Bay, Punta Moreno to Punta Garcia.

ⓔ Magnificent Frigatebird *Fregata magnificens*

The larger of the two frigatebirds found in Galápagos, up to 1.10 m long and with a wingspan of up to 2.45 m. Frigatebirds have the largest wingspan-to-weight ratio of any species of bird and are extremely able and skilled fliers. The male (upper left photo) is entirely black with a purplish sheen on its back and a red goular, or throat, pouch which is only visible during the breeding season. The female (upper right photo) is slightly larger than the male and has a white breast and shoulders, but is otherwise completely black. Immatures (middle right photo) have a white head and neck.

Frigatebirds eat a wide range of food including fish, small crustaceans and newly hatched Green Turtles (*Chelonia mydas*) which they pick up off the beach almost as soon as they emerge from the nest, and sometimes before. They may fish directly from the surface of the sea, or will frequently chase other species, such as the Blue-footed Boobies (*Sula nebouxii*) or Red-billed Tropic Birds (*Phaeton aethereus*) and force it to disgorge its recent catch, often actually catching hold of the tail feathers of both of these species, shaking them until they disgorge their catch, and then catching the disgorged fish before it hits the water.

An insubstantial nest of twigs is built for breeding, in low trees or shrubs close to the shore, often using twigs stolen from other frigatebirds. The courtship includes an acrobatic aerial display and the male pumping up his large, bright red, goular pouch and uttering an unworldly ullulating trill. A single egg is laid which is incubated by both parents for some 42 days. The young fledge after some 90 days.
Best viewed: Throughout the islands, inshore and at their breeding sites. North Seymour; Floreana – Gardner; Isabela – Punta Moreno; San Cristóbal – Wreck Bay, Kicker Rock, Punta Pitt; Genovesa.

ⓡ Great Frigatebird *Fregata minor ridgwayi*

The adult (pair, middle photo; male bottom left photo) is indistinguishable from the Magnificent Frigatebird except when seen close up. The Great Frigatebird has a greenish sheen on its back, while the Magnificent has a purplish one. The juvenile (bottom right photo) has rust-coloured patches on the head and breast. It is less likely to be seen in coastal waters as it feeds at sea on fish and squid. Like the Magnificent Frigatebird, it is involved in kleptoparasitism, stealing from anyone and everyone. Both species also feed on sea lion placenta.

Courtship is similar to the Magnificent Frigatebird but the egg takes 55 days to incubate. The young are dependent on the parents for up to a year after fledging. The feeding technique is much more difficult to master than that of the inshore-fishing Magnificent Frigatebird. The Spanish name of *Pajaro Pirata* translates as 'Pirate Bird'. An apt description.
Best viewed: At sea throughout the islands. Española – Punta Suarez; North Seymour; Genovesa; San Cristóbal– Punta Pitt; Fernandina – Punta Espinosa.

(e) Swallow-tailed Gull *Larus furcatus*

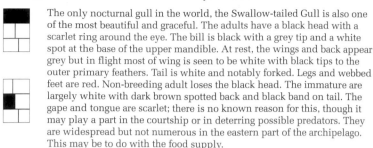

The only nocturnal gull in the world, the Swallow-tailed Gull is also one of the most beautiful and graceful. The adults have a black head with a scarlet ring around the eye. The bill is black with a grey tip and a white spot at the base of the upper mandible. At rest, the wings and back appear grey but in flight most of wing is seen to be white with black tips to the outer primary feathers. Tail is white and notably forked. Legs and webbed feet are red. Non-breeding adult loses the black head. The immature are largely white with dark brown spotted back and black band on tail. The gape and tongue are scarlet; there is no known reason for this, though it may play a part in the courtship or in deterring possible predators. They are widespread but not numerous in the eastern part of the archipelago. This may be to do with the food supply.

The Swallow-tailed Gull is the only night-feeding gull. It leaves the nest site at dusk and fishes well out to sea, generally some 15–30 km from land. Little is known about its feeding habits, but it may have special visual and sonar facilities. Its diet consists largely of small fish and squid. They possibly make use of the phosphorescence of these light-emitting animals in the water. In this context, the red ring around the eye may help them locate their prey more precisely, red being commonly associated with improved night vision. When it returns to the nest site, the white spot at the base of the upper mandible may help the young to locate the food source. Additionally, the fact that the young are white (the only gull to have white young) may help the adult locate them.

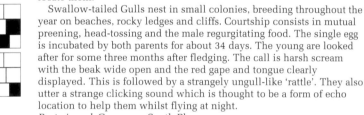

Swallow-tailed Gulls nest in small colonies, breeding throughout the year on beaches, rocky ledges and cliffs. Courtship consists in mutual preening, head-tossing and the male regurgitating food. The single egg is incubated by both parents for about 34 days. The young are looked after for some three months after fledging. The call is harsh scream with the beak wide open and the red gape and tongue clearly displayed. This is followed by a strangely ungull-like 'rattle'. They also utter a strange clicking sound which is thought to be a form of echo location to help them whilst flying at night.

Best viewed: Genovesa; South Plaza.

ⓔ Lava Gull *Larus fuliginosus*

A completely dark gull, the Lava Gull's head and wings are almost black. The rest of the body is dark grey though paler on the belly. They have white upper and lower eyebrows, which vary between individuals, and red eyelids. The legs and bill are black while the inside of the mouth or gape is scarlet. This is quite often seen as they frequently emit long raucous gull-like calls with their bills wide open. The immature bird is largely brown.

The Lava Gull is primarily a scavenger and nest robber. It will also eat lizards and newly hatched iguanas and turtles, and will on occasion catch fish and small crustaceans in shallow lagoons and beaches.

A solitary nester on sheltered beaches and lagoons, the two olive, heavily blotched eggs of the Lava Gull blend in with their surroundings and are difficult to pick out. Incubation takes around 30 days and the young fledge at about 60 days. They are then looked after by the adults for a short period. Being scavengers, immature Lava Gulls are more naturally self-sufficient than some species with more specialised feeding habits. While the total population is thought to be only around 400 pairs, they are not in immediate danger but are obviously vulnerable especially in view of their ground nesting.
Best viewed: Widespread. South Plaza; Santa Cruz – Puerto Ayora, Bahia Tortuga; Isabela – Villamil; Genovesa.

ⓜ Franklin's Gull *Larus pipixcan*

A small gull (37 cm) that is found in Galápagos mainly during the northern winter and therefore in non-breeding plumage. The wings and back are grey with a grey patch behind the eye. The rest of the plumage is white, with dark bill and legs with just a hint of red. In breeding plumage, the head is black with white eyelids, the legs and bill dark red. Wings in flight show white tips to the primary feathers, followed by a broader band of black, and then a white band. The rest of the wing is mid to dark grey.

Franklin's Gull is not known to breed in Galápagos.
Best viewed: Widespread from October to March.

ⓜ Laughing Gull *Larus atricilla*

This is not a common gull. In winter plumage, the Laughing Gull is similar to Franklin's Gull but larger (42 cm). In flight, it is distinguishable from Franklin's Gull by completely dark wing tips. First-year birds are rather browner on the head, neck and breast than Franklin's Gull. The bill is clearly larger with a more downcurved upper mandible than the bill of Franklin's Gull; this is the best way of distinguishing the two species in non-breeding plumage when not in flight. Breeding plumage similar to Franklin's Gull, apart from the wings.

The Laughing Gull is not known to breed in Galápagos.
Best viewed: Widespread from October to March.

(es) Brown Noddy *Anous stolidus galapagensis*

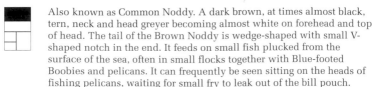

Also known as Common Noddy. A dark brown, at times almost black, tern, neck and head greyer becoming almost white on forehead and top of head. The tail of the Brown Noddy is wedge-shaped with small V-shaped notch in the end. It feeds on small fish plucked from the surface of the sea, often in small flocks together with Blue-footed Boobies and pelicans. It can frequently be seen sitting on the heads of fishing pelicans, waiting for small fry to leak out of the bill pouch.

The Brown Noddy breeds throughout the year on rock ledges and small caves in cliffs, generally in small colonies, often quite close to the water. Courtship includes a lot of nodding and bowing, hence the common name. A single off-white blotched egg is laid on the bare rock. They breed less than once a year.
Best viewed: Widespread throughout the islands. South Plaza; Santa Cruz – Puerto Ayora; Rábida; Isabela – Tagus Cove; Bartolomé.

(r) Sooty Tern *Sterna fuscata*

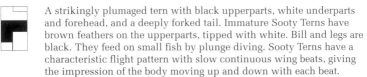

A strikingly plumaged tern with black upperparts, white underparts and forehead, and a deeply forked tail. Immature Sooty Terns have brown feathers on the upperparts, tipped with white. Bill and legs are black. They feed on small fish by plunge diving. Sooty Terns have a characteristic flight pattern with slow continuous wing beats, giving the impression of the body moving up and down with each beat.

The Sooty Tern is found only on the northern islands of Darwin and Wolf, where it breeds in large numbers.
Best viewed: Darwin; Wolf. Rarely seen elsewhere in the islands.

(m) Royal Tern *Sterna maxima*

Large (51 cm) tern seen in Galápagos only during the northern winter, in non-breeding plumage. Royal Terns have large orange bills, white forehead, black further back on the head, turning into a distinct crest. Generally white underparts and grey wings and mantle, but black primary feathers. Tail deeply forked, but less so than the Sooty Tern. Legs and feet are black.

The Royal Tern is not known to breed in Galápagos.
Best viewed: Isabela – Quinta Playa. From January to March.

(m) Common Tern *Sterna hirundo*

Small, slim tern with grey mantle and wings. Black primary feathers. The head has an incomplete black cap and the bill is black, sometimes with a red base. In breeding plumage, the black cap is complete and the bill scarlet with a black tip. The feet and legs of the Common Tern are scarlet. Underparts are white, with a tail deeply forked.

The Common Tern is not known to breed in the Galápagos. It is seen only in small numbers from December to March.
Best viewed: Southern islands.

COASTAL BIRDS

ⓡ Great Blue Heron *Ardea herodias*

The largest heron in the islands, the Great Blue stands nearly 1-m high with a wingspan of 175 cm. It is largely grey on the wings and back, the underparts being paler. The head is black and white, the breast streaked, with rufous and black on the folds of the wings. The thighs are rufous. It has distinctive head plumes during the breeding season. The legs are long and dark grey. The bill is yellow but darker on top. In flight, the neck is pulled back in an S-shape.

The Great Blue Heron feeds on small fish, crabs, lizards, young iguanas and young birds.

Breeding occurs throughout the year on a large untidy platform of twigs in mangroves or sometimes on cliffs. It is a solitary nester, laying two or three eggs which hatch after 28 days. Incubation and feeding is shared by both parents.

Best viewed: On beaches and lagoons on all the main islands.

ⓡ Great Egret *Casmerodius albus*

Also known as the Common Egret. A large elegant all-white heron, at 85-cm tall it is slightly smaller than the Great Blue Heron. The bill is large and yellow and the feet and legs black. Feeding habits of the Great Egret are similar to the Great Blue Heron, but it additionally will eat locusts, grasshoppers and other insects.

The Great Egret breeds in small colonies near the shore, generally in mangroves. The clutch is normally two eggs.

Best viewed: Lagoons and intertidal zones on Santa Cruz, San Cristóbal, Isabela, Santiago and Floreana. Also found in the highlands of cattle-farming areas.

ⓜ Snowy Egret *Leucophoyx thula*

Small (60 cm) all-white heron (though larger than the Cattle Egret) with slender black bill and yellow lores (the area of skin just behind bill). The legs are black with yellow feet. Can be differentiated from the Cattle Egret by its black bill and black legs.

The Snowy Egret is not known to breed in Galápagos.

ⓡ Cattle Egret *Bubulcus ibis*

Probably the most recent natural arrival in Galápagos as part of a worldwide expansion of this species. It was first recorded in 1964, and is now known to breed in several locations. The Cattle Egret is the smallest (50 cm) all-white heron found in Galápagos. The bill is yellow, the legs and feet also yellow in the adult but darker in immature birds. Breeding birds have buff tinge to the head and back.

The Cattle Egret feeds on locusts, grasshoppers and other insects, and also lizards and probably the young of iguanas and Green Turtles.

A colonial nester laying two or three eggs, first known to have bred in 1986. It is too early to say if this species will have a significant impact on any other species in Galápagos.

Best viewed: Agricultural areas on San Cristóbal, Santa Cruz, Floreana and Isabela. By mangroves and lagoons, and on South Plaza.

(e) Lava Heron *Butorides sundevalli*

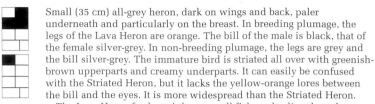

Small (35 cm) all-grey heron, dark on wings and back, paler underneath and particularly on the breast. In breeding plumage, the legs of the Lava Heron are orange. The bill of the male is black, that of the female silver-grey. In non-breeding plumage, the legs are grey and the bill silver-grey. The immature bird is striated all over with greenish-brown upperparts and creamy underparts. It can easily be confused with the Striated Heron, but it lacks the yellow-orange lores between the bill and the eyes. It is more widespread than the Striated Heron.

The Lava Heron feeds mainly on small fish, crabs, lizards and insects. When fishing from mangrove roots or rocks, it may jump or dive into the water to ensure the capture of its prey. Often seen stalking Sally Lightfoot crabs on coastal rocks.

The Lava Heron is a solitary nester in mangroves on the coast or around lagoons. It is quite territorial. Nesting can be year round but generally starts between September and March. The clutch size is two or three eggs.

Best viewed: On coast and in mangrove lagoons throughout the islands.

(r) Striated Heron *Butorides striatus*

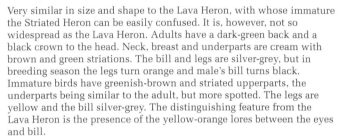

Very similar in size and shape to the Lava Heron, with whose immature the Striated Heron can be easily confused. It is, however, not so widespread as the Lava Heron. Adults have a dark-green back and a black crown to the head. Neck, breast and underparts are cream with brown and green striations. The bill and legs are silver-grey, but in breeding season the legs turn orange and male's bill turns black. Immature birds have greenish-brown and striated upperparts, the underparts being similar to the adult, but more spotted. The legs are yellow and the bill silver-grey. The distinguishing feature from the Lava Heron is the presence of the yellow-orange lores between the eyes and bill.

The Striated Heron feeds on small fish, crabs, lizards and insects. Breeding habits are very similar to the Lava Heron, but it is recorded as nesting only on Isabela, Santa Cruz, Fernandina, Pinta and Pinzón.

Best viewed: Mangrove lagoons and on the coast.

(es) Yellow-crowned Night Heron *Nyctanassa violacea*

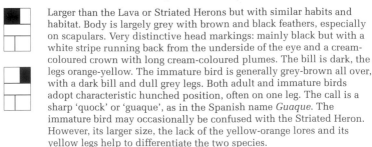

Larger than the Lava or Striated Herons but with similar habits and habitat. Body is largely grey with brown and black feathers, especially on scapulars. Very distinctive head markings: mainly black but with a white stripe running back from the underside of the eye and a cream-coloured crown with long cream-coloured plumes. The bill is dark, the legs orange-yellow. The immature bird is generally grey-brown all over, with a dark bill and dull grey legs. Both adult and immature birds adopt characteristic hunched position, often on one leg. The call is a sharp 'quock' or 'guaque', as in the Spanish name *Guaque*. The immature bird may occasionally be confused with the Striated Heron. However, its larger size, the lack of the yellow-orange lores and its yellow legs help to differentiate the two species.

Feeding is on crabs, scorpions, locusts and other insects caught mainly at night. It favours mangrove lagoons and towns or villages with streetlights which attract the painted locust, *Schistocerca melanocera*, and other insects.

The Yellow-crowned Night Heron is a solitary nester. A nest of twigs is built in low mangrove or under a rock. A clutch of two to four blue-green eggs is incubated by both parents.

Best viewed: Widespread on coast and occasionally inland. Not found on Darwin and Wolf.

(r) Greater Flamingo *Phoenicopterus ruber*

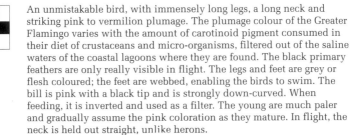

An unmistakable bird, with immensely long legs, a long neck and striking pink to vermilion plumage. The plumage colour of the Greater Flamingo varies with the amount of carotinoid pigment consumed in their diet of crustaceans and micro-organisms, filtered out of the saline waters of the coastal lagoons where they are found. The black primary feathers are only really visible in flight. The legs and feet are grey or flesh coloured; the feet are webbed, enabling the birds to swim. The bill is pink with a black tip and is strongly down-curved. When feeding, it is inverted and used as a filter. The young are much paler and gradually assume the pink coloration as they mature. In flight, the neck is held out straight, unlike herons.

Nests are built in small colonies in a number of saline coastal lagoons. The nest of mud is conical-shaped and some 20–25-cm high to enable the adult to incubate comfortably with its long legs. The chick leaves the nest soon after hatching and its initially straight bill starts to curve after three weeks or so. Breeding is often disrupted by El Niño when the water level rises and floods the nests. Flamingoes live for up to 30 years but do not start breeding until they are 5-years old. The population is thought to number less than 500 individuals.

Best viewed: Isabela – Villamil, Punta Moreno; Santa Cruz – Turtle Bay, Las Bachas; Floreana – Punta Cormorant; Rábida; Santiago – Espunilla.

ⓟ ⓜ Pied-billed Grebe *Podilymbus podiceps*

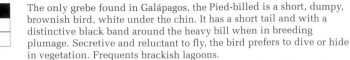

The only grebe found in Galápagos, the Pied-billed is a short, dumpy, brownish bird, white under the chin. It has a short tail and with a distinctive black band around the heavy bill when in breeding plumage. Secretive and reluctant to fly, the bird prefers to dive or hide in vegetation. Frequents brackish lagoons.

The Pied-billed Grebe is not known to have bred in Galápagos, but may well have done so. Sightings are year round, including immature individuals.

Best viewed: Santa Cruz – Turtle Bay; Floreana – Punta Cormorant; Isabela – Villamil; San Cristóbal – highlands.

ⓔ White-cheeked Pintail *Anas bahamensis galapagensis*

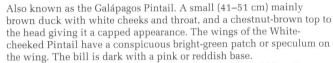

Also known as the Galápagos Pintail. A small (41–51 cm) mainly brown duck with white cheeks and throat, and a chestnut-brown top to the head giving it a capped appearance. The wings of the White-cheeked Pintail have a conspicuous bright-green patch or speculum on the wing. The bill is dark with a pink or reddish base.

This duck feeds on the surface of the water and by dabbling. It may also dive in deeper freshwater lakes and ponds. It is found on both saltwater and freshwater lagoons, ponds and both permanent and temporary lakes.

An opportunistic breeder, nesting occurs when conditions are suitable. Up to ten pale-brown eggs are laid in a well-hidden nest at the edge of the pond, lagoon or lake. The female incubates for 25 days and once hatched the chicks are able to feed for themselves.

Best viewed: Santa Cruz – Puerto Ayora, Turtle Bay, Las Bachas; Isabela – Villamil, Quinta Playa; Santiago – Puerto Egas; San Cristóbal – El Junco.

ⓜ Blue-winged Teal *Anas discors*

Slightly smaller (37–41 cm) than the White-cheeked Pintail, the female duck is all-brown with a paler head and neck, and darker cap. Males are more chestnut-brown with distinctive white crescent on the side of the head and a smaller white patch near the tail. Both sexes have a distinctive blue patch on the wings as well as a green speculum. The bill is dark, almost black. It is found mainly on inland freshwater ponds, and less commonly on coastal lagoons in similar locations to the White-cheeked Pintail.

It feeds on the surface and by dabbling. The Blue-winged Teal is not known to breed in Galápagos, but the presence of groups of both sexes suggests it may have, or will do so shortly.

Best viewed: Santa Cruz – Purto Ayora, Turtle Bay, Las Bachas; Isabela – Villamil, Quinta Playa; Santiago – Puerto Egas; San Cristóbal – El Junco.

(es) American Oystercatcher *Haematopus palliatus*

Heavily built shorebird. Underparts white, and breast, head, wings and back black. A white wing patch and rump are visible in flight. Striking, long, powerful red bill, laterally flattened to help open bivalves. Eyes yellow with a red ring around them. Feet and legs flesh coloured. The call is a shrill 'kle-e-ep'. Nesting takes place between October and March. The chicks leave the nest immediately on hatching.
Best viewed: Widespread throughout the islands.

(r) Black-necked Stilt *Himantopus mexicanus*

Also known as the Common Stilt. Elegant very long-legged wader. Distinctive plumage. Underparts white, upperparts mainly black with white forehead and patch behind the eyes. Legs and feet red. Bill long, straight, slender, pointed and black. Feeds on small invertebrates and fish. Breeds between December and June and courtship is preceded by an elaborate and acrobatic air dance. Four green-brown eggs are laid.
Best viewed: Coastal lagoons throughout the islands.

(m) Semi-palmated Plover *Charadrius semipalmatus*

Small, stocky shorebird, largely grey-brown with white underparts, white neck ring, forehead and a line over the eyes. Legs and feet dull orange-yellow. Bill dark with an orange base. Immature birds have all-dark bill. Breeding plumage similar with black on the upper breast, cheeks and forehead. A pale wingbar is visible in flight. Characteristic behaviour is to run a few metres and then stop. The call is a sharp 'chi-we'.
Best viewed: Throughout the islands from August to April.

(m) Black-bellied Plover *Pluvialis squatarola*

Also known as the Grey Plover. Breeding plumage jet-black underparts and breast, contrasting with silver-grey back and wings. Winter plumage much less striking, with grey-and-white upperparts and pale-grey underparts. The bill, legs and feet are black. In flight, a differentiating feature is the black patch under the wings where they join the body.
Best viewed: Coastal Lagoons throughout islands.

(m) Ruddy Turnstone *Arenaria interpres*

Small (24 cm) stocky wader with short legs. Breeding plumage, tortoise-shell back and wings, black-and-white patterned head, white underparts. Winter plumage grey or brown back and head, white underparts and dark breast. Bill dark with orange base in adults, all-dark in immatures. It appears to be up-turned. Legs orange-yellow, paler in winter. Feeds on small molluscs and crustaceans. Not known to breed in Galápagos.
Best viewed: Widespread throughout the islands.

(m) Wandering Tattler *Heteroscelus incanus*

Medium-sized (28 cm) strong-legged wader. Back and wings slate-grey. Breast and underparts heavily barred in the breeding plumage, breast grey and underparts white in winter plumage. Bill is dark, of medium length and heavy. Legs and feet yellow. Not known to breed in Galápagos.
Best viewed: Widespread on coasts throughout the islands.

ⓜ Western Sandpiper *Calidris mauri*

A small pale sandpiper. The winter plumage is almost indistinguishable from the Semi-palmated Sandpiper but the Western has an appreciably longer bill with a hint of a down-curve at the tip. Breeding plumage a much more rufous colour on back and head. Bill, legs and feet are black. This bird is not known to breed in Galápagos.
Best viewed: Beaches and coastal lagoons, December to March.

ⓜ Least Sandpiper *Calidris minutilla*

The commonest of the 'peep' sandpipers in Galápagos. Upperparts and head are much darker and browner than the Western or Semi-palmated Sandpipers. Winter plumage has red-brown cap. Bill black, very short and sharp. Legs are yellow, which distinguishes Least from the other two, which have black legs. The Least Sandpiper is not known to breed in Galápagos.
Best viewed: Beaches and coastal lagoons, December to March.

ⓜ Solitary Sandpiper *Tringa solitaria*

A medium-sized (22 cm) wader with dark upperparts and white underparts, breast grey in winter plumage but barred in breeding. Fine white band above and around the eyes. Bill is dark, the legs greenish-yellow. Not to be confused with the Lesser Yellowlegs. Bobs a little like yellowlegs. In flight, distinctive black-and-white barring to sides of tail. This bird is not known to breed in Galápagos.
Best viewed: Highlands, December to March.

ⓜ Spotted Sandpiper *Actitis macularia*

A small (19 cm) neat wader. In winter plumage, it has olive-brown upperparts and white underparts. Bill is short, sharp and dark. Legs are dull orange-yellow. White eyestripe above eyes. Breeding plumage has dark brown spots on the breast and flanks. In flight, narrow white wingbar and white sides to the tail are visible. Characteristic short glide after several short wing beats. Watch for bobbing or teetering movements. It is not known to breed in Galápagos.
Best viewed: Beaches and coastal lagoons, December to March.

ⓜ Sanderling *Calidris alba*

A small tide-line wader, frequently seen following waves up and down the beach rather like a clockwork toy. Winter plumage is largely white with a grey back and head; dark primary feathers. Breeding plumage much darker on the back with brown and black. Marked white wingbar in flight, the underside of the wing is very white! Bill, legs and feet are black. Not known to breed in the islands but is present all-year round.
Best viewed: Widespread on beaches.

ⓜ Short-billed Dowitcher *Limnodromus griseus*

Snipe-like wader. Winter plumage generally grey, upperparts darker. Distinctive pale eyestripe and barring on tail, particularly visible in flight. Long, thin, dark, pointed bill. Breeding plumage reddish brown. Legs are olive-yellow. This bird is not known to breed in Galápagos.
Best viewed: Coastal lagoons and beaches.

ⓜ Willet *Catoptrophorus semipalmatus*

Large (38 cm) non-descript wader, especially in winter plumage. Grey-brown back and head, paler undersides and neck. Long, heavy black bill. Legs dark in winter, bluish in breeding plumage, which is more barred on the back and flanks. In flight, black-and-white wing pattern shows on both upper- and undersides of wings. Not known to breed in Galápagos. *Best viewed:* Beaches and coastal lagoons, December to March.

ⓜ Whimbrel *Numenius phaeopus hudsonicus*

Also known as the Seven Whistler. Large (42 cm), brown, long-legged wader with long, markedly down-curving bill. Underparts are pale brown; upperparts darker. Crown is striped dark and pale brown. Commonest large wader in the islands. Not known to breed but present all year. *Best viewed:* Beaches, coastal lagoons and highlands, best on Isabela.

ⓜ Greater Yellowlegs *Tringa melanoleuca*

Large (36 cm) brown wader. Long, yellow legs and long, thin, pointed bill. Dark on top pale underneath with brown flecked breast. White eyeline in front of and above eyes. In flight, shows white rump and pale tail, but no wingbar. Not known to breed in Galápagos. *Best viewed:* Beaches and coastal lagoons.

ⓜ Lesser Yellowlegs *Tringa flavipes*

Smaller (27 cm) than Greater, and commoner. Similar plumage to Greater, with distinctive yellow legs, long, fine, pointed bill, white rump, pale tail and no wingbar. Not known to breed in Galápagos. *Best viewed:* Beaches, coastal lagoons and highlands, December to March.

ⓜ Surfbird *Aphriza virgata*

Plump plover-like wader. In winter, slate-grey back and breast, underparts white. Breeding plumage, brown above with golden scapulars, breast white with dark markings. Bill dark with orange base. Legs stout and yellow. In flight, note white wingbar, white rump and black tail tip. *Best viewed:* Rocky coasts, December to March.

ⓜ Red-necked Phalarope *Phalaropus lobatus*

Small (20 cm) swimming wader. Winter plumage dark grey and white, black crown and distinctive black eye patch. Legs dark, bill short and dark. Phalaropes hold their head in a distinctively upright way, with bill parallel to water. Swims in circles to assist catching small fish and crustaceans. Distinctive white wingbars in flight. Not known to breed in Galápagos. *Best viewed:* At sea and coastal lagoons, December to March.

ⓜ Wilson's Phalarope *Phalaropus tricolor*

Less common and slightly larger (24 cm) than Red-necked, with longer bill and generally paler. The dark eye patch less noticeable, white eye-stripe narrower and more distinctive. No wingbar but white rump and dark end to the tail. Legs yellowish. Not known to breed in Galápagos. *Best viewed:* Mangrove lagoons especially on Santa Cruz.

LAND BIRDS

ⓔ Galápagos Hawk *Buteo galapagoensis*

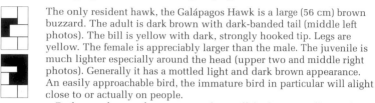

The only resident hawk, the Galápagos Hawk is a large (56 cm) brown buzzard. The adult is dark brown with dark-banded tail (middle left photos). The bill is yellow with dark, strongly hooked tip. Legs are yellow. The female is appreciably larger than the male. The juvenile is much lighter especially around the head (upper two and middle right photos). Generally it has a mottled light and dark brown appearance. An easily approachable bird, the immature bird in particular will alight close to or actually on people.

Both a predator and a scavenger, they will feed on virtually anything, especially young iguana, lizards, birds, especially doves and finches, rats (endemic and introduced), centipedes, locusts and on carrion such as dead goats, donkeys or sea lions and frequently on sea lion placenta.

The Galápagos Hawk nests on all the major islands apart from Genovesa, which it has probably never reached, and San Cristóbal and Floreana, as a result of eradication by humans. The nest is a large untidy pile of twigs and branches in a tree or on a rocky outcrop. A territory will have several nests, only one of which will be used at a time. Each female will mate with up to four males, all of whom help with incubation and rearing the young. This is known as 'co-operative polyandry', and clearly increases the chances of reproductive success. Two or three eggs are laid and hatch after some 50–60 days. The young birds are expelled from the territory after three to five months and spend two years or more in non-territorial areas before breeding. It is these immature birds that are most likely to approach humans. While breeding only takes place in the arid zone, individuals are frequently observed in all areas. There are thought to be only some 120–150 'pairs' but around 800 individual birds. This makes it a very vulnerable species.
Best viewed: South Plaza; Española – Punta Suarez and Gardner Bay; Fernandina – Punta Espinosa; Santa Fé.

ⓜ Osprey *Pandion haliaetus*

Also known as the Fish Eagle. Though not a common bird, the Osprey may be seen near mangrove lagoons. A large (60 cm) hawk, the Osprey is dark brown above, with white underparts, a head largely white with a black mark through the eyes and cheek. The tail is barred, black-brown above, black-white on underside. It has very long (150–180 cm) broad wings, often held with a marked crook in them. The Osprey fishes by plunge diving feet first.

The Osprey is not known to breed in Galápagos, though an occasional bird will stay over the summer.
Best viewed: Santa Cruz; San Cristóbal; Isabela.

ⓜ Peregrine Falcon *Falco peregrinus*

The only falcon recorded in Galápagos. The Peregrine Falcon is slate-grey above with near-black head and distinctive sideburns. Breast and underparts are light grey with darker spots and barring. The tail is narrow and barred. The bill is yellow and hooked with a dark tip. The legs are yellow. Immature birds are similar but brown. A powerful flyer, the Peregrine Falcon catches birds on the wing, and is known to attack boobies, tropic birds, gulls, shorebirds and finches.

The Peregrine Falcon is not known to breed in Galápagos
Best viewed: Widespread but uncommon near cliffs and bird colonies.

ⓔⓢ Barn Owl *Tyto alba punctatissima*

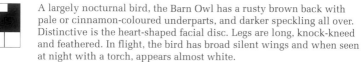

A largely nocturnal bird, the Barn Owl has a rusty brown back with pale or cinnamon-coloured underparts, and darker speckling all over. Distinctive is the heart-shaped facial disc. Legs are long, knock-kneed and feathered. In flight, the bird has broad silent wings and when seen at night with a torch, appears almost white.

The Barn Owl feeds entirely at night on rats, mice, small birds and larger insects.

Barn Owls are known to nest in all months of the year. Preference is for the arid and transitional zones but it will also nest in the highlands. It nests in holes, especially lava tubes and other volcanic features. The clutch of three eggs is incubated for about 30 days and the young fledge after 10–12 weeks.
Best viewed: At night on Santa Cruz, San Cristóbal and Isabela. (Visitors are not allowed ashore on the other islands at night!)

ⓔⓢ Short-eared Owl *Asio flammeus galapagoensis*

A dark brown owl, much more likely to be seen than the nocturnal Barn Owl. It has some lighter streaking above, paler underneath with dark markings. The dark facial disc emphasises the yellow eyes. The bill is dark, and the legs feathered. The short ear tufts are difficult to see. It is most likely to be seen in flight, hunting.

The Short-eared Owl feeds mainly on small birds, and particularly preys on storm petrel colonies, rats and mice (introduced) as well as some larger insects.

Nests on all the major islands apart from Fernandina. It prefers highlands. The nests are in open ground. The bird lays three or four eggs, though normally only two chicks survive to fledging.
Best viewed: Genovesa; highlands of Santa Cruz; San Cristóbal; Floreana; Isabela.

ⓔ Galápagos Dove *Zenaida galapagoensis*

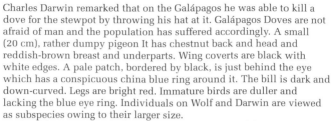

Charles Darwin remarked that on the Galápagos he was able to kill a dove for the stewpot by throwing his hat at it. Galápagos Doves are not afraid of man and the population has suffered accordingly. A small (20 cm), rather dumpy pigeon It has chestnut back and head and reddish-brown breast and underparts. Wing coverts are black with white edges. A pale patch, bordered by black, is just behind the eye which has a conspicuous china blue ring around it. The bill is dark and down-curved. Legs are bright red. Immature birds are duller and lacking the blue eye ring. Individuals on Wolf and Darwin are viewed as subspecies owing to their larger size.

The Galápagos Dove feeds on whatever is most readily available, including insect larvae, seeds, pollen, and cactus fruit. It is a reluctant flier, which explains Darwin's ability to knock it down with his hat! The call is a rather annoying soft 'cooing' by the males.

The Galápagos Dove nests all-year round depending on food supply, but mainly in the rainy season, February to June, when food is most abundant. Typical pigeon courtship including an aerial display and much bowing and cooing. It nests on the ground under an overhanging rock ledge or in Opuntia cactus, sometimes using old mockingbird nests. The normal clutch is two eggs, with a two-week incubation period and a further two weeks to fledging.

Best viewed: Drier parts of all the main islands.

ⓔ Galápagos Rail *Laterallus spilonotus*

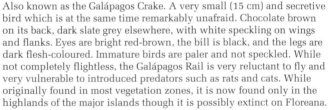

Also known as the Galápagos Crake. A very small (15 cm) and secretive bird which is at the same time remarkably unafraid. Chocolate brown on its back, dark slate grey elsewhere, with white speckling on wings and flanks. Eyes are bright red-brown, the bill is black, and the legs are dark flesh-coloured. Immature birds are paler and not speckled. While not completely flightless, the Galápagos Rail is very reluctant to fly and very vulnerable to introduced predators such as rats and cats. While originally found in most vegetation zones, it is now found only in the highlands of the major islands though it is possibly extinct on Floreana.

The Galápagos Rail feeds on small invertebrates and seeds.

Ground nesting occurs on the major islands, and has been recorded in all months of the year though predominantly in the period June to February. Up to five eggs are laid in a covered nest. Incubation takes up to 25 days and the young birds reach maturity after a further 12 weeks or so.

Best viewed: Highland areas of Santa Cruz, San Cristóbal and Isabela.

ⓡ Paint-billed Crake *Neocrex erythrops*

Slightly larger (20 cm) than the Galápagos Rail, the Paint-billed Crake has dark grey plumage, a yellow bill with a red base and red legs. It flies rather more readily more than the Galápagos Rail but is not keen to do so!

The Paint-billed Crake feeds on insects and other invertebrates.

Nests are found in thick vegetation, the bird laying six or seven eggs, which hatch within three weeks. The young leave the nest immediately. The main breeding period is December to May.

Best viewed: Farming zones: Santa Cruz; San Cristóbal; Floreana; Isabela.

ⓡ Common Gallinule *Gallinula chloropus*

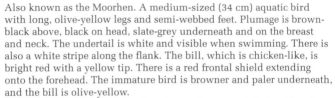

Also known as the Moorhen. A medium-sized (34 cm) aquatic bird with long, olive-yellow legs and semi-webbed feet. Plumage is brown-black above, black on head, slate-grey underneath and on the breast and neck. The undertail is white and visible when swimming. There is also a white stripe along the flank. The bill, which is chicken-like, is bright red with a yellow tip. There is a red frontal shield extending onto the forehead. The immature bird is browner and paler underneath, and the bill is olive-yellow.

The Common Gallinule feeds on invertebrates, mainly in soil and leaf litter. It flies reluctantly.

The bird nests between May and October, close to the shore of a pond or lagoon, or in mangroves. Seven or more eggs are laid in a clutch. The young leave the nest as soon as all the eggs have hatched.

Best viewed: Coastal lagoons and mangroves on Santa Cruz, Isabela, San Cristóbal and Floreana. San Cristóbal – El Junco, La Toma.

ⓜ Belted Kingfisher *Ceryle alcyon*

A large (33 cm), strikingly plumaged bird and the only kingfisher found in Galápagos. Plumage is grey-blue above, white underparts. A blue-grey band extends across the breast. Neck white, head blue-grey with prominent crest and white spot just in front of eyes. The female has an additional cinnamon band across the abdomen. The outer tail feathers are barred dark grey and white. The primary feathers are black. The bill is long, stout and sharp.

The Belted Kingfisher feeds by plunge-diving either after hovering or directly from a branch.

The Belted Kingfisher is not known to breed in Galápagos.

Best viewed: Mangrove lagoons on Isabela and Santa Cruz.

ⓡ Dark-billed Cuckoo *Coccyzus melacoryphus*

A slender, elegant, long-tailed, skulking bird. Chestnut-brown above, grey-black cap to head, white below the eye. Underparts are pale beige with more rufous coloration on breast and neck. The bill is black and slightly downcurved. The tail is long, brown and with white tips to outer tail feathers.

The Dark-billed Cuckoo likes thickly vegetated areas, and feeds on insects.

Though it is known to breed in Galápagos, no record exists of any nests.

Best viewed: On all major islands. Santa Cruz – Puerto Ayora. The Charles Darwin Research Station is one of the best places to see it.

Mockingbirds

There are four species of mockingbird found in Galápagos; all have very similar plumage and all are endemic. They are very adaptable, especially to humans, and can be quite demanding. They will eat almost anything including seeds, insects and other invertebrates, baby turtles, sea-lion placenta, eggs and even ticks off the Land Iguanas on Santa Fé. They are excellent mimics and have even learnt to imitate the recently introduced Smooth-billed Ani.

ⓔ Galápagos Mockingbird *Nesomimus parvulus*

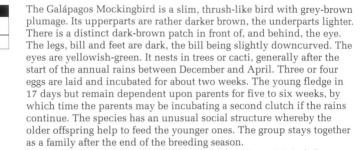

The Galápagos Mockingbird is a slim, thrush-like bird with grey-brown plumage. Its upperparts are rather darker brown, the underparts lighter. There is a distinct dark-brown patch in front of, and behind, the eye. The legs, bill and feet are dark, the bill being slightly downcurved. The eyes are yellowish-green. It nests in trees or cacti, generally after the start of the annual rains between December and April. Three or four eggs are laid and incubated for about two weeks. The young fledge in 17 days but remain dependent upon parents for five to six weeks, by which time the parents may be incubating a second clutch if the rains continue. The species has an unusual social structure whereby the older offspring help to feed the younger ones. The group stays together as a family after the end of the breeding season.
Best viewed: Santa Cruz; South Plaza; Santiago; Santa Fé; Isabela; Fernandina; Pinta; Marchena; Genovesa; Darwin; Wolf.

ⓔ Charles Mockingbird *Nesomimus trifasciatus*

Virtually identical to *N. parvulus* but with red-brown eyes, the Charles Mockingbird has rather browner plumage with conspicuous dark patches on the side of the breast. It is found exclusively on the small islands of Champion and Gardner, off Floreana. It was previously found on Floreana (English name Charles) itself, but it has become extinct there, presumably through the depredations of cats and rats. The total population is probably in the region of 150 individuals.
Best viewed: Champion; Gardner by Floreana.

ⓔ Hood Mockingbird *Nesomimus macdonaldi*

Slightly larger than the other mockingbirds, the Hood Mockingbird also is at times rather scrawny looking. The tail feathers have less white on them than other species. The longer legs are distinctive, and the bill more down-curved. The eyes are hazel. Outside the breeding season it may gather in large groups of up to 40 individuals. It is well known to follow tourists and is quite reluctant to fly. Found only on Española (English name Hood) and neighbouring Gardner island. When boats anchor at Gardner, they nearly always receive a delegation of mockingbirds.
Best viewed: Española; Gardner by Española.

ⓔ Chatham Mockingbird *Nesomimus melanotis*

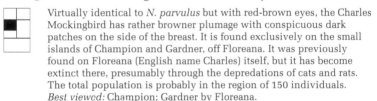

Very similar to other species, the Chatham Mockingbird's plumage is mid-way between that of *N. parvulus* and *N. macdonaldi*. The eyes are greenish-yellow. It is found exclusively on San Cristóbal.
Best viewed: San Cristóbal.

(r) Vermilion Flycatcher *Pyrocephalus rubinus*

The adult male Vermilion Flycatcher is unmistakable, with brilliant undersides, breast, neck and cap. The back is black and there is a black eyeband running back to, and joining, the black on the nape of the neck. The bill, legs and feet are also black. The female is much less colourful, having yellow underparts, an off-white breast and neck and a brown head and back. The bill, neck and feet of both sexes are black. The immature bird resembles the female.

The Vermilion Flycatcher feeds on insects mainly caught on the wing, but it is also known to feed on the ground.

The bird breeds mainly during the warm season, December to May, on the coast, but may nest year all round in the highlands. It is known to breed frequently during heavy El Niño years.

Best viewed: Widespread on main islands in dry areas and in highlands.

(e) Galápagos Flycatcher *Myriarchus magnirostris*

Also known as the Large-billed Flycatcher. Slightly larger than the Vermilion Flycatcher, and with a superficial resemblance to the female or immature bird of that species, the Galápagos Flycatcher has a mid-brown back and head, grey breast and pale-yellow underparts. The bill, legs and feet are dark, the bill being appreciably larger than that of the Vermilion Flycatcher. A double wingbar is visible on the closed wing.

The Galápagos Flycatcher feeds on flying insects and also larvae. It will often approach very close to humans and even accept insects from the hand.

Nests are constructed during the warm season, December to May, generally in a hole in a tree cactus or lava rock.

Best viewed: Widespread on all main islands, except Genovesa. Commoner in dry zones.

(es) Yellow Warbler *Dendroica petechia aureola*

A small (12 cm) bright-yellow bird commonly seen in all areas of the major and many of the smaller islands, particularly where it is dry. The adult Yellow Warbler has bright yellow underparts and head, is more olive-yellow above, and the wings have dark primary feathers and primary coverts. The male has red streaking on the crown and on the flanks. The bill and legs are dark. The bill is finely pointed, typical of most warblers.

Immatures are greyer, with very pale underparts; some yellow is always visible. It feeds on insects and is often seen feeding on flies in the intertidal zone. Frequently, it is seen entering houses to feed.

Nesting takes place during the warm season, December to April, and is largely dictated to by the annual rains (El Niño). In a major El Niño, breeding will take place several times. The nest is cup-shaped and generally located well off the ground in the canopy of a tree or bush. Two or three buff-spotted eggs are incubated by the female. The young are fed by both parents.

Best viewed: Widespread on all major islands and many small ones.

ⓘ Smooth-billed Ani *Crotophaga ani*

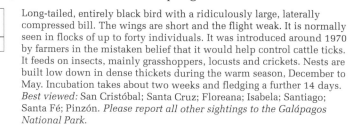

Long-tailed, entirely black bird with a ridiculously large, laterally compressed bill. The wings are short and the flight weak. It is normally seen in flocks of up to forty individuals. It was introduced around 1970 by farmers in the mistaken belief that it would help control cattle ticks. It feeds on insects, mainly grasshoppers, locusts and crickets. Nests are built low down in dense thickets during the warm season, December to May. Incubation takes about two weeks and fledging a further 14 days. *Best viewed:* San Cristóbal; Santa Cruz; Floreana; Isabela; Santiago; Santa Fé; Pinzón. *Please report all other sightings to the Galápagos National Park.*

ⓟ Bobolink *Dolichonyx oryzivorus*

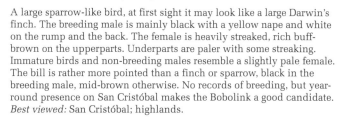

A large sparrow-like bird, at first sight it may look like a large Darwin's finch. The breeding male is mainly black with a yellow nape and white on the rump and the back. The female is heavily streaked, rich buff-brown on the upperparts. Underparts are paler with some streaking. Immature birds and non-breeding males resemble a slightly pale female. The bill is rather more pointed than a finch or sparrow, black in the breeding male, mid-brown otherwise. No records of breeding, but year-round presence on San Cristóbal makes the Bobolink a good candidate. *Best viewed:* San Cristóbal; highlands.

ⓔ Galápagos Martin *Progne modesta modesta*

The only resident member of the swallow family. Males are almost entirely blue-black, with slightly paler underwings. The wings are pointed and the tail narrow, with a shallow fork. Females are similar but dark brown below. Flight is typical of other martins: a series of quick wing-beats followed by a glide. The Galápagos Martin feeds on insects, always caught while on the wing. Widespread, but not common, most frequently seen in highland areas. Not found in the northern islands. *Best viewed:* Highland areas on the major islands.

ⓜ Purple Martin *Progne subis*

Completely dark-coloured martin, easily confused with the Galápagos Martin. However, the Purple Martin is larger, 19 cm as opposed to 15 cm for the Galápagos Martin. Males are all dark with a steely-blue sheen; the female is duller and with a grey forehead and greyish underparts. The immature bird is grey-brown above and on the head, with pale underparts. Not known to breed in Galápagos. *Best viewed:* San Cristóbal; Española.

ⓜ Barn Swallow *Hirundo rustica*

A long-winged swallow with a deeply forked tail. Dark blue above and on the head. Underparts are pale buff, the forehead and throat a rich cinnamon, with a narrow blue chest band. The immature bird is less strikingly marked and lacks the chest band; the immature tail also lacks long outer feathers. Flight is fast and often close to the ground or water. It feeds on insects, always on the wing. *Best viewed:* Widespread, but uncommon during northern winter.

Finches

There are 13 species of finch in the Galápagos, collectively known as 'Darwin's finches'. No other group of birds, indeed no other group of animals, has had such a profound impact on the development of human thought and our understanding of our place in our world, than these little brown and black birds. When Charles Darwin visited the Galápagos in 1835, he collected specimens of the animals and plants that he encountered. Among these were specimens of these finches. Surprisingly, for someone who was normally so careful, he neglected to label them precisely. When he returned home to England to examine and catalogue his collection, he started to appreciate that these little birds were something rather special. They were what we now know to be one of the finest examples of adaptive radiation. Fortunately for Darwin, he was not the only person collecting on the 'Beagle'. Both Captain Fitzroy and the ship's surgeon, Simms Covington, had collected finches and had labelled them carefully.

As Darwin gradually came to appreciate the significance of the finches, he could see clearly that all these little brown birds were essentially similar. This has since been confirmed by DNA testing. Each species was fitted into its own particular ecological niche: the small, medium and large seed eaters, the nectar eaters, the fruit and insect eaters and, most surprising of all, the tool-using bird. All had developed from a common ancestor as a result of isolation and a relative lack of pressure from predators.

Today, it is easy for us to see how the finches of Galápagos, Darwin's finches, help to explain how life has developed and evolved. What is extraordinary, was that Charles Darwin should see this over 150 years ago without the benefit of the technology and facilities that we have today. So when you have the opportunity to observe these finches at first hand, make sure that you appreciate the role that they have played in the history of human thought.

There are 13 species of Darwin's finches. They are almost all identifiable by their beaks. Where this is not easy, identification can be by location: they tend to live on different islands, or inhabit different parts of the same island. In general, the males are dark brown or black and the females are mid-brown. On the whole, they have been unaffected by the arrival of man, though inevitably cats and rats affected their survival rate and breeding success. Also, the change of habitat in the highlands due to farming can have an impact on populations, for example of tree finches. The one species that is seriously threatened is the Mangrove Finch, owing to destruction of its habitat. The table opposite will help to identify them.

(e) Large Ground Finch *Geospiza magnirostris*

Much the largest (16.5 cm) of the ground finches, it is easily identified by its disproportionately large beak, which is as deep as it is long, and is ideally adapted for cracking large, hard seeds. It tends to be solitary in contrast to *G. fortis* which often feeds in small groups. The adult male is black with white or buff tips to undertail coverts. Female grey brown, paler underneath and streaked, especially on throat and breast.

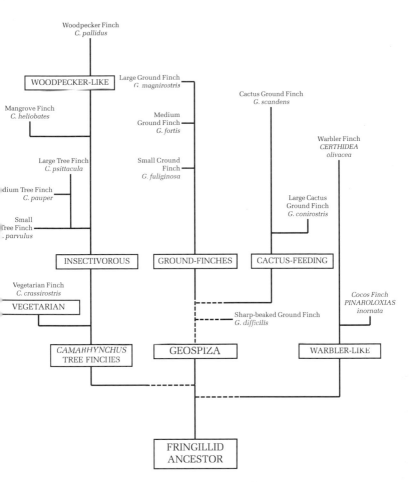

Woodpecker Finch
C. pallidus

WOODPECKER-LIKE

Large Ground Finch
G. magnirostris

Cactus Ground Finch
G. scandens

Mangrove Finch
C. heliobates

Medium
Ground Finch
G. fortis

Warbler Finch
*CERTHIDEA
olivacea*

Large Tree Finch
C. psittacula

Small Ground
Finch
G. fuliginosa

dium Tree Finch
C. pauper

Large Cactus
Ground Finch
G. conirostris

Small
Tree Finch
. parvulus

INSECTIVOROUS

GROUND-FINCHES

CACTUS-FEEDING

Vegetarian Finch
C. crassirostris

*Cocos Finch
PINAROLOXIAS
inornata*

VEGETARIAN

Sharp-beaked Ground Finch
G. difficilis

CAMARHYNCHUS
TREE FINCHES

GEOSPIZA

WARBLER-LIKE

FRINGILLID
ANCESTOR

Finch family tree (after Lack).

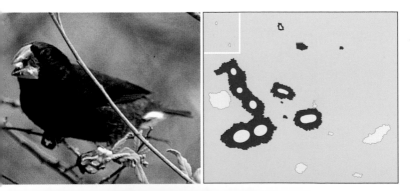

ⓔ Medium Ground Finch
Geospiza fortis

Intermediate in size (12.5 cm)
between the Large and Small
Ground Finches, it has a heavy bill
but one that is much more pointed than
the Large. The beak size varies considerably,
even on the same island. The plumage is
virtually identical to that of the Large
Ground Finch. It tends to feed in flocks rather
than individually. This species also feeds on the
ectoparasites of tortoises and iguanas. Very well
adapted to urban areas.

ⓔ Small Ground Finch *Geospiza fuliginosa*

The smallest (11.5 cm) of the ground finches.
Very similar in plumage to the Large and the
Medium Ground Finches but with a short
stubby beak. Can be confused with the
Sharp-billed Ground Finch, but it is
much commoner. Has developed an interesting
relationship with the reptiles, feeding off their
ectoparasites. The tortoises and iguanas will often raise
themselves up to make it easier for the finches to clean
their legpits and undersides.

ⓔ Sharp-beaked Ground Finch *Geospiza difficilis*

Similar to Small Ground Finch but larger (12.5 cm) and
with a sharper more pointed beak, however, overlap
of species only occurs in the highlands of
Santiago, Fernandina and Pinta. On
Darwin and Wolf the species has
developed an interesting feeding habit,
probably in response to a relative paucity of food
and moisture. It feeds on the bird lice found in the
feathers of the Masked Boobies that nest there, and
also pecks at the base of the back feathers until it draws
blood, and then drinks the blood. They are also known to roll booby eggs
out of the nest to break them and consume the contents. The Sharp-billed
will also feed on the ectoparasites of tortoises and iguanas. Some think that
the separate populations represent distinct races.

ⓔ Cactus Ground Finch
Geospiza scandens

One of the more easily recognisable
finches (14 cm), it has a longer, more downcurved
beak than the other ground finches and is frequently
seen feeding on the flowers of the Opuntia cactus. This
often leaves it with a dusting of yellow pollen on the
head. It also nests in the Opuntia rather than in trees and
shrubs. The plumage is similar to the other ground finches.

ⓔ Large Cactus Ground Finch
Geospiza conirostris

The Large Cactus Ground Finch (15 cm) has two distinct races or subspecies, one found on Española, the other on the northern islands of Genovesa, Darwin and Wolf. It is not found on the same islands as its smaller cousin, *G. scandens*, and the southern population has a much heavier beak than *G. scandens*, while the northern population has a similar but straighter beak. It is less specialised in feeding on Opuntia than *G. Scandens*.

ⓔ Vegetarian Finch *Platyspiza crassirostris*

One of the largest finches (16 cm) with a distinctive plumage. The adult male is all black with a pale or yellowish belly. However, many individuals have only the head and back black. The female is brown above, with an olive rump and whitish or yellowish underparts, with dark streaking on breast and sides. Found mainly in transitional and humid zones. Beak short, deep and broad.

ⓔ Large Tree Finch *Camarhynchus psittacula*

The largest (15 cm) of the tree finches, the adult male has a black head, breast, neck and part of the back, the rest of the upperparts are grey/brown, the underparts pale tinged with yellow. The female is grey-brown above with underparts pale or yellowish. The beak is quite distinctive: stout and with strongly curved upper and lower surfaces giving it a parrot-like appearance. Found mainly in the humid zone.

ⓔ Medium Tree Finch *Camarhynchus pauper*

A smaller tree finch (12 cm) with a more pointed beak than Large Tree Finch, this species is found only in the humid zone on Floreana. The adult male has the head, neck and upper breast black; the back and tail is olive green. The undersides are pale or yellowish. The female is olive-green above and pale yellowish below.

ⓔ Small Tree Finch *Camarhynchus parvulus*

The smallest (11 cm) of the tree finches, the adult
male has the head, neck and part of the back
black. The rest of the upperparts are grey and
the underparts pale yellowish. In common
with other tree finches, the adult male
plumage varies and some individuals have
only a black head and neck. The female is grey
brown with pale or yellowish underparts, sometimes
with the suggestion of a pale eye ring and a stripe
behind the eye. Found mainly in the Humid and Transitional Zones.

ⓔ Woodpecker Finch *Cactospiza pallidus*

Quite a large finch (18 cm). The plumage of the sexes
is similar with an olive or brown back and a
rather paler underside. The beak is
elongated but strong, curving down at
the end quite sharply. This is very
distinctive when birds are breeding as
the beak usually turns black, which
contrasts with the generally olive plumage.
Possibly the best known of all the finches due to its
habit of using a tool, generally a cactus spine or a twig
to dig beetle larvae out of rotten wood. Found mainly in
the Humid and Transitional Zones.

ⓔ Mangrove Finch *Cactospiza heliobates*

Very similar in appearance and size (14 cm) to the
Woodpecker Finch, the Mangrove Finch is the
most endangered of all the bird species in
Galápagos, It is restricted to the
mangrove swamps or forests of
southern Isabela which have been
considerably reduced by man. The
population is now down to some 40–50 pairs.
The sexes are similar having brown upperparts with
an olive rump and underparts pale with some spotting
on the breast. The beak is similar to the Woodpecker Finch but less heavy.
This species also uses tools to assist in its feeding.

ⓔ Warbler Finch *Certhidea olivacea*

Easily the smallest (10 cm) of the finches, for some
time there was disagreement about whether this
was a finch at all. It is now accepted as one.
The sexes are similar. The back is olive-
green to pale grey and the underparts
pale buff. Some adult males have an orange
throat patch. The beak is fine and warbler-like. It
can be confused with the Yellow Warbler, but is
smaller and lacks any yellow. It is the only one of the
finches with any real song. The calls of the other finches are a variety of
finchy noises but rarely melodic.

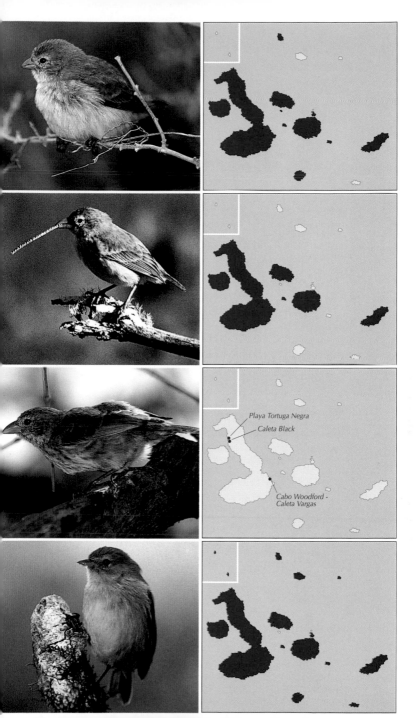

Playa Tortuga Negra

Caleta Black

Cabo Woodford -
Caleta Vargas

REPTILES

One of the most significant features of the wildlife of Galápagos is that the land animals are predominantly reptiles whereas in most of the world, mammals are dominant. Reptiles are dominant in Galápagos owing to the isolation of the islands. The only native land mammals are the rice rats and they are in severe danger of being wiped out by their larger cousin, *Rattus rattus*, the Brown or Ship Rat, introduced by man. It is generally accepted that the islands have never been connected to the mainland of South America, so all the native animals have had to make a crossing of at least 1,000 km from the continent, to reach the islands. Reptiles are much better equipped than most mammals for such a journey, owing to their ability to survive long periods without water. As a result, until the arrival of man, the reptiles of Galápagos were unchallenged and developed into the fascinating varieties that we can see today.

One of the early visitors to Galápagos remarked that the loudest noise inland in the Galápagos is a hiss! This is almost true, as none of the reptiles found there – tortoises, iguanas, lizards, geckos and snakes – makes any appreciable noise. However, the mating male tortoise does emit a rhythmical snoring or grunting noise which can be heard from quite some distance. For the most part, identifying the reptiles is a fairly straightforward job. The particular subspecies will, as a rule, be identified by location as much as by any distinctive features.

Tortoises

The islands are named after the tortoises. *Galápago* is an old Spanish word for 'saddle' and several of the species, especially on the low-lying islands, have carapaces (shells) shaped very much like a Spanish saddle. When Charles Darwin visited the islands in 1835, the Vice Governor, an Englishman by the name of Lawson, told him that he was able to tell which island a tortoise came from by the shape of its shell. This is largely true and was a factor that helped Darwin in developing his theory of evolution. The Galápagos tortoise populations are a good example of 'adaptive radiation'.

The tortoises can be divided into two groups:

- the saddleback tortoises, which live on generally low islands, Pinta, Pinzón and Española;
- the dome-shaped tortoises, which live on the larger higher islands where there is an extensive moist area.

It is generally accepted that the saddleback shell evolved in species needing to reach high up into the vegetation to feed, while the dome-shaped animals evolved by remaining at or near ground level where there was plenty of suitable food. In spite of their very distinct apparent differences, the two tortoises are considered as being a single species with 14 different varieties.

ⓔ Galápagos Giant Tortoise
Geochelone elephantophus

The estimated population is thought to be around 15,000 individuals. The Galápagos Giant Tortoise measures up to 1.5 m over the carapace and up to 250 kg in weight. There are thought to have been 14 races or subspecies of Galápagos tortoise before the arrival of man. However, three of them are either extinct or may never have existed. The surviving subspecies vary in numbers from the Pinta tortoise represented by 'Lonesome George', the last survivor (which now resides at the Charles Darwin Research Station (CDRS) in Puerto Ayora on Santa Cruz) to the Alcedo tortoise from the central volcano of Isabela, which numbers over 5,000.

The reproductive cycle is determined to a large extent by the climate. The dome-shaped tortoises inhabit islands with humid areas where they live for most of the year. Mating takes place towards the end of the warm season (March and April). Copulation, which may take several hours, is accompanied by loud snoring or grunting noises from the

male. The sound of mating tortoises is familiar to many researchers and National Park wardens. It is often described as the loudest noise in the Galápagos bush. The female then heads off to the lowlands where she locates a suitable area, generally with a reasonable depth of earth, digs a shallow pit up to 30-cm deep, and lays a clutch of up to 20 leathery eggs which look like large ping-pong balls. She then covers up the nest, urinates on it and tamps it down as an additional protection.

Incubation takes between 120 and 140 days and after struggling to the surface, the young tortoises hastily locate the nearest cover to escape their potential predators. These include herons, snakes, owls, hawks and, if those were not enough, several species introduced by man, viz. cats, rats and dogs.

We do not know the full life-span of the Galápagos Giant Tortoise, though it is thought to be at least 150 years. Most races reach sexual maturity at the age of 20–25 years. We do know that their rate of

growth is controlled by the availability of food, wet years producing faster growth. This is traceable by means of the rings on the individual scutes (plates) of the tortoise carapace or shell. One Isabela tortoise at the CDRS put on 175 kg in 15 years!

Many of the populations of tortoises have been badly affected by the activities of man.

The early buccaneers and whalers found them a handy source of fresh meat, as they would stay alive for long periods without water. They were also killed for the oil that is produced by rendering down their fat reserves. One race is known to be extinct, *G. e. galapagoensis* from Floreana. It is possible that species also existed on the islands of Fernandina, Santa Fé and Rábida. One live specimen was found on Fernandina in 1906, and another on Rábida by the same expedition. Skeletal

remains were found on Santa Fé, although it is known that tortoises were taken there by man. The taxonomy of the Galápagos Giant Tortoise is subject to considerable debate. It may also be referred to as

Geochelone nigra spp.

Best viewed: While there are still 11 subspecies of Galápagos tortoise, visitors are only likely to see the Santa Cruz, San Cristóbal and Alcedo tortoises in the wild. You may see others at the tortoise breeding centres in Puerto Ayora (Santa Cruz) and Villamil (Isabela).

TORTOISE	BEST VIEWED	ISABELA spp	BEST VIEWED
G. e. porteri	Santa Cruz	*G. e. vandenburgi*	V. Alcedo
G. e. Darwini	Santiago	*G. e. vicina*	V. Cerro Azul
G. e. ephippium	Pinzón	*G. e. guntheri*	V. Sierra Negra
G. e. chatamensis	San Cristóbal	*G. e. microphyes*	V. Darwin
G. e. hoodensis	Española	*G. e. becki*	V. Wolf
G. e. abingdoni	Pinta		

Isla Santa Cruz The population of dome-shaped tortoises *G. e. porteri* on Santa Cruz is the second largest in the islands. They have managed to live in harmony with the farmers who now farm much of their moist and humid habitat. Some farmers charge visitors to come onto their land to view tortoises, an excellent example of sustainable use of natural resources. There are some 3,000 tortoises on Santa Cruz, divided into two populations by an area of farmland. The one in the west is appreciably larger than the one in the east. Dogs, and to a lesser extent pigs and cats, are a threat to this race.

G. e. porteri

Isla Isabela There are five distinct races on the island of Isabela, each restricted to one of the five large-shield volcanoes. Each volcano is separated from the next by a lava flow, impassable to tortoises. This is an excellent example of species variation owing to topographical isolation. Since the volcanoes on Isabela have extensive moist areas, all the tortoises are essentially dome-shaped. There is, however, considerable variation and large elderly males may develop a more saddleback shape in some races. Early reports suggest saddleback tortoises were found on Volcan Wolf, but this has never been verified.

The species *G. e. vandenburgi* is found only on Volcan Alcedo, the middle and lowest volcano on Isabela. The tortoise is dome-shaped and this is the largest single population of tortoises in the islands, with over 5,000 individuals. The tortoises are found largely on the southern rim of the caldera, especially around an area of fumarolic activity where there are a number of shallow pools. Their survival in such numbers is severely threatened by the very large feral goat population. The goats appear to have crossed Perry Isthmus, which separates Alcedo from Sierra Negra, in 1969. The goat population is now in the region of 100,000. Plans are afoot to eliminate the feral goats, but this will take at least five years and may not be completely successful.

G. e. vandenburgi

Found only on Volcan Cerro Azul, the main population of *G. e. vicina* near Caleta Iguana, was virtually exterminated in the 1950s and 1960s owing to its living near to the coast. Since 1979, they have been bred in captivity by the CDRS. Numbers are now thought to be in the region of 700. Four were killed in the volcanic eruption of June 1998. Feral pigs and dogs are their main threat.

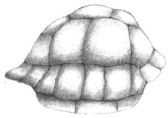

G .e. vicina

G. e. guntheri is found only on Volcan Sierra Negra and was previously one of the most numerous in the islands, but was reduced to perhaps 100–200 individuals by whalers around the end of the nineteenth century. The population has now recovered to over 2,000. Sierra Negra is the only inhabited volcano on Isabela and farmland divides the population into two. Feral pigs, dogs and cats are the main threat.

Volcan Darwin is a rather drier volcano than the others on Isabela because of the fact that it is lower than most and in the rain shadow of Volcan Alcedo. It is not surprising that the population of *G. e. microphyes* is smaller

G. e. guntheri

than on the other volcanoes, numbering
around 1,000 individuals. Cats and,
more recently, goats are the major
threat.

Being appreciably higher than its
neighbour Darwin, to the south, Volcan
Wolf has a rather larger moist and
humid area than its neighbour to the
south and the population size of
G. e. becki is uncertain. However, it may be

G. e. microphyes

in the region of 1,500 to 2,000 individuals. Owing to the nesting areas
being close to the coast at Punta Albermarle and Puerto Brava in Banks
Bay, this species is still suffering the predations of man. Cats and goats
are probably a lesser threat.

G. e. becki

G. e. darwini

Isla Santiago The Santiago
population of *G. e. darwini*, which
now stands at 500–700 tortoises, is
one that was seriously depleted by
man; Porter in 1815 recorded taking 14
tons (about 500 individuals) on one visit!
The Santiago race is of intermediate
dome–saddleback shell shape, with some
of the large males having quite saddlebacked
carapaces. Until recently, their breeding success has
been limited owing to the presence of feral pigs. The
pig population has now largely been removed and once the problem of
feral goats has been solved, the tortoise population should thrive.

Isla Pinzón This small island has very
rough terrain and virtually no moist or
humid region. The population of the
species *G. e. ephippium* was reduced
to only 120 old individuals by the
1950s, having failed to reproduce for
many years owing to predation on
the eggs and hatchlings by black rats
introduced to the island. Captive breeding
was started by the CDRS in 1965 and
the population is now some 500. The
problem of the black rats has not yet been solved.

G. e. ephippium

Isla San Cristóbal The original population of *G. e. chatamensis*, which
inhabited the southern end of San Cristóbal, is now extinct. There is a

G. e. chatamensis

second population of saddlebacks at the northern end, numbering up to 1,000 individuals. This may in fact be a separate race as it appears to be morphologically distinct from the specimen found at the south end of the island, by which the species was first described. Feral dogs and goats are its main threat.

Isla Española The Española race *G. e. hoodensis* has a very pronounced saddleback carapace. The survival of this race is a great conservation success. In 1964, the entire population consisted of only three males and twelve females. These were taken to the CDRS in 1965 and were the first Galápagos tortoises to be bred in captivity. In March 2000 the 1,000th young tortoise was returned to the island and with the eradication of feral goats on the island their future appears to be secure.

G. e. hoodensis

Isla Pinta

The smallest population of tortoises in the world belongs to *G. e. abingdoni*. Only one member of this saddleback race survives. 'Lonesome George' was discovered in 1971 and now lives – as its name suggests – a rather lonely but much observed life at the CDRS in Puerto Ayora, Santa Cruz. There appears to be no likelihood of finding him a mate, though it is possible that DNA research may identify a mate among the many unidentified Galápagos tortoises around the world.

G. e. abingdoni

Turtles

(r) (es?) Galápagos Green Turtle *Chelonia mydas agassisi*

By far the commonest species of turtle found in the Galápagos. It is thought to be a subspecies of the Pacific Green Turtle and the only turtle to breed in the islands. They spend most of their lives in shallow lagoons and waters around the islands, though they are frequently spotted in the open sea between the islands. The shell is generally dark green to black, but it does vary and can be an attractive yellow tortoiseshell colour.

The Green Turtle is almost entirely herbivorous. However, little work has been done on the Galápagos subspecies to confirm its feeding habits. Mating normally takes place in November and December and it is common to see a mating couple bobbing about offshore, the smaller male clinging to the larger female while another male waits his turn. The females come ashore at night, on sandy beaches from December to June, and having excavated a large pit with a smaller egg chamber at the bottom lay some 50–80 eggs at a time. The eggs are then covered up and left to incubate for about three months. A female may come ashore up to eight times over a two-week period. The temperature within the nest determines the sex of the hatchlings. Over 30°C, the young tend to be females; below 30°C they are more likely to be males.

Within the nest, the eggs may be attacked by a beetle, *Trox suberosus*. Once hatched, the young turtles are prey to everything from ghost crabs to sharks. They normally emerge at night; if they emerge during the day, few survive to make it to the water. Frigate birds, in particular, spot them as they come out of the nest, and pick them up with amazing precision.

(ro) Hawksbill Turtle *Eretmochelys imbricata bissa*

Appreciably smaller than the Galápagos Green Turtle, but with a much more amber-brown carapace, the source of 'tortoiseshell'. The plastron or underside of the turtle is yellow. Not common, but seen regularly. It is not easy to distinguish unless a good view is obtained. Size and colour are good indicators. The Hawksbill is omnivorous and its diet consists largely of seaweed, crabs, shellfish and jellyfish.

(oo) Leatherback Turtle *Dermochelys coriacea*

The largest turtle in the world, an average adult is 1.5m–1.8-m long and weighs up to 500 kg. The largest specimens are up to 2 m or more and weigh 600–700 kg. It can have a 'flipper span' of up to 3 m. In contrast to the other marine turtles, the Leatherback does not have a hard bony carapace but has tough leathery skin, characterised by longitudinal ridges. It is dark brown with white or yellow spotting, especially on the sides and flippers. Its size, ridges and carapace make it relatively easy to identify. It prefers the open sea more than other turtle species and feeds largely on jellyfish and other soft-bodied marine animals.

(oo) Olive Ridley Turtle *Lepidochelys olivacea*

The smallest turtle found in Galápagos, the Olive Ridley grows to little more than 75 cm in length and has an olive-green carapace. These are its two most distinctive features. Like all marine turtles, it is found throughout the tropics, but is not known to breed in Galápagos.

Lizards

ⓔ Marine Iguana *Amblyrhynchus cristatus*

The Galápagos Marine Iguana is the world's only sea-going lizard, and is found on all of the main islands. There are seven races or subspecies which vary considerably in size and colour from island to island. The ones on Española are the most brightly coloured. Northern Isabela boasts the largest (up to 1.3 m in length) and Genovesa the smallest (up to 75 cm in length). The males are larger and more brightly and distinctively coloured than the females. They are largely black or dark grey. However, the males take on a red or red-green tinge during the mating season. This is particularly evident in the Española race. Some races look to have lichens growing on them, such are the variations in their skin colour. Marine Iguanas have a pronounced crest which is most prominent on the head but runs all the way down their back and tail.

Because it is ectothermic, or cold-blooded, and yet feeds in the cool waters of the Humboldt and Cromwell currents, it must warm up by basking in the sun on the black lava rocks, both before and after feeding trips. To avoid overheating, which would occur if its body temperature exceeded 35°C, it varies its position in relation to the sun, often facing directly into it to reduce its exposure.

The Marine Iguana lives largely on land but feeds inshore and in the intertidal zone at depths of up to about 10 m. It feeds almost entirely on red and green algae but is also known to consume its own faeces as well as those of sea lions and crabs. This diet results in a high intake of salt. To eliminate this excess of salt, they spit out brine through their nostrils. This snorting is the only noise that they make.

The Marine Iguana can remain submerged for 10 minutes or more. It does not generally venture more than 50 m offshore. During a strong El Niño, when its food supply is severely affected, the population can suffer a very severe drop.

The timing of the mating season varies on different islands but generally starts in December to January, with egg-laying towards the end of the warm season, March and April. The female excavates a nest in the sand, a burrow up to 1-m long, then lays a clutch of up to four leathery elongated eggs, which take between three and four months to incubate. The young are 10-cm long when they emerge and almost entirely black. They are very vulnerable to predation by frigatebirds, herons, hawks and snakes as well as feral cats and dogs on land, and by moray eels and other predators in the water. Survival is quite an achievement. Once they are mature, their only real enemies are hawks and feral cats and dogs.
Best viewed: Common throughout the islands on rocky coasts and cliffs.

SUBSPECIES	ISLANDS	CHARACTERISTICS
A. c. cristatus (1, 3, 4)	Fernandina	The first three races form a closely related group in the central and western islands
A. c. hassi (2)	Santa Cruz	
A. c. albemarlensis (5, 6)	Isabela	Largest in size
A. c. mertensi (7)	San Cristóbal; Santiago	
A. c. sielmanni	Pinta	
A. c. venustissimus (8, 9)	Española	Most brightly coloured
A. c. nanus (10, 11)	Genovesa	Very small, dark colour

Note: numbers relate to photograph positions as indicated by the symbol on the left.

ⓔ Land Iguana *Conolophus subcristatus*

There are two species of land iguana in the Galápagos: *C. subcristatus* is the more widespread while *C. pallidus* is found only on Santa Fé. They number between 5,000 and 10,000 individuals, and measure up to 1 m in length and 13 kg in weight. They live in small colonies, in marked contrast to when Darwin visited the islands in 1835 and had trouble pitching his tent owing to the number of iguana burrows! Evidence from the Seymour population indicates that the normal lifespan is over 60 years. The reduction in population is most probably the result of predation by man and introduced animals such as dogs, pigs, cats and rats. Land Iguanas vary in colour but are generally a pale to dark yellow, occasionally coming close to ochre. On some islands, the colonies are restricted to suitable isolated habitats such as Cerro Dragon on Santa Cruz, an old tuff cone (rock formed from volcanic ash) which makes it easy for the iguana to excavate burrows for egg-laying. Elsewhere they are more widespread. On some islands such as Fernandina, the females make long journeys to the nesting zones, some of which are within the caldera and constitute a major challenge for the hatchlings when they appear. The colony on Seymour was introduced from Baltra in the 1930s. The Baltra population subsequently became extinct during the period that the island was used as a military base by US forces during and after the Second World War. Recently, individuals have been reintroduced to Baltra from Seymour, an interesting example of accidental conservation.

Adult Land Iguanas feed mainly on pads and fruit from the Opuntia cactus, but they also eat other plants and insects. Young iguanas, in contrast, feed mainly on insects and other arthropods, and become largely vegetarian as they mature. They have even been observed taking finch nestlings.

The reproductive cycle of the Land Iguana is linked to climate, like the Marine Iguana. Mating takes place towards the end of the year, with egg-laying in January to March. Mating is a fairly violent affair with the male seizing a receptive female by the back of the neck prior to copulation. The young face the same formidable range of predators as the Marine Iguana on land, but do not have the added threat of marine predators. They are though fewer in number than the Marine Iguana. This may be a result of a more restricted habitat, but is more probably owing to predation by man and introduced species such as feral pigs, dogs and cats.
Best viewed: South Plaza; Santa Cruz – Cerro Dragon; Seymour.

ⓔ Santa Fé Land Iguana *Conolophus pallidus*

This species is found only on the island of Santa Fé. It is similar to *C. subcristatus* though the males tend to be more brightly coloured and have more pronounced crests.
Best viewed: Santa Fé – Barrington Bay.

ⓔ Hybrid Iguana

Marine and Land Iguana do hybridise from time to time. The result, interestingly, looks like what might be presumed to be the mainland ancestor of both. It is dark skinned with regular bands of paler markings. The spinal crest is much smaller and the feet are somewhat webbed. The head more resembles the marine parent than the terrestrial one, but it feeds on cactus pads rather than seaweed! It is likely that the hybrid is sterile.

(e) Lava Lizard *Microlophus* spp.

There are seven species of the genus *Microlophus* in the Galápagos. They are found on all the major islands apart from Genovesa.
M. albemarlensis is found on ten islands in the centre and west of the archipelago, while the six other species are island specific and apart from *M. duncanensis* on Pinzón, are found on the outer and eastern islands.

Identifying a Lava Lizard is straightforward. The only possible confusion would be with a very young Marine or Land Iguana or a gecko. Iguanas are more heavily built, especially around the head. Marine Iguanas are much darker than most Lava Lizards, except for those on Fernandina, and Land Iguanas are much paler than almost all Lava Lizards. The palest Lava Lizards are much smaller than recently hatched Land Iguanas. The native geckos are smaller than adult Lava Lizards, paler in colour and are nocturnal. The introduced geckos are a similar size to Lava Lizards, but paler and with wider and flatter heads. They are also nocturnal.

Male and female Lava Lizards are quite distinct. The male is generally much larger (15–20-cm, exceptionally 30-cm, long) and has rougher and more patterned skin, with a very distinct spinal crest. He has a clearly visible black or yellow throat. The female is smaller (12–18-cm long) and smoother with a less patterned skin and a red or orange throat; this is often very bright and distinctive. Males in particular are often to be seen displaying (doing 'push-ups') on the top of rocks or National Park trail markers! You can, however, note considerable variations in the size and colour of *M. albemarlensis* on the ten islands it inhabits. This may be associated with the local geology and vegetation. Those on Fernandina (black lava) tend to be darker and smaller than those on Santa Cruz (where there is little black lava).

Lava Lizards are omnivorous, eating mainly insects and some plant food, especially in the dry season. On Bartolomé, the flowers of *Tiquila* are an important source of food. Cannibalism is not unknown. Their chief predators are hawks, snakes, herons, centipedes and mockingbirds.

Breeding takes place mainly in the warm season with clutches of three to six eggs being laid in deep burrows. Several females may use the same area and each female may lay several clutches three or four weeks apart. The eggs take about three months to hatch and the young are only 3–4-cm long. They are very hard to find. Females take only nine months to reach sexual maturity, while males take three years.
Best viewed: On all major islands, except Genovesa, mainly in lowlands.

SPECIES	BEST VIEWED
M. albemarlensis (3, 4, 5, 6)	Isabela, Santa Cruz, Fernandina, Santiago, Baltra, Santa Fé, Rábida, Seymour, Daphne Major and Plaza Sur
M. bivittatus (7, 8, 10)	San Cristóbal
M. grayi (1, 2, 12)	Floreana
M. habellii	Marchena
M. delanonis (9, 11)	Española
M. duncanensis	Pinzón
M. pacificus	Pinta

Note: numbers relate to photograph positions as indicated by the symbol on the left.

Geckos

There are six endemic species of gecko in Galápagos and three introduced species. The endemic species can be identified by location, though *P. leei* has been identified at Villamil on Isabela. The introduced species are all larger than the endemic species.

ⓔ Galápagos Leaf-toed Gecko *Phyllodactylus galapagoensis*

Grows to 50 mm. Pale creamy brown with darker blotches and markings. Often seen without a tail which can be regenerated. Geckos have pads on their toes covered in microscopic hairs, which enable then to climb vertical surfaces, even glass, or walk on the ceiling. They are nocturnal and largely insectivorous, though they do eat their own discarded skin. Widespread but infrequently seen except in inhabited areas where they are often found in houses.

ⓔ San Cristóbal Leaf-toed Gecko *Phyllodactylus leei*

Darker than *P. galapagoensis* and smaller; found only on San Cristóbal. Breeding in both species is in October and November. A single egg is laid under a rock or dead tree, sometimes in a tree. The same nest may be used by several females on different occasions. The young have to fend for themselves from hatching.

ⓘ *Phyllodactylus reissi*

This species is a native of Ecuador and is widespread in the coastal areas in and around Guayaquil from where most freight for Galápagos originates. It was first reported in Puerto Ayora in 1979. It is a pale greyish colour with indistinct, irregular and diffuse darker spots or blotches. The belly is pale yellow or whitish. At 75 mm, it is much larger than the native and endemic geckos. Anecdotal evidence points to it spreading and supplanting the endemic *P. galapagoensis*, at least in Puerto Ayora.

ⓘ *Lepidodactylus lugubris*

Originally from South-East Asia, this species arrived in Galápagos via Ecuador. It is similar in size to the native and endemic species and has been reported from both Santa Cruz and San Cristóbal.

ⓘ *Gonatodes caudiscutatus*

A native of western Ecuador, this recently arrived gecko has so far been reported only from Puerto Baquerizo Moreno on San Cristóbal.

GECKO	STATUS	BEST VIEWED
P. leei	Endemic	San Cristóbal
P. gilberti	Endemic	Wolf
P. barringtonensis	Endemic	Santa Fé
P. galapagoensis	Endemic	Isabela, Santa Cruz, Fernandina, Santiago
P. bauri	Endemic	Floreana, Pinta
P. tuberculosus	Endemic	San Cristóbal
P. reissi	Introduced	Santa Cruz
L. lugubris	Introduced	Santa Cruz, San Cristóbal
G. caudiscutatus	Introduced	San Cristóbal

Snakes

There are four species of snake found in Galápagos. They are all endemic and are found in the Coastal and Arid Zones. They feed on Lava Lizards, geckos, grasshoppers, young iguanas and rats. They also prey on young finch and mockingbird nestlings. They are constrictors and so not poisonous and are not at all aggressive. Little is known of the reproductive process of these reptiles, but it is probably like that of similar species elsewhere in the world.

ⓔ Hood Racer *Philodryas hoodensis*

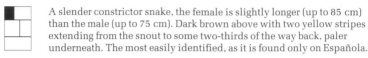

A slender constrictor snake, the female is slightly longer (up to 85 cm) than the male (up to 75 cm). Dark brown above with two yellow stripes extending from the snout to some two-thirds of the way back, paler underneath. The most easily identified, as it is found only on Española.

ⓔ Banded Galápagos Snake *Antillophis slevini*

Clearly identifiable as it is banded rather than striped, with bands of dark brown and pale creamy-yellow virtually the whole length of the body. The smallest snake in the islands with males up to 52 cm and females up to 42 cm. Found only on Fernandina, Isabela and Pinzón.
Best viewed: Fernandina – Punta Espinosa; Isabela – Punta Moreno, Tagus Cove, Urvina Bay; Pinzón.

ⓔ Striped Galápagos Snake *Antillophis steindachneri*

A small snake but slightly larger than *A. slevini* with males up to 61 cm and females up to 54 cm. Dark brown with two clear pale creamy-yellow stripes along the back, starting from the back of the head and extending to the tail. Found only on Baltra, Seymour, Rábida, Santiago and Santa Cruz.
Best viewed: Seymour; Rábida; Santiago – Sullivan Bay, Puerto Egas; Santa Cruz – Tortuga Bay.

ⓔ Galápagos Racer *Alsophis biseralis*

This species is divided into three subspecies. They are all appreciably longer than the other three endemic snakes and are generally dark brown with usually a striped pattern, but are often also spotted. They can be distinguished by location:

Eastern Galápagos Racer *A. b. biseralis*: male to 80 cm, female to 85 cm, found only on Floreana and San Cristóbal

Central Galápagos Racer *A. b. dorsalis*: male to 102 cm, female to 95 cm, very variable in pattern, often pale with dark irregular spots over entire dorsal area. Found on Baltra, Bartolomé, Rábida, Santa Cruz, Santa Fé and Santiago.

Western Galápagos Racer *A. b. occidentalis*: the longest snake in Galápagos with males up to 125 cm and females to 110 cm. Much darker than the other two subspecies and spotted or almost banded in appearance. Found only on Isabela and Fernandina.

AQUATIC MAMMALS

Excluding whales, there have only ever been 14 species of native mammals (sea and land) in Galápagos and eight of these are rice rats, of which five are now extinct.

Of the other six species, two are dolphins, two bats and the others are the fur seal and sea lion. This paucity of mammals is clearly the result of the isolation of the islands and the fact that mammals are far less well adapted to endure the rigours of a 1,000-km or more crossing from the mainland of South and Central America. Nevertheless, the most enduring image that many visitors take home with them is that of the Galápagos Sea Lion, which is found throughout the archipelago.

(n) Galápagos Sea Lion *Zalophus californianus wollebacki*

1	2
3	
4	5
6	

1 Male
2 Female
3 Harem
4 Group resting
5 Female and pup
6 Pup suckling

A subspecies of the California Sea Lion, the Galápagos Sea Lion is the largest animal found on land in the islands. While the normal population is estimated to be around 50,000, this can be severely reduced by a major El Niño event which seriously affects their food supply. The species also suffers from a virus known as 'sea lion pox', which is thought to be transmitted by mosquitoes. An epidemic of this pox erupts from time to time but does not appear to be a real threat to the species. They live very largely on fish and can be found out to sea, anywhere around the islands. As a rule they prefer sandy beaches. They are very well adapted to humans and frequently have to be removed from the small landing stages and docks found at many visiting sites or in the island ports. Male or bull sea lions, which are easily distinguished from the females by their larger size (up to 250 kg) and distinctive bump on the head, have well-defined territories that they guard jealously, especially during the mating season.

The mating season varies from island to island but is generally between June and September. A dominant bull will have a territory often consisting of a beach or bay, which will include a group of cows, immature sea lions and pups, loosely referred to as a 'harem'. While sea lions are generally very approachable, care should be taken with the bulls, which are naturally more aggressive than the cows and which should definitely be avoided during the mating season. It is not for nothing that they are referred to as 'beachmasters'. Successful males guard their territory jealously from other males, fights are frequent and can be quite bloody. The harem may consist of only a few cows or may be very much larger, up to thirty or so. The barking of the patrolling bull sea lion is one of the enduring sounds of Galápagos.

Mating normally takes place in the water and within four weeks of the cow giving birth, but owing to 'delayed implantation' the egg is not actually implanted in the womb for two months, thus allowing for an annual cycle. Gestation takes about nine months and the single pup grows rapidly on a diet of the mother's very rich milk. The pups start fishing for themselves at about five months; in the meantime they stay in the nursery with the other young and are only allowed to swim and play in the shallow water, often with human visitors. They show a total lack of fear of humans, often climbing into dinghies or onto a ship's boarding platform, or even onto the deck.

Identifying features: Largest land animal on the islands. Male is much larger than the female and has a distinctive bump on the head. Larger than a fur seal and has a longer snout.

Best viewed: Widespread on the coast throughout the archipelago.

(e) Galápagos Fur Seal *Arctocephalus galapagoensis*

The Galápagos Fur Seal, like the Galápagos Sea Lion is not a true seal (family Phocidae). It is technically a 'fur sea lion'. Both the fur seal and the sea lion have small but visible ears and use their front flippers for swimming. Indeed, they seem to 'fly' through the water using their flippers like a bird uses its wings. The fur seal is easily distinguished from the sea lion by its smaller size and much shorter snout, giving their head a rather bear like appearance, hence its Latin name, *Arcto* = bear, *cephalus* = head.

The exact population of fur seals is unknown, in part because they are far more difficult to count than sea lions owing to their preferred resting places, but it is thought to number about 25,000. They are found almost entirely on rocky shores where there is deep water immediately offshore. Sea lions on the other hand, owing to their size, coat and diet, enjoy sandy beaches and shallower water. Fur seals being appreciably smaller than sea lions are much more able to clamber up steep rocky shores. The very bulk of adult sea lions makes this much more difficult. The thick coat of fur seals means that they prefer to lie in the shade rather than the full sun. Their feeding requirements also dictate a different location. Squid are found in deeper waters, so fur seals are generally found around the outer shores of the archipelago rather than in the middle.

Fur seals feed on fish and squid, diving to depths of up to 100 m. They hunt mainly at night. This is partly because it is the time when the squid come closer to the surface and partly because they are less likely to be attacked by sharks at night. Fur seals fish much less when the moon is full; this is, again, thought to be linked to the availability of food and the likelihood of attack from sharks. It is quite common to see scars from shark attacks on both sea lions and fur seals.

The breeding season is from August to November with mating taking place during this period. If a cow has just given birth she will mate immediately, but owing to 'delayed implantation', fertilisation of the egg will not take place for another couple of months. She will probably not give birth the following year. Pups are suckled for two or three years and cows generally manage to raise at best one pup every two years. In contrast, sea lions frequently raise a pup each year.

Fur seals were hunted almost to extinction during the nineteenth century because of their valuable fur. They have made a remarkable comeback and are now a great deal more common than even thirty years ago. They are not currently under threat but would be if their food source were to be overfished.

Identifying features: Smaller than the sea lion and with a shorter snout. The head is bear-like.

Best viewed: Always on rocky costs, never on sandy beaches.

CETACEANS – Whales and Dolphins

Cetaceans, an order of entirely aquatic mammals, is divided into two major groups. The baleen whales include most of the larger species and feed on plankton and other small marine animals. The toothed whales, which include the large Sperm Whale and all the dolphins and porpoises, feed on fish, squid, other cetaceans and marine mammals, such as sea lions and fur seals.

Some 24 species of whale and dolphin have been recorded in Galápagos, and it is almost certain that other species are present from time to time, but identification is difficult and often impossible. Most visitors will see at least one species, the Bottlenose Dolphin, and if you are observant, especially on the longer passages between the islands, and to the west of Isabela, you may well see other species. The best identifier for the larger baleen whales is the shape of their 'spout', and species such as the Humpback, Sperm and the Orca, have distinctive features that make identification relatively easy. The illustrations here should help you if you are fortunate enough to get a good view. The precise status within the islands of most species is uncertain, and so they are marked with the periodicity of viewing. None is known, or likely, to be endemic, but the commonest dolphins and the Orca are probably resident in the islands.

Baleen Whales

(oo) Sei Whale *Balaenoptera borealis*

A very large baleen whale. It has a dark steel grey back with the pleated throat and chest being appreciably paler. The Sei (pronounced 'say') feeds quite close to the surface and when it 'blows' it does not arch its back appreciably or show its flukes, giving the whale a very gentle appearance and disappearance. Most easily confused with the Blue and Bryde's Whales. It is much smaller than the Blue, and does not arch its back as much as Bryde's.
Size: Males 15–18 m; females 16–20 m.
Weight: 12–29 tons.
Identifying features: Notice the slow, gentle blow, with gently arched back, no roll and flukes never shown. The spout is an inverted cone up to 3-m high. It has a single ridge on the head, and a uniformly dark appearance. The fin is up to 60-cm high and strongly hooked.

(ro) Bryde's Whale *Balaenoptera edeni*

Also known as the Tropical Whale. Very similar in shape and form to the Sei, Bryde's (pronounced *bree-dahs*) is smaller and less muscular. It is a deep diver and often shows the head on surfacing, followed by a distinctly arched roll of the back. The head has three distinctive ridges and the back is blue-grey compared to the Sei's steel grey. This whale is known to approach boats and is the baleen whale that you are most likely to see.
Size: Males 12–14 m; females 13–15 m.
Weight: 12–20 tons.
Identifying features: Faster blow with a distinctly arched back. The flukes are rarely shown, but it has a tendency to roll on re-entry. The fin is up to 45-cm long and quite pointed. The spout is narrow, up to 4-m high. Three ridges on the head are diagnostic if you get a good view.

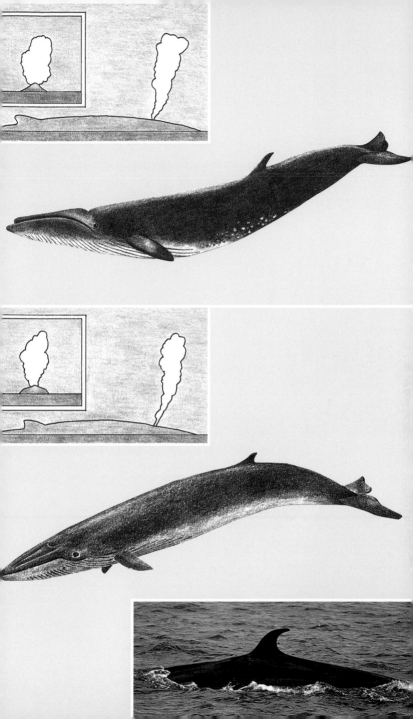

⓸ Minke Whale *Balaenoptera acutorostrata*

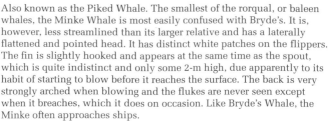

Also known as the Piked Whale. The smallest of the rorqual, or baleen whales, the Minke Whale is most easily confused with Bryde's. It is, however, less streamlined than its larger relative and has a laterally flattened and pointed head. It has distinct white patches on the flippers. The fin is slightly hooked and appears at the same time as the spout, which is quite indistinct and only some 2-m high, due apparently to its habit of starting to blow before it reaches the surface. The back is very strongly arched when blowing and the flukes are never seen except when it breaches, which it does on occasion. Like Bryde's Whale, the Minke often approaches ships.
Size: Males 8–9.5 m; females 8–10.2 m.
Weight: 6–9 tons.
Identifying features: Small size and pointed head with one central ridge. The fin appears at the same time as a minimal spout. White patches on the flippers. Back strongly arched when diving; fins and flukes never show except when breaching.

⓸ Humpback Whale *Megaptera novaeangliae*

This is the most easily identified of the baleen whales. It has a broad rounded head with a string of fleshy tubercles or knobs in place of the median ridge and further rows of knobs, all of which have protruding hairs, along each edge of the jaw. The body is blackish with white throat grooves. It is heavily built and narrows rapidly to the tail. The flippers are very large, up to 5-m long, mottled black on top and white underneath, and are heavily scalloped along the trailing edge. The spout is distinctively a broad bushy balloon up to 3-m high. The fin is short and squared and appears only as the body humps up to dive down. Most distinctively, the tail flukes, which are white underneath and also heavily scalloped on the trailing edge, are raised clear of the water on sounding or diving. The Humpback also frequently breaches, leaping clear of the water; this is also known as 'sky hopping'. While this species does not normally actively approach ships, it does not appear to object to being approached by ships or small boats.
Size: Males 14.5–17.5 m; females 15–19 m.
Weight: 30–48 tons.
Identifying features: Knobbly head, humped back, square fin, long flippers with white undersides. Shows flukes when diving. Spout, broad and bushy to a height of 3 m.

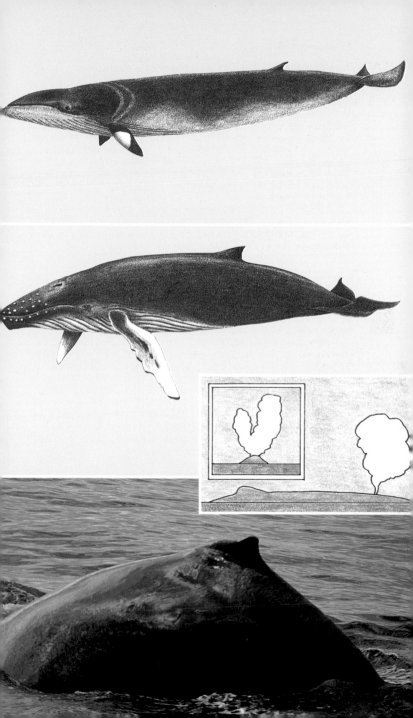

Toothed Whales

(ro) Sperm Whale *Physeter macrocephalus*

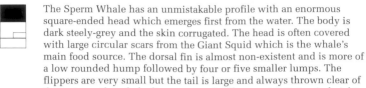

The Sperm Whale has an unmistakable profile with an enormous square-ended head which emerges first from the water. The body is dark steely-grey and the skin corrugated. The head is often covered with large circular scars from the Giant Squid which is the whale's main food source. The dorsal fin is almost non-existent and is more of a low rounded hump followed by four or five smaller lumps. The flippers are very small but the tail is large and always thrown clear of the water as the whale dives or sounds. The spout is 3–5 m in height and is directed forward at an angle of 45° and to the left as the blowhole is located on the front of the head and is offset from the median line.

Size: Males 15–20 m; females 11–17 m.
Weight: Males 36–38 tons; females 20–30 tons.
Identifying features: Large square head, angled spout, minimal dorsal fin, humped back and flukes clear of water on sounding.

(ro) (pr) Orca *Orcinus orca*

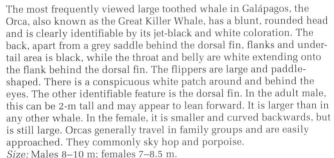

The most frequently viewed large toothed whale in Galápagos, the Orca, also known as the Great Killer Whale, has a blunt, rounded head and is clearly identifiable by its jet-black and white coloration. The back, apart from a grey saddle behind the dorsal fin, flanks and under-tail area is black, while the throat and belly are white extending onto the flank behind the dorsal fin. The flippers are large and paddle-shaped. There is a conspicuous white patch around and behind the eyes. The other identifiable feature is the dorsal fin. In the adult male, this can be 2-m tall and may appear to lean forward. It is larger than in any other whale. In the female, it is smaller and curved backwards, but is still large. Orcas generally travel in family groups and are easily approached. They commonly sky hop and porpoise.

Size: Males 8–10 m; females 7–8.5 m.
Weight: Males up to 7 tons; females up to 4.5 tons.
Identifiable features: Black-and-white coloration; large dorsal fin.

(ro) (pr) Shortfin Pilot Whale *Globicephala macrorhynchus*

Also known as Pacific Pilot Whale. Often seen in groups of up to 30 or 40 individuals cruising on the surface, this is the only pilot whale found in Galápagos. Shorter and much slimmer than the Orca, it is almost all black apart from a grey anchor-shaped blaze on the belly which is hard to see. The head is round and melon-shaped and is clearly visible every time the whale breathes. The dorsal fin is long, rounded and back-curving. They are indifferent to ships and are often seen in the company of Bottlenose or Common Dolphins.

Size: Male 5.5–6.75 m; females 4.25–5 m.
Weight: Male up to 3 tons; females up to 1.5 tons.
Identifying features: All black, rounded head, long back-curving dorsal fin; travel in large groups often cruising on the surface.

(ro) (pr) Bottlenose Dolphin *Tursiops truncatus*

The Bottlenose, the most commonly observed dolphin in Galápagos, frequently rides the bow wave of ships and yachts. It is mid-grey on the back and paler underneath. Its name stems from the short (7–8 cm) beak. The dorsal fin is 15–20-cm high and strongly back curved. Bottlenose Dolphins generally travel in groups, often 20 or 30 strong, and often school with Common Dolphins and Shortfin Pilot Whales. They frequently leap well clear of the water, sometimes landing noisily on their sides. This may be a means of ridding themselves of ectoparasites. They are quite often seen with large remora or sucker fish attached to their flanks.
Size: 3–4.2 m. Males slightly larger than females.
Weight: 200–300 kg. Exceptionally to 650 kg.
Identifying features: Colouring, short beak, large back-curved dorsal fin and habit of playing around ships and riding the bow wave.

(ro) Common Dolphin *Delphinus delphis*

Very much smaller and sleeker than the Bottlenose, the Common Dolphin has a dark-grey back and undertail. The underside is largely white, but there is an elaborate pattern of pale grey and buff on the flanks, which varies with individuals but generally has an hourglass appearance. A dark stripe runs forward from the flipper to the chin. The dorsal fin is large but more upright than the Bottlenose and more pointed than the Striped. The beak is longer than the Bottlenose. Common Dolphin also enjoy riding the bow wave of ships and travel in large groups, often of several hundred individuals.
Size: 2.1–2.6 m.
Weight: 80–135 kg.
Identifying features: Buff and grey flank markings, long beak, upright dorsal fin, small size, speed and manoeuvrability.

(ro) Striped Dolphin *Stenella coeruleoalba*

Slightly larger than the Common Dolphin, but smaller than the Bottlenose. The Striped Dolphin is the least common of the three and rarely bow-rides. It is darkish brown on the back with very varied flank markings, but always has a dark line from the eye, along the flank to the anus. The underside is largely white. The beak is shorter than the Common Dolphin, but in both species it is always dark. It is best distinguished from the Common by its more rounded dorsal fin and the fact that the dark line running forward from the flipper is to the eye and not the chin. It is also distinguished by its reluctance to bow-ride.
Size: 2.4–3 m.
Weight: 100–130 kg.
Identifying features: Rounded dorsal fin, black lateral line, black line from eye to flipper.

(ro) Risso's Dolphin *Grampus griseus*

Mid-grey above and with a bulging forehead and short head. It has a tall slightly curved dorsal fin. The skin is distinctively scratched and scarred.
Size: 2.6–3.8 m
Weight: 300–500 kg.
Identifying features: Grey scarred skin, bulging forehead and tall dorsal fin.

LAND MAMMALS
Rats

The isolation of Galápagos has ensured that only one family of terrestrial mammal has ever made it to the islands of its own accord. The Galápagos Rice Rat holds the world record for sea crossings by terrestrial mammals.

Of the probable eight different species of rice rat, only two, possibly three, now remain. Apart from *M. curiori* the others appear to have been forced to extinction by the arrival of humans and their ever-present companion, *Rattus rattus*, the Black or Ship Rat!

(ip) Black or Ship Rat *Rattus rattus*

An ever-present companion of man, it can be either dark black-brown or mid-brown (photo below left). The tail is appreciably longer than the body. A widespread pest and disease carrier.

(ip) Brown Rat *Rattus norvegicus*

A more recent arrival in Galápagos, but more aggressive than the Black Rat. It is larger, with pale brown fur, lighter underneath (photo below right). Distinguished from Black Rat by the tail which is shorter than the overall body length. It is a serious threat to the biodiversity of the islands.

(e) Galápagos Rice Rat *Oryzomys bauri*

Small (10 cm), long, brown rat with black bulging eyes and bat-shaped ears. They are fearless and are easily observed on Santa Fé where they are particularly in evidence towards sunset. The population has burgeoned since the goats were removed in the late 1960s. This resulted in a remarkable re-growth of the native vegetation and a corresponding increase in habitats for the rats. They live mainly in holes in the ground and under rocks, but can also be found in the giant Opuntia cacti. They are omnivorous, feeding on seeds and small insects, probably also on carrion. Breeding is generally restricted to the warm season between December and April. Up to four young are raised.
Best viewed: Santa Fé.

(e) Fernandina Rice Rat *Nesoryzomys narboroughii*

Virtually indistinguishable from the Galápagos Rice Rat on Santa Fé, it is easily identified simply by it being on Fernandina.
Best viewed: Fernandina.

(e) Darwin's Rice Rat *Nesoryzomys fernandinae*

This species has recently been identified from fragments of skeleton found in the droppings of owls on Fernandina, an island that is very largely covered in relatively recent lava, so that the vegetation is in 'islands'. It is quite possible that these two species have developed in isolation on these islands of vegetation.

ⓔ Giant Galápagos Rice Rat *Megaoryzomys curiori*

This rat has been identified from sub-fossil remains that are at least 100,000 years old. We have no further details or records! The other extinct species of rice rat are: *O. swarthi* (Santiago); *O. galapagoensis* (San Cristóbal); *O. indefessus* (Santa Cruz); *O. darwini* (Santa Cruz).

Bats

ⓔ Galápagos Bat *Lasiurus brachyotis*

The Galápagos Bat is most closely related to the Red Bat (*L. borealis*) of South America and is locally abundant on Santa Cruz and San Cristóbal where it is found in both the highlands and lowlands. It roosts in mangroves or other dense shrubs during the daytime. It is smaller than the Hoary Bat. It is entirely insectivorous and feeds generally within 8 m of the ground, between dusk and sunrise. Little is known of its further distribution in the islands or of its biology.
Best viewed: Santa Cruz – Puerto Ayora; San Cristóbal – Puerto Baquerizo.

ⓝ Hoary Bat *Lasiurus cinerius*

The Hoary Bat is widespread in North America. It has attractive red-brown fur with white tips and a buff-coloured throat. It is found on both Santa Cruz and San Cristóbal. It can be easily distinguished from the Galápagos Bat with a bat detector as their calls are quite distinct! During the day, it is most likely to be found hanging in mangroves or occasionally in caves. This bat is insectivorous, but feeds more than 8 m above the ground. It is not known to breed in the islands, but may well do so.
Best viewed: Santa Cruz – Puerto Ayora; San Cristóbal – Puerto Baquerizo.

INVERTEBRATES

Galápagos, being oceanic islands, has relatively few species of higher animals. The same is true of the invertebrates. We have a reasonable degree of knowledge about the higher animals, albeit with some surprising gaps, but our knowledge of the invertebrate life of the islands is very patchy indeed, much of it derived from the various large expeditions that visited the islands at the end of the nineteenth and in the first part of the twentieth century. It is only now that the Charles Darwin Research Station is working on producing more comprehensive papers on the various families of invertebrates found in Galápagos.

Boats at Puerto Ayora. Boats are the main source of introduced invertebrate species.

By their very nature, being very small, you will not see many invertebrates unless they bite or annoy you. There are, for example, 202 species of oribatid mites currently known to exist in Galápagos (Schatz 1998), but you are unlikely to see any of them unless you have a microscope with you. This guide will not therefore seek to attempt to illustrate more than a very small percentage of the nearly 2,500 known species of terrestrial and freshwater invertebrates found in Galápagos. There are many more species to be discovered here. It is sadly true that many species have already become extinct, largely due to the activities of humans, and more will follow. This is a particularly damaging loss as probably more than 50 per cent of all invertebrate species found in the islands are endemic.

INSECTS

Two-thirds of invertebrates found in Galápagos are insects (over 1,700 species). However, only a small percentage of these are likely to be seen, and fewer still will be identified by the casual visitor. Many of the species

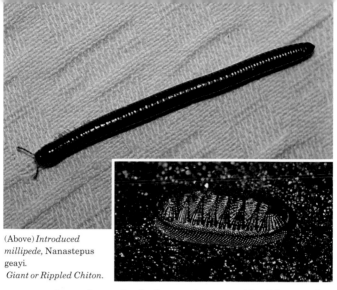

(Above) *Introduced millipede,* Nanastepus geayi.

Giant or Rippled Chiton.

are present in numbers only after heavy rains, or at night. Others need to be searched for. Do not, therefore, be disappointed at not seeing as many insect species as you might have expected. This may also mean that you are visited by fewer mosquitoes!

Butterflies

These are probably the most easily seen and attractive of the insects you are likely to see. Until recently it was thought that there were only eight species of butterfly in Galápagos. However, recent research by the CDRS has discovered some 12 new records. This is a good indication of the current paucity of knowledge about the insect fauna of the islands. It is not possible to be precise about the distribution and behaviour of any of the butterflies or moths as very little work has been done on them. All observations should be noted and reported to the CDRS.

An unidentified butterfly, photographed in Galápagos.

(es) Galápagos Sulphur Butterfly *Phoebis sennae marcellina*

The most easily identified butterfly in the islands, lemon or sulphur-yellow with wingspan of 7 cm, frequently seen on Muyuyu and Parkinsonia. Caterpillars feed on Flat-fruited Senna *Senna pistaciifolia*. Small subspecies of the species that occurs throughout the western hemisphere.
Best viewed: Found on all the main islands at all altitudes.

(es) Galápagos Silver Fritillary *Agraulis vanillae galapagensis*

Slow-flying butterfly with a wingspan of 5 cm. Black and orange with silver spots on the underside of wing. Found in all zones, principally after rain. Caterpillars frequently found on Passion Flower *Passiflora foetida*.
Best viewed: Widespread but uncommon.

(n) Painted Lady *Vanessa cardui* and *Vanessa virginensis*

Similar to their namesakes elsewhere, but smaller, orange, red and black above with pastel-coloured underwings. The two species are similar and not easy to tell apart. *V. virginensis* has two large eye-like marks. It also appears to be restricted to Isabela.
Best viewed: Widespread but uncommon.

(n) Monarch Butterfly *Danaus plexippus*

The largest of the Galápagos butterflies with a wingspan of 10 cm, the wings are a rich red-brown, with a heavy black-veined pattern and black edging. It became established in the islands after the introduction of Milkweed *Asclepias curassavica*. First recorded by William Beebe in 1923.
Best viewed: Widespread, but not common, after rain.

(n) Queen Butterfly *Danaus gilippus*

Slightly smaller than Monarch, the Queen has similar coloration but less dramatic markings, especially on the upper sides of the wings where the veins are less obvious. Found mainly on Isabela.
Best viewed: Isabela, Baltra.

(e) Galápagos Blue Butterfly *Leptodes parrhasioides*

An unmistakable very small, blue butterfly. Male has violet-bluish upper surfaces to the wings, dark brown below. Female has greyer upper surfaces with blue dusting especially near the body; undersides similar to male. Both sexes have two to four dark spots, often ringed with blue, at the rear inner edge of the hind wings.
Best viewed: Widespread after rain.

(e) Large Tailed Skipper *Urbanus galapagensis*

A small brown 'tailed' butterfly. Wings brown with a greenish-olive gloss with whitish-yellow spots on the forewings. Dark brown line around the edge of the wings; rear wings have distinct 'tails' which are slightly darker than the rest of the wings. Sexes similar though female is slightly larger, 5 cm as opposed to 4.5 cm in the male. 'Tails' on female also slightly longer, 6 mm as opposed to 5 mm in the males.
Best viewed: Uncommon, found in the Humid Zone on major islands.

Moths

The fact that we have more information of the moths than of the butterflies of Galápagos, is probably due to their being largely nocturnal and being attracted to lights. Even so we have very little knowledge of the distribution, biology and life cycle of most species and there is a great deal of work to be done in this area. Of the more than 300 species of lepidoptera known to exist in Galápagos, the vast majority are moths. Around 30 per cent of moth species are endemic and a further 15 per cent are likely to be endemic subspecies.

(es) Green Hawkmoth *Eumorpha labruscae*

A large bright green hawkmoth (sphinx moth), one of twelve species of this family found in Galápagos. It is frequently attracted to lights, and can be seen feeding hummingbird-like on the nectar of many plants in the settlements. It is widespread in the islands, even being attracted to the lights of ships at sea.

(es) Galápagos Hawkmoth *Manduca rustica galapagensis*

A fairly common hawkmoth with a wingspan of 9 cm. It shows considerable variation in basic colouring from dark brown to gold and even to white, but with an overall mottled appearance. The forewings have a number of longitudinal bands running in from the wingtips across them. The hindwings are darker in colour and hairy at the thorax ends. Most commonly seen at night when attracted to lights.

(n) Fringed Noctuid *Ascalapha odorata*

This is the largest of 84 species of noctuid moth recorded in Galápagos. The largest moth in the islands, it has a wingspan of up to 15 cm. It has a varied brown and white coloration which is excellent camouflage on rocks and lichen-covered trees. Widespread, generally appearing around dusk.

(n) Crimson Speckled Footman Moth *Utethesia ornatrix*

An attractive day-flying moth with grey-white forewings and reddish or orange underwings. Frequently seen in the highlands where they can be quite numerous. At rest the wings are folded close to the body. Larvae probably feed on *Crotalaria*. There are three other species of this genus in Galápagos and they are hard to distinguish in the field. *Best viewed:* Widespread in the Humid Zone.

(e) Indefatigable Hawkmoth *Xylophanes norfolki*

A small brown hawkmoth with a wingspan of 6–7 cm. Found only in the highlands of Santa Cruz. The forewing pattern distinguishes it from *X. tersa*, a native species found on San Cristóbal and Santiago. *Best viewed:* Santa Cruz – Los Gemelos.

Ants, Flies and Bees

ⓘⓟ Little Red Fire Ant *Wasmannia auropunctata*

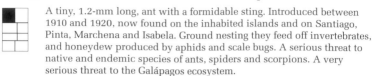

A tiny, 1.2-mm long, ant with a formidable sting. Introduced between 1910 and 1920, now found on the inhabited islands and on Santiago, Pinta, Marchena and Isabela. Ground nesting they feed off invertebrates, and honeydew produced by aphids and scale bugs. A serious threat to native and endemic species of ants, spiders and scorpions. A very serious threat to the Galápagos ecosystem.

ⓘⓟ Tropical Fire Ant *Solenopsis geminata*

Similar to *W. auropunctata*, slightly larger and less widespread but equally aggressive and the only ant able to compete successfully with it. It may affect the reproductive success of the Giant Tortoise, Land Iguana and birds. Large numbers of their stings can kill animals as large as black rats and can cause illness in humans.

ⓘ Longhorn Ant *Paratrechina longicornis*

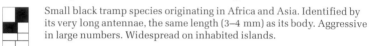

Small black tramp species originating in Africa and Asia. Identified by its very long antennae, the same length (3–4 mm) as its body. Aggressive in large numbers. Widespread on inhabited islands.

ⓔ Galápagos Carpenter Ant *Camponotus macilentus*

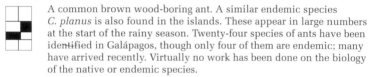

A common brown wood-boring ant. A similar endemic species *C. planus* is also found in the islands. These appear in large numbers at the start of the rainy season. Twenty-four species of ants have been identified in Galápagos, though only four of them are endemic; many have arrived recently. Virtually no work has been done on the biology of the native or endemic species.

ⓔ Galápagos Green-eyed Horsefly *Tabanus vittiger*

Largest fly in Galápagos (12 mm) with bright iridescent green eyes. Body is dark with reddish longitudinal lines, wings are translucent. Female feeds on the blood of iguanas, tortoises and sea turtles as well as humans. Male feeds on pollen, nectar and plant sap. Larvae live in the mud of lagoons and brackish ponds. You are likely to feel this species before you see it!

ⓘⓟ Biting Blackfly *Simulium bipunctatum*

Introduced to San Cristóbal in 1989, this biting fly causes large painful welts in humans. Found on other islands but needs running water to complete the breeding cycle, so may not be able to establish permanently.

ⓔ Galápagos Carpenter Bee *Xylocopa darwini*

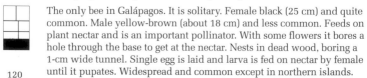

The only bee in Galápagos. It is solitary. Female black (25 cm) and quite common. Male yellow-brown (about 18 cm) and less common. Feeds on plant nectar and is an important pollinator. With some flowers it bores a hole through the base to get at the nectar. Nests in dead wood, boring a 1-cm wide tunnel. Single egg is laid and larva is fed on nectar by female until it pupates. Widespread and common except in northern islands.

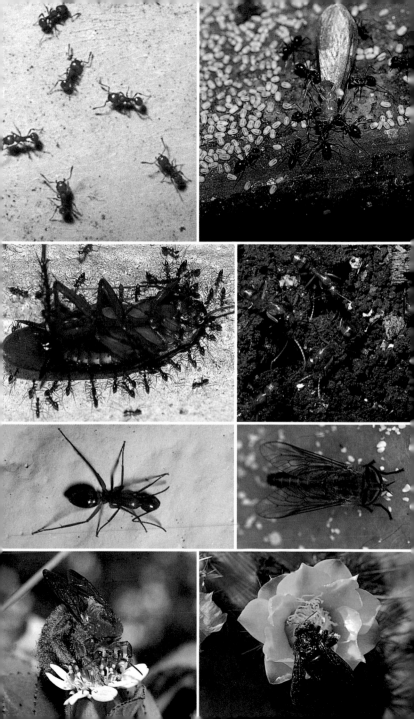

Wasps, Bugs, Beetles and Cockroaches

ⓘ Yellow Paper Wasp *Polistes versicolor*

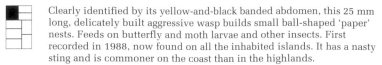

Clearly identified by its yellow-and-black banded abdomen, this 25 mm long, delicately built aggressive wasp builds small ball-shaped 'paper' nests. Feeds on butterfly and moth larvae and other insects. First recorded in 1988, now found on all the inhabited islands. It has a nasty sting and is commoner on the coast than in the highlands.

ⓘₚ Dark Paper Wasp *Brachygastra lecheguana*

First reported in 1994, this small, 12-mm long wasp has a pale brown-and-black banded abdomen. Feeds on butterfly and moth larvae and other insects. Nests are larger than *P. versicolor* and contain many females. Frequently swarms in large numbers.

There are a small number of endemic wasps in the Galápagos. These are rarely seen and are likely to have been affected by the presence of the two recently introduced species.

ⓔ Spotless Ladybug *Cyloneda sanguinea*

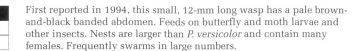

A bright-red spotless ladybug found on most of the major islands. It is an important predator and lives on a wide range of soft-bodied insects such as aphids and scale bugs.

ⓘₚ Cottony Cushion Scale *Icerya purchasi*

A white almost circular insect with a rather furry appearance. It feeds off plant juices and is potentially a serious threat to the native flora. It has been found on 44 different species of plant, 15 of them endemic, on nine different islands. Its rapid dispersal since its introduction in 1982 is only partly accounted for by human agents, as it has probably spread to uninhabited islands by wind dispersal.

ⓝ Giant Long-horn Beetle *Stenodontes molarius*

The largest beetle in Galápagos, growing to some 6 cm in length with a fearsome pair of mandibles or pincers, over 1-cm long. Wing cases covering the abdomen are almost black. Eggs are laid in dead wood. The larvae bore long tunnels in the wood. The adults probably feed on fruit, plant sap, nectar and pollen. The pincers are larger in the male than the female and are used in both sexes for digging into trees and plants, and in the males for fighting other males for females.

ⓘ ⓔ Cockroaches

There are at least 18 species of cockroach in Galápagos. Eleven are recent introductions and five are endemic including two blind (*Chorisoneura* spp.) and three flightless species (*Ischnoptera* spp.). The endemic species are from the family Blattellidae. Many of the species are found in and around human habitation; they have a particular liking for ships. There is no evidence that the introduced species have displaced the native and endemic species, or that they have had any impact on other invertebrates. They feed on litter and detritus and are food for birds and invertebrates.

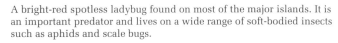

Dragonflies, Grasshoppers and Crickets

(n) Spot-winged Glider *Pantala hymenaea*

Large (8–9 cm) dragonfly with reddish abdomen, often with a dark tip. Wings translucent with large brown spot on inner end of the hindwing. Nymphs develop in fresh or brackish water and often in as little as five weeks. A strong flier it is known to migrate long distances. It feeds on other insects and is frequently seen darting about over ponds and lagoons as it hunts its prey. This is one of eight species of dragonfly and damselfly found in Galápagos. Only one, *Aeshna galapagoensis* is endemic.

(e) Galápagos Field Cricket *Gryllus abditus*

Large (up to 5 cm) dark-coloured cricket, the long sharp rear end is not a stinging organ, but an ovipositor. This is lacking in the male. The head is shiny black and the hindlegs are dark brown. The wings extend beyond the end of the abdomen. There are eight species of *Gryllus* in the islands, *G. abditus* is the commonest. *G. galapageius* is similar with reddish brown hindlegs. Both are winged, the others are all flightless.
Best viewed:

G. abditus	Isabela, Santiago, San Cristóbal, Española, Floreana, Santa Cruz
G. galapageius	Santa Cruz, Santa Fé
G. isabela	Isabela and Fernandina
G. genovesa	Genovesa

(e) Large Painted Locust *Schistocerca melanocera*

Large (up to 8 cm) colourful grasshopper, particularly abundant after heavy rains. Head and thorax have irregular yellow markings, wings have reddish veins. Hindlegs are red above, yellow below and black on the sides. The immature or nymph stages are bright green, turning brown and then multicoloured. *S. melanocera* is more widespread than *S. literosa*. *Best viewed:* All islands except Española.

(e) Small Painted Locust *Schistocerca literosa*

Smaller than *S. melanocera*, up to 5 cm long and less colourful. It is pale brown with darker brown splotches making it well camouflaged. *Best viewed:* All islands.

(e) Galápagos Flightless Grasshopper *Halemus robustus*

One of four flightless species of this genus. A rather dumpy looking grasshopper due to the lack of wings. You will need to look carefully for these as they are well camouflaged with the brown coloration.

(n) Squeak Bug *Eburia lanigera*

Common beetle that gets its name from its ability to squeak or 'stridulate' when picked up. This is a defence mechanism to protect it from being eaten by birds. Body is about 25 mm long but with very long antennae and long legs. Fairly uniform grey in colour with yellowish spots. Attracted to lights and often found in considerable numbers.

SPIDERS, SCORPIONS, CENTIPEDES, MILLIPEDES

(n) Giant Huntsman *Heteropoda venatoria*

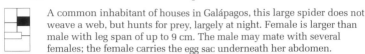

A common inhabitant of houses in Galápagos, this large spider does not weave a web, but hunts for prey, largely at night. Female is larger than male with leg span of up to 9 cm. The male may mate with several females; the female carries the egg sac underneath her abdomen.

(e) Galápagos Black Widow *Latrodectus apicalis*

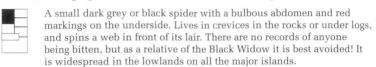

A small dark grey or black spider with a bulbous abdomen and red markings on the underside. Lives in crevices in the rocks or under logs, and spins a web in front of its lair. There are no records of anyone being bitten, but as a relative of the Black Widow it is best avoided! It is widespread in the lowlands on all the major islands.

(e) Zig-zag Spider *Neoscona cooksoni*

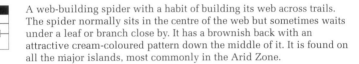

A web-building spider with a habit of building its web across trails. The spider normally sits in the centre of the web but sometimes waits under a leaf or branch close by. It has a brownish back with an attractive cream-coloured pattern down the middle of it. It is found on all the major islands, most commonly in the Arid Zone.

(n) Silver Argiope *Argiope argentata*

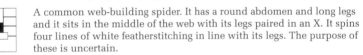

A common web-building spider. It has a round abdomen and long legs and it sits in the middle of the web with its legs paired in an X. It spins four lines of white featherstitching in line with its legs. The purpose of these is uncertain.

(n) Star Spider *Gasteracantha servillei*

A web builder with a remarkable black-and-yellow, shell-like abdomen with six pointed spines. Most commonly found in the Coastal Zone, among mangroves and other shore vegetation.

(e) Galápagos Centipede *Scolopendra galapagensis*

This large centipede has a dark brown body, reddish legs and an impressive pair of fangs with which it poisons its prey. It grows up to 30 cm long. Found in the Arid Zone and is largely nocturnal. It preys on other invertebrates, lizards and even small birds. It is a favoured food of the Galápagos Hawk *Buteo galapagoensis*. There are at least eight species of centipede in Galápagos, the others are all very much smaller.

(es) Galápagos Scorpion *Hadruroides maculatus galapagoensis*

A small scorpion (up to 10 cm), common in the Coastal and Arid Zones. This species is a yellowy-brown colour with quite heavy pincers; the endemic *Centruroides exsul* is darker brown and has finer pincers. Feeds largely on other invertebrates. A favoured food of Lava Lizards.

MOLLUSCS

(e) Bulimulid Land Snails

A remarkable example of speciation is to be found in the 66 identified species of land snail of the genus *Bulimulus*. All are endemic and are thought to have developed from an original parent species. They are found on all the major islands and in all vegetation zones. Santa Cruz had 24 different species, *Bulimulus gilderoyi* being confined to a single valley in the highlands. They vary in size from 6 to 25 mm in length, and in colour from white through dull brown, to dark brown and even black.

They are under increasing threat, especially on the inhabited islands, from the destruction of their habitat for farming and the introduction of predators such as the Little Red Fire Ant and the Black Rat. Over half of the surviving species are now endangered.

Marine Molluscs

1	2
3	4
5	6
7	

1 Horse Conch
2 Chief Rocksnail
3 Slender Triton
4 Cowries
5 Crowned Cone
6 Grinning Tun
7 Zebra Auger

Some 800 species of intertidal and shallow water molluscs have been identified in Galápagos of which some 18 per cent are endemic. You may be able to identify some intertidal molluscs whilst walking along the coast, in particular the **Giant** or **Rippled Galápagos Chiton** *Chiton goodallii* (see photo p.115) is quite common. This is a large black-shelled mollusc that grows up to 15 cm long with a segmented shell. It makes an excellent meal and is therefore uncommon anywhere near inhabited areas. You may also come across the **Wide-mouthed Purpura** *Plicopurpura patula pansa* which is also found on intertidal rocks and has an attractive orange and white aperture. This shell is named from the purple dye that used to be extracted from it and was used to dye the purple robes of Roman emperors.

On the beach you will often come across worn shells, members of the cone family are quite common. The **Diadem** or **Crowned Cone** *Conus diadema* is a plain chestnut-brown cone and usually easily identified. Live cones are extremely poisonous, and they inject their poison through a harpoon-like organ. Watch out also for cowrie shells with their unmistakable double-lipped opening. The spotted **Little Deer Cowrie** *Cypraea cervinetta* is one of the commonest.

You may also find on the beach, or see while snorkelling or diving, the **Chief Rocksnail** *Hexaplex princeps* (up to 25 cm). It is whitish with reddish purple lines, with a series of large blunt spines. It is often entirely covered with soft corals and algal growth. It feeds on molluscs and barnacles, and drills holes through the shells to kill them. If you come across a long slender shell with zebra-like markings, it is the **Zebra Auger** *Terebra strigata*, a member of the *Terebridae* family (up to 12 cm). They are best seen in sandy bays; Santa Fé is probably the best location.

The two largest shells that you are likely to see in the islands are the **Grinning Tun** *Malea ringens* and the **Galápagos Horse Conch** *Pleuroploca princeps*. The former grows up to 24 cm long and is barrel-shaped. It lives on sandy bottoms in fairly shallow water, up to 8 m. The latter is longer, up to 40 cm, and more slender with a long orange opening. The animal is an amazing crimson colour with iridescent blue-purple spots.

The **Slender Triton** *Cymatium pileare macrodon* is another quite common shell found on beaches. The live shell is covered with a coarse hair. The shell is quite elongated and grows up to 11 cm in length and is characterised by three ribs or thickenings of the shell, which run up it longitudinally.

CRABS

ⓔ Sally Lightfoot Crab *Grapsus grapsus*

A dramatic scarlet and orange crab growing up to 20 cm across, often seen in large numbers. The underside is white, often bluish; juveniles are much darker, starting almost black, with small orange spots, becoming redder with each successive change of shell. They are predators and scavengers. Juveniles feed largely on algae and animal detritus, while adults feed on other crabs, including their own species, and small crustaceans. Their common name comes from their ability to 'walk on water' as they scurry from one rock to another.

ⓝ Hairy Rock Crab *Geograpsus lividus*

A fairly common rock crab with a dull orange carapace and hairy legs. A voracious predator which feeds on the small fish that inhabit the tide pools. Widespread but tends to hide in cracks or algae.
Best viewed: On rocky shorelines where there are tide pools.

ⓝ Velvet-fingered Ozius *Ozius verreauxi*

A neat, compact, blue-grey crab with a very smooth carapace up to 85 mm across. Claws of different size, one to hold its main prey, snails, the other to eat the flesh. Not uncommon but hides in cracks in the rocks.

ⓝ Fiddler Crab *Uca helleri*

Small, reddish brown crab up to 8 cm across. It has one very large claw, and one very small one. The male waves this large claw about during the courtship ritual, a little like a violinist's bow. It lives colonially in burrows amongst the roots of mangroves and feeds on algae and bacteria found on and around the roots.

ⓝ Ghost Crab *Ocypode gaudichaudii*

The commonest of a number of species of ghost crab. A small (10 cm) flesh-coloured crab. The eyes are on stalks which are raised when in the open, and lowered into the carapace in their burrows. Lives in the sand in the intertidal zone. They are omnivorous. They leave large numbers of little balls of sand that they have searched through for algal and animal detritus.

ⓝ Semi-terrestrial Hermit Crab *Coenobita compressus*

Hermit crabs have no hard carapace, but inhabit mollusc shells. As they grow they move to a larger shell. This species is light brown. Its external parts, head, claws and legs are laterally compressed. A common scavenger of the beach and in the littoral zone.

ⓔ Galápagos Hermit Crab *Calcinus explorator*

A small dark brown-to-black hermit crab with red-edged appendages. Another scavenger which is widely distributed and found mainly on rocks in the intertidal zone.

SEA URCHINS AND SEA STARS

Sea urchins and sea stars are echinoderms, or 'spiny skinned', which have rotational symmetry. Sea urchins have hard globular-shaped shells covered with spines. Sea stars are flattened and have a generally softer exterior covered with spikes or bristles rather than spines.

(n) Pencil-spined Sea Urchin *Eucidaris thouarsii*

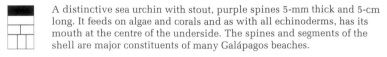

A distinctive sea urchin with stout, purple spines 5-mm thick and 5-cm long. It feeds on algae and corals and as with all echinoderms, has its mouth at the centre of the underside. The spines and segments of the shell are major constituents of many Galápagos beaches.

(e) Green Sea Urchin *Lytechinus semituberculatus*

A small sea urchin to 6 cm in diameter, with lime-green spines up to 15-mm long. Found mainly below the low-tide mark, but also in tidal pools. Frequently found washed up on sandy beaches.

Crowned Sea Urchin *Centrostephanus coronatus*

Black urchin with very long (12 cm), very sharp, spines, which break off easily and are slightly poisonous. A nocturnal carnivorous species found throughout the islands, best seen at very low tide or while snorkelling.

(n) White Sea Urchin *Tripneustes depressus*

A medium-sized urchin growing up to 10 cm in diameter with short, white or pale brown spines to 1 cm. They are normally found below the low-tide level, but can be seen during spring tides grazing, often in large numbers, on algae on exposed rocks.

(es) Sand Dollar *Micropora galapagensis*

An almost flat urchin, growing to 15 cm in diameter and up to 2-cm thick. It is pale-cream coloured to match its sandy habitat and has a clearly marked five-arm pattern on its upper surface. The spines are virtually non-existent. Often found washed up on beaches.

(n) Chocolate Chip Sea Star *Nidorellia armata*

Also known as the Spiny Sunstar, this five-armed starfish is common on rocky coastlines. It grows to 15 cm in diameter and is a generally orange-yellow coloration with a regular pattern of dark-brown short sturdy spines. It normally lives below the low-tide mark.

(n) Sea Cucumber *Holothuria* spp.

A soft-bodied relative of the starfish, it is a dark brown-to-black sausage-shaped animal, growing up to 20 cm in length. The largest member of the family in Galápagos, the Giant Sea Cucumber *Isostichopus fuscus* which is covered in yellow-brown bumps, has been the object of a commercial fishery since 1993 and its numbers have decreased substantially. It feeds on small gastropods and invertebrates as well as general detritus.

VEGETATION ZONES

There are seven generally accepted vegetation zones in Galápagos, all of them quite distinct:

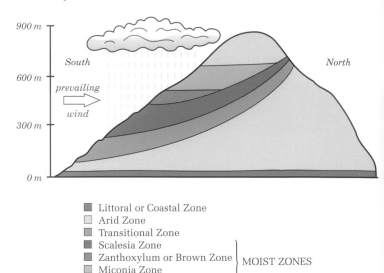

- Littoral or Coastal Zone
- Arid Zone
- Transitional Zone
- Scalesia Zone
- Zanthoxylum or Brown Zone ⎫
- Miconia Zone   ⎬ MOIST ZONES
- Pampa or Fern-sedge Zone ⎭

These zones are largely dictated by the climate, which in turn is largely dictated by altitude and position on each island. In very general terms, the higher up the wetter the climate. In addition, the south sides of the islands are very much wetter than the north. This is because the prevailing wind for much of the year is from the south-east which results in the north side of the islands being in a rain shadow. Not all the large islands have quite the same vegetation zones owing to a variety of factors, in particular their height and location in relation to other islands. They also vary in age and in the composition of the underlying rock. Isla Isabela is a very interesting case in point, because while it consists of five large shield volcanoes with heights varying from 1,123 m (3,650 ft) on Volcan Alcedo in the middle to 1,704 m (5,540 ft) on Volcan Cerro Azul in the south. Each volcano has quite distinct vegetation. On Alcedo, there is virtually no bare lava. It is covered largely in volcanic ash and pumice and has only the lower five zones as it is itself relatively low. The two volcanoes to the north, Darwin and Wolf, have relatively smaller moist zones as they lie in the rain shadow of the rest of the islands. Cerro Azul, which is the extreme south-west of the islands, has the Transitional Zone on the coast and an Arid Zone on the rim which rises above the clouds and so receives only a small amount of precipitation in the garua season.

There are also very distinct differences between the flora of the islands, Isabela and Fernandina and the rest of the archipelago. These are the younger islands and are thought to have less well-developed soils than the older islands such as Santa Cruz, Santiago and San

Cristóbal. For the purpose of describing the vegetation zones, Santa Cruz has been used as the guide. While farming has damaged many of the zones, some irrevocably, it is still possible to see aspects of all of the zones quite clearly and, in addition, it is the island most likely to be visited by all visitors. It is also the one where visitors are most likely to visit the interior.

The Littoral or Coastal Zone

As its name suggests, this zone is immediately along the shore line and may extend 50 m to 100 m inland. The plants found here are not so much dependent upon the climate as on their ability to tolerate salt and to live on the edge of the sea. Many of the plants in this zone are evergreen, such as the several species of mangrove, and are characterised by heavy waxy, or fleshy succulent leaves.

Not many of the plants here are endemic and all will probably have arrived on the ocean currents.

The Arid Zone

This is the area that most visitors will become most accustomed to as it is also the habitat and breeding area for several of the animal species. On the south side of the islands, this may extend up to less than 100 m in altitude, while on the north side of the larger islands, it may extend up to an altitude of over 500 m. The smaller and lower islands are entirely in the Arid Zone. The most characteristic plants in the zone are the endemic Palo Santo tree (*Bursera graveolens*) whose silver-coloured bark contributes to the characteristic greyness of the zone, and the Opuntia cactus (*Opuntia* spp.) which varies from a low cluster of pads to 30-ft high brown-barked trees. You will also find a number of evergreen shrubs such as *Croton scouleri* and other drought-resistant plants. When the annual 'El Niño' rains come, the zone turns green very quickly, and many of the plant species of the zone, which are annuals, suddenly appear, flower and die within a period of six to eight weeks.

(Top left) *Arid Zone.* (Top right) *Brackish pool in Arid Zone.*
(Above) *Transitional Zone.*

The Transitional Zone

This is the zone between the dry and moist zones and is found at a much lower altitude (80–100 m) on the southern slopes of the larger islands than on the northern sides, and even at sea level in south-western Isabela. On some medium-sized islands such as Pinzón, Rábida and Pinta and Marchena, it is the only zone apart from the Littoral and Arid Zones. It is dominated by larger deciduous trees such as Guayabillo (*Psidium galapageium*), Pega-pega (*Pisonia floribunda*) and the amazing hardwood Matazarno (*Piscidia cathagenensis*). All three of these are endemic. With no canopy to shut out light, there are a number of shrubs in this zone, some of which are evergreen. Many lichens and mosses attach themselves to the trees. While no species is dominant in this zone, all the species found here are also found in either the Arid Zone below or in the Scalesia Zone above. It has the greatest diversity of species of any of the vegetation zones.

The Scalesia Zone

Starting at around 180–200 m, this, the first of four moist zones, is a lush cloud forest and is characterised by the largest of the 20 members of the *Scalesia* genus found in the Galápagos, *Scalesia pedunculata*. While *S. pedunculata* is dominant on Santa Cruz, San Cristóbal, Floreana and Santiago, it is replaced on Isabela and Fernandina by *Scalesia cordata*, and *Scalesia microcephala*, another good example of inter-island variation, possibly related to soil and climate differences. Scalesia form dense stands with trees up to 15 or even 20 m in height; from afar, they appear like a bright-green hummocky bog. Underneath the canopy the trunks and branches are encrusted with epiphytes: mosses, liverworts, ferns, bromeliads and orchids. Epiphytes (plants which grow on another plant, but do not parasitise them) are characteristic of the moist zones of the Galápagos as a result of the long periods when the upper reaches of the higher islands are shrouded in cloud and mist. Many species of vine also flourish with the Scalesia forests. Much of this zone has been destroyed on the inhabited islands. It is the best area for agriculture, being well watered by the garua during the cool season. There is still a good area of Scalesia forest at the western end of Santa Cruz close to the airport road by the pit craters knows as Los Gemelos (The Twins).

(Top) *Scalesia Zone.*
138   (Above) *Brown Zone.*

The Zanthoxylum or Brown Zone

Very little of this zone survives on Santa Cruz owing to agriculture. It is the zone between the densely wooded Scalesia Zone and the shrubby Miconia Zone. The dominant plant is *Zanthoxylum fagara*, more commonly known as Cat's Claw or Wait-a-Minute bush owing to its very sharp hooked spines. These are covered in epiphytes and it is these that give the zone its brown appearance. *Zanthoxylum* and *Scalesia* are both very susceptible to attack by goats and have been seriously damaged on Santiago and Alcedo. Ironically, where there are human populations, the goats are much less of a problem. However, farming has more than made up for that.

The Miconia Zone

Starting at between 400 and 500 m, this zone is only found on Santa Cruz and San Cristóbal, on the southern, windward, slopes. It is dominated by *Miconia robinsoniana*, a shrub growing up to 5-m high. It forms a dense thicket which provides a perfect nesting area for the Hawaiian or Dark-rumped Petrel. Unfortunately, the area has been invaded on Santa Cruz by the imported Quinine Tree *Cinchona succirubra*, a serious threat to the whole zone. On San Cristóbal, the stands of *Miconia* are less dense and are interspersed with other shrubs, while on Isabela and Fernandina, *Miconia* is entirely absent and replaced by a variety of other shrubs such as *Baccharis*, *Darwiniothamnus*, *Hyptis* and *Dodonea*.

The Pampa or Fern-sedge Zone

The highest zone of all is the Pampa Zone. Like upland moorlands worldwide, the vegetation here is almost entirely composed of mosses, grasses and ferns, most of which are no more than 30-cm high. One exception is the Galápagos Tree Fern, *Cyathea weatherbyana*, which grows up to 3-m tall but is generally found in

Miconia Zone.

gullies and ravines or inside small craters and potholes, where there is better water retention during the dry season. There are also four species of orchid in this zone. Lichens are also abundant in this area, brightening it up with their varying shades of green, grey, yellow, orange and red.

139

(Top) *Pampa Zone.*

(Above) *Bog pond in Pampa Zone.*

SOILS

Given the importance of soil in determining the plants that will thrive in any area, it is surprising that very little work has been done on the soils of the islands. Laruelle (1966) worked on Santa Cruz and identified five different zones, which correspond approximately to the vegetation zones. The soils in the lower zones are neutral or moderately basic, and those above increasingly more acidic. Soil zones 1 and 2 are identified with the Coastal to Transitional Zones. Soil zones 3 and 4 are found with the Scalesia and Zanthoxylum Zones, and soil zone 5, where the increasingly acidic soils are found, with the Miconia and Pampas Zones.

This is an area where further research is needed – understanding all aspects of the biology of the islands is an essential prerequisite to being able to preserve them.

ECOLOGICAL ZONES

While the vegetation divides up into seven zones, there are three basic ecological zones in Galápagos. The first is the Coastal Zone, characterised by animals and plants which depend on the proximity of the sea. The Arid and Transitional Zone is characterised by long periods of drought and a relative lack of moisture. The animals and plants found here can survive long periods without water. Thirdly there is the Humid Uplands Zone, where there may be periods of drought, but as a general rule the plants and animals here are adapted to a relative abundance of water.

PLANTS

This guide will not attempt to provide you with an exhaustive list of the plants found in Galápagos, but it will help you to identify the commoner species that you are likely to see whilst visiting the islands. It will also help you to appreciate that while the differences between the plants on the various islands are not always as dramatic or well publicised as those in the Animal Kingdom, they are equally important in helping us to understand the very special nature of the Galápagos.

In the first instance, the very paucity of species is important. There are only some 600 Native species, subspecies, and varieties (taxa) of vascular plant in Galápagos; this compares with over 20,000 in mainland Ecuador. This lack of species is simply due to the isolation of the islands. Within this relative paucity of species, some 250 are Endemic, in other words found nowhere else. This is a remarkably high proportion. These endemic species have 'developed' or evolved from an original 110 species that arrived here by natural means. Most of these plants are closely related to ones found on the mainland.

'Adaptive radiation' is a term often used in relation to the development of the 13 species of Darwin's finch, or the 14 subspecies of giant tortoise. Adaptive radiation is, however, equally evident in the plant world. There are 20 taxa of the genus *Scalesia*, a member of the daisy family, and 14 taxa of the genus *Opuntia*, a widely distributed member of the cactus family. The average visitor to Galápagos will get a better chance to see and identify several different plant taxa from the same genus than they will different animal taxa from the same genus. Keep your eyes open and look out for the differences that Darwin noted and that helped him to reach his revolutionary conclusions.

Coastal (Littoral) Zone Plants

The plants found in this zone need to be very tolerant of salt. Many of them are at times entirely or partially covered by sea water. To cope with this, they have special glands in the leaves which excrete the salt. You can often see or taste this.

ⓝ Red Mangrove *Rhizophora mangle*

The commonest of the four mangroves found in Galápagos, it is easily recognised by its thick, dark green, waxy leaves and often delicate stilt or prop roots. These external roots support the tree so that the trunk itself is generally not in the water. With prop roots, the main trunk gradually diminishes in size the closer it gets to the water or beach. The flowers are individual, have four petals and are on short stalks. These develop into 15–25-cm long fruits or seedlings which fall off and float away to develop elsewhere. Found on sheltered beaches and in coves and lagoons throughout the islands, it normally grows up to 7-m high, but on Isabela, either side of the Perry Isthmus, it can grow to 15 or 20 m.
Best viewed: Santa Cruz – Puerto Ayora, Tortuga Bay, Turtle Cove and Caleta Negra; Isabela – Elizabeth Bay, Punta Garcia and Puerto Villamil; Fernandina – Punta Espinosa; Genovesa – Darwin Bay; Bartolomé.

ⓝ Black Mangrove *Avicennia germinans*

The largest mangrove in the islands, reaching heights of up to 25 m. It is slightly less common than the red mangrove, but is found throughout the islands. It takes its English name from the grey, at times almost black, bark. It is also found on beaches and lagoons but has a conventional root system sending out finger-like breathing roots (pneumatophores) which stick up out of the sand or mud and help to anchor the beach. These pneumatophores help to provide the plant with oxygen, as the soil is often waterlogged. It has smaller, more pointed leaves than the red mangrove. They have a grey tinge, darker above than underneath. The leaves often have a thin layer of salt on them, excreted by glands which help the mangrove to cope with the salt water. The black mangrove has clusters of small white flowers with 5 petals which develop into flattened drop-shaped fruit and which, like those of the red mangrove, are dispersed by the sea.
Best viewed: Santa Cruz – Puerto Ayora, Tortuga Bay, Las Bachas; Santiago – Espumilla Beach; Floreana – Punta Cormoran; Fernandina; Isabela – Elizabeth Bay; Rábida.

ⓝ White Mangrove *Laguncularia racemosa*

This species is best identified by its paler oval leaves with dots on the underside. Its flowers, which have five petals, form inconspicuous small greenish-white clusters. The fruits are pale green and flask-shaped. It grows as a shrub or tree up to 10 m in height. Though not common it is often found together with red mangroves in lagoons or brackish-water swamps but not on beaches.
Best viewed: Santa Cruz – Puerto Ayora, Tortuga Bay, Turtle Cove; Santiago – Espumilla Beach, Sullivan Bay; Fernandina – Punta Espinosa; Bartolomé; Isabela – Elizabeth Bay, Puerto Villamil, Punta Garcia, Punta Moreno.

⓷ Button Mangrove *Conocarpus erectus*

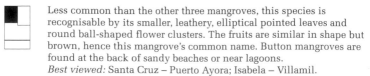

Less common than the other three mangroves, this species is recognisable by its smaller, leathery, elliptical pointed leaves and round ball-shaped flower clusters. The fruits are similar in shape but brown, hence this mangrove's common name. Button mangroves are found at the back of sandy beaches or near lagoons.
Best viewed: Santa Cruz – Puerto Ayora; Isabela – Villamil.

⓷ Leatherleaf *Maytenus octogona*

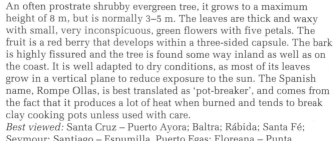

An often prostrate shrubby evergreen tree, it grows to a maximum height of 8 m, but is normally 3–5 m. The leaves are thick and waxy with small, very inconspicuous, green flowers with five petals. The fruit is a red berry that develops within a three-sided capsule. The bark is highly fissured and the tree is found some way inland as well as on the coast. It is well adapted to dry conditions, as most of its leaves grow in a vertical plane to reduce exposure to the sun. The Spanish name, Rompe Ollas, is best translated as 'pot-breaker', and comes from the fact that it produces a lot of heat when burned and tends to break clay cooking pots unless used with care.
Best viewed: Santa Cruz – Puerto Ayora; Baltra; Rábida; Santa Fé; Seymour; Santiago – Espumilla, Puerto Egas; Floreana – Punta Cormoran; Bartolomé; South Plaza.

⓷ Saltbush *Cryptocarpus pyriformis*

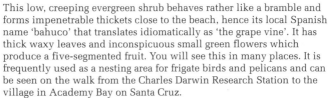

This low, creeping evergreen shrub behaves rather like a bramble and forms impenetrable thickets close to the beach, hence its local Spanish name 'bahuco' that translates idiomatically as 'the grape vine'. It has thick waxy leaves and inconspicuous small green flowers which produce a five-segmented fruit. You will see this in many places. It is frequently used as a nesting area for frigate birds and pelicans and can be seen on the walk from the Charles Darwin Research Station to the village in Academy Bay on Santa Cruz.
Best viewed: Santa Cruz – Puerto Ayora, Tortuga Bay; Española – Punta Suarez, Gardner Bay; North Seymour; Genovesa – Darwin Bay; Floreana – Punta Cormoran and Post Office Bay; Rábida; Santiago - Espumilla Beach and Sullivan Bay; Bartolomé; Isabela – Tagus Cove; Rábida; Santa Fé.

(n) Saltwort *Batis maritima*

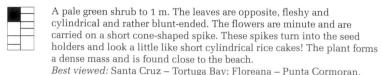

A pale green shrub to 1 m. The leaves are opposite, fleshy and cylindrical and rather blunt-ended. The flowers are minute and are carried on a short cone-shaped spike. These spikes turn into the seed holders and look a little like short cylindrical rice cakes! The plant forms a dense mass and is found close to the beach.
Best viewed: Santa Cruz – Tortuga Bay; Floreana – Punta Cormoran.

(n) Scorpion Weed *Heliotropium curassavicum*

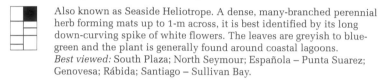

Also known as Seaside Heliotrope. A dense, many-branched perennial herb forming mats up to 1-m across, it is best identified by its long down-curving spike of white flowers. The leaves are greyish to blue-green and the plant is generally found around coastal lagoons.
Best viewed: South Plaza; North Seymour; Española – Punta Suarez; Genovesa; Rábida; Santiago – Sullivan Bay.

(n) Salt Sage *Atriplex peruviana*

A small salt-tolerant shrub, growing up to 1 m in height, with leathery round to rhomboid, grey-green, alternate leaves. The flowers are small and yellow-brown and grow in clusters at the end of the branches.
Best viewed: Española – Punta Suarez; North Seymour.

(n) Sea Grass *Sporobolus virginicus*

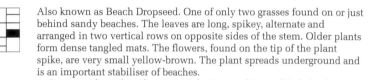

Also known as Beach Dropseed. One of only two grasses found on or just behind sandy beaches. The leaves are long, spikey, alternate and arranged in two vertical rows on opposite sides of the stem. Older plants form dense tangled mats. The flowers, found on the tip of the plant spike, are very small yellow-brown. The plant spreads underground and is an important stabiliser of beaches.
   *S. pyramidatus,*found on Española, Fernandina and Isabela, does not creep and the leaves are not arranged so precisely.
Best viewed: Santa Cruz – Puerto Ayora, Las Bachas, Tortuga Bay; Floreana – Post Office Bay, Punta Cormoran; Santiago – Sullivan Bay; Genovesa; Española – Gardner Bay.

(n) Desert Plum *Grabowskia boerhaaviaefolia*

Low shrub growing to 2.5 m, bark whitish on new growth, turning brown with age. The branches are often thickly encrusted with lichens. Pale-green slightly elongated leaves. Small white trumpet-shaped flowers 3–5-mm long, produced in clusters at the branch ends producing a small red-orange berry.
Best viewed: South Plaza; Española – Punta Suarez.

(e) Galápagos Clubleaf *Nolana galapagensis*

A low shrub to 1.5 m. The dense clusters of short, pale-green sometimes yellowish, fleshy, club-shaped leaves, give the plant the appearance of a succulent. The flowers are small, white and bell-shaped. Found very close to the shore at a number of visiting sites.
Best viewed: San Cristóbal – Punta Pitt; Santa Cruz – Tortuga Bay.

(n) Ink Berry *Scaevola plumieri*

Also known as Sea Grape. A compact but spreading shrub, growing to about 1 m, found on or close to the beach. The leaves are alternate, waxy, almost circular. The flowers are white with long narrow petals. The fruit looks like a large blackcurrant but starts off green.
Best viewed: Floreana – Post Office Bay, Punta Cormoran; Santa Cruz – Tortuga Bay; Isabela – Villamil.

(e) Galápagos Carpetweed *Sesuvium edmonstonei*

A low-lying perennial herb with fat, fleshy cylindrical leaves, The flowers are small, white and star-shaped. The plants are green after rain but turn a spectacular orange-red during the dry or garua season. The seeds are black and contained in a small oval capsule.
Best viewed: South Plaza; Sombrero Chino; North Seymour; Española – Punta Suarez; Santiago – Sullivan Bay; Genovesa.

(n) Common Carpetweed *Sesuvium portulacastrum*

Also known as Sea Purslane. Very similar to the Galápagos Carpetweed *Sesuvium edmonstonei,* but with flatter rather more pointed leaves and a pink rather than white flower. This species also forms dense carpets and turns red in the garua season.
Best viewed: Santa Fé; North Seymour; Santa Cruz – Puerto Ayora, Tortuga Bay; Isabela – Punta Moreno.

(n) Beach Morning Glory *Ipomoea pes-caprae*

An unmistakable perennial with its long creepers stretching 10 m or more, found on sandy beaches and dunes. Leaves leathery and oval to elliptical. The attractive purple-mauve trumpet flower is typical of the genus, producing large oval seed-pods containing a number of hairy seeds. An important stabiliser of beaches and sand dunes.
Best viewed: Española – Gardner Bay; Genovesa; Santa Cruz – Puerto Ayora, Tortuga Bay; Bartolomé; Isabela – Elizabeth Bay, Punta Albemarle.

(e) Galápagos Shore Petunia *Exedeconus miersii*

This annual herb is easily identified by its large trumpet-shaped white flowers. It will only appear during the rainy season, when it forms dense mats. The leaves are large and oval with indented edges. The stems are hairy and sticky. The seed capsule is egg-shaped.
Best viewed: Española – Punta Suarez; Floreana – Post Office Bay, Punta Cormoran; Genovesa – Darwin Bay; Fernandina – Punta Espinosa; Isabela – Tagus Cove, Urvina Bay.

(n) Morning Glory *Ipomoea triloba*

A commonly seen vine in both the Arid and Transitional Zones after heavy rains. It has large (up to 10 cm) three-lobed leaves and attractive trumpet-shaped, pink, lavender or purple flowers (occasionally white).
Best viewed: Santa Cruz – inland from Puerto Ayora.

Arid and Transitional Zone Plants

There are no clear boundaries between the seven different vegetation zones. The Transitional Zone, by its very nature, includes plants from the Arid and the Humid Zones. Most visitors will see more of these two zones than any others. The zones as described exist only on the southern or windward slopes of the islands. On the northern slopes, which are in a rain shadow, the Arid and Transitional Zones extend much higher up. The best place to observe this is on the airport road on Santa Cruz, where in less than a kilometre, you move from the moist Scalesia Zone to the Arid Zone.

Cacti

The large family Cactaceae are succulents: plants with fleshy leaves or stems or both. Cacti are generally characterised by extremely sharp spines. These are actually the leaves and also their main defence against herbivorous predators. Galápagos cacti vary in size from the Lava Cactus, which rarely exceeds 60 cm in height, to the large Prickly Pear and Candelabra Cacti both of which can reach heights of 8–12 m.

ⓔ Lava Cactus *Brachycereus nesioticus*

The smallest of the Galápagos cacti, found exclusively on barren lava fields, it is usually one of the first plants to colonise a fresh lava flow. It consists of a number of short spiny cylinders or stems up to 60 cm in length. The individual stems do not branch, but it is easy to see how an individual stem may have grown in several stages. The younger stems and spines are a fresh greenish yellow, gradually turning grey to black with age. The individual plants or clumps may be as much as 2 m or more across. It flowers very briefly, the large creamy white flowers opening before dawn and shrivelling within a few hours. The fruits are dark brown up to 3.5-cm long and with yellow spines.
Best viewed: Santiago – Sullivan Bay; Bartolomé; Isabela – Punta Moreno; Fernandina – Punta Espinosa; Genovesa – Prince Philip's Steps; Sombero Chino.

ⓔ Candelabra Cactus *Jasminocereus thouarsii*

This large candelabra-shaped cactus grows up to 7 or 8 m high and is found mainly in the Arid Zone. The arms are made up of fluted, very spiny cylindrical sections, which become woodier with age. The bright red-pink flowers open before dawn, these turn into reddish-purple globular-shaped fruit up to 50-cm long which are edible. When the plant or part of it dies, the hollow woody 'skeleton' is left behind. There are three varieties of this species:
J. thouarsii. var. thouarsii
Is found on San Cristóbal, Floreana and Corona del Diablo.
J. thouarsii. var. delicatus
Is found on Santa Cruz, South Plaza and Santiago
J. thouarsii var. sclerocarpus
Is found only on Isabela and Fernandina.

Best viewed: Santa Cruz – Puerto Ayora; Sombrero Chino; Floreana – Punta Cormoran, Corona del Diablo.

ⓔ Giant Prickly Pear Cactus *Opuntia* spp.

The most widely distributed and numerous of the islands' cacti,
Opuntia are an excellent example of adaptive radiation, there being six
different species divided into 14 different varieties. There are
considerable variations from island to island. The tallest, *Opuntia
echios* var. *gigantea* found on Santa Cruz may grow to 12 m; while on
Santa Fé *O. echios* var. *barringtonensis* has a girth of up 2.60 m. On
North Seymour, *O. echios* var. *zacana* and on Rábida *O. galapageia* var.
profusa look like a heap of jumbled pads.

When young, the tree species have a trunk covered with a fearsome
display of spines facing outwards and downwards. As they develop,
the spines give way to a beautiful rich brown bark. However unlike
Jasminocereus, opuntias do not become woody and if you find a fallen
one you can see how the trunk is made up of layer upon layer of a
fibrous honeycomb material. The pads (the spines are the leaves and
the pads are the stem) also have a wonderfully delicate pattern. Both of
these are sometimes used as decorative material.

While there is no conclusive evidence, it seems reasonable to suppose
that the large, trunked species of *Opuntia* evolved in response to
competition for light, and also as a protection from predators, mainly
tortoises and Land Iguanas. It is certainly true that for the most part,
where there are tall, trunked varieties, there are also tortoises, and
islands such as Marchena and Rábida, which have no tortoises, have
low or prostrate forms, often with virtually no spines, or only soft ones.

Opuntia spp. are very important in the Galápagos ecosystem. The pads
and fruit provide an important part of the diet of tortoises and Land
Iguanas. Doves and mockingbirds also enjoy the fruits which are from 4 to
7 cm long. The two Cactus finches, *Geospiza scandens* and *G. conirostris*,
are dependent upon the cactus flowers, fruits and seeds, and even extract
water from the pads. In an environment not noted for its flowering plants,
the flowers are an important source of nectar for insects. *Opuntia* may
flower at any time of the year, the flowers are bright yellow and multi-
petalled, and emerge from the end of the already formed, top-shaped fruit.
In some species the flowers turn pinkish-orange with time.

Best viewed: Widespread throughout the Arid Zone and into the
Transitional Zone on most islands.

O. echios var. *barringtonensis*

This is found only on the island of Santa Fé, and is distinguished by its
immense trunks. The fruits of this variety are up to 7-cm long. Santa Fé
has never had a tortoise population but does have its own species of
Land Iguana which may have impacted on the evolution of this variety
of cactus in the same way that tortoises are thought to have elsewhere.

O. echios var. *echios*

Found on Baltra, Daphne, South Plaza and the northern parts of Santa
Cruz. On South Plaza the variety is tall and treelike, up to 4 m in height,
but elsewhere the shrubby variety is found. The fruits are top-shaped.
There are no tortoises on any of these islands apart from Santa Cruz, but
Land Iguanas are found on South Plaza and northern Santa Cruz.

O. echios var. *gigantea*

The tallest of the *Opuntia* varieties, growing up to 12 m in height, it
occurs only on Santa Cruz, noticeably around Puerto Ayora. Both
tortoises and Land Iguanas are found here.

O. echios var. inermis
A tree-like variety found only on Volcan Sierra Negra on Isabela. It grows to a height of 6 m. The best place to see this variety is around the town of Villamil. Tortoises and Land Iguanas are found here.

O. echios var. zacana
A shrubby form 1–2 m in height, found only on North Seymour, often close to the Dwarf Palo Santo tree *Bursera macrophylla*. There have never been tortoises on this island, but there are Land Iguanas.

Opuntia galapageia var. galapageia
A relatively short (to 4 m) trunked variety found on Pinta and Santiago. On Pinta in particular, the trunk often tapers quite markedly to a point about 2–3 m up where it branches into a dense mass of pads giving it the appearance of a giant mushroom. There are, or were, tortoises and Land Iguanas on both islands.

Opuntia galapageia var. macrocarpa
A trunked variety found only on Pinzón. This is another island with its own tortoise population but no Land Iguanas.

Opuntia galapageia var. profusa
A shrubby variety found only on Rábida. It has soft spines and produces a very large number of fruit, hence its scientific name. This island has never had a tortoise or Land Iguana population.

Opuntia helleri
A low-growing shrubby species found on the northern islands of Darwin, Wolf, Marchena and Genovesa. None of these islands has had a tortoise or Land Iguana population. The spines are often soft and wavy.

Opuntia insularis
A short-trunked and sometimes shrubby variety, found on Fernandina and Isabela. It cohabits on Cerro Azul with *O. saxicola* and on Sierra Negra with *O. echios inermis*. It differs from the latter in being rather taller, up to 6 m and having longer spines, 5–8 cm and top-shaped fruits. There are, or were, tortoise and Land Iguana populations on both islands.

Opuntia saxicola
A rare trunked variety found only on Volcan Cerro Azul, Isabela, an island with both tortoise and Land Iguana populations.

Opuntia megasperma var. megasperma
This trunked variety is found only on Floreana and the Corona del Diablo. This species has the largest seeds of any of the species, up to 13-mm long. Floreana has had both tortoise and iguana populations in the past.

O. megasperma var. orientalis
Another very thick and heavily tapering trunked variety found only on San Cristóbal and Española. Both islands have tortoise populations but there are no Land Iguanas on Española.

O. megasperma var. mesophytica
Found only on San Cristóbal and its offshore islands. This trunked variety is found at higher elevations and has a thinner trunk and smaller seeds than *O. m. orientalis*. San Cristóbal has both tortoise and Land Iguana populations.

Arid and Transitional Zone Trees

(n) Palo Santo *Bursera graveolens*

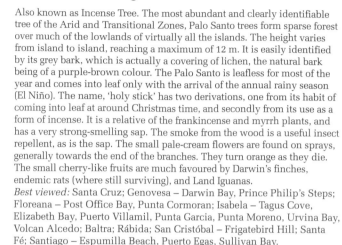

Also known as Incense Tree. The most abundant and clearly identifiable tree of the Arid and Transitional Zones, Palo Santo trees form sparse forest over much of the lowlands of virtually all the islands. The height varies from island to island, reaching a maximum of 12 m. It is easily identified by its grey bark, which is actually a covering of lichen, the natural bark being of a purple-brown colour. The Palo Santo is leafless for most of the year and comes into leaf only with the arrival of the annual rainy season (El Niño). The name, 'holy stick' has two derivations, one from its habit of coming into leaf at around Christmas time, and secondly from its use as a form of incense. It is a relative of the frankincense and myrrh plants, and has a very strong-smelling sap. The smoke from the wood is a useful insect repellent, as is the sap. The small pale-cream flowers are found on sprays, generally towards the end of the branches. They turn orange as they die. The small cherry-like fruits are much favoured by Darwin's finches, endemic rats (where still surviving), and Land Iguanas.
Best viewed: Santa Cruz; Genovesa – Darwin Bay, Prince Philip's Steps; Floreana – Post Office Bay, Punta Cormoran; Isabela – Tagus Cove, Elizabeth Bay, Puerto Villamil, Punta Garcia, Punta Moreno, Urvina Bay, Volcan Alcedo; Baltra; Rábida; San Cristóbal – Frigatebird Hill; Santa Fé; Santiago – Espumilla Beach, Puerto Egas, Sullivan Bay.

(e) Dwarf Palo Santo *Bursera malacophylla*

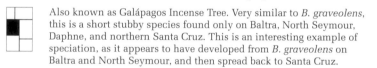

Also known as Galápagos Incense Tree. Very similar to *B. graveolens*, this is a short stubby species found only on Baltra, North Seymour, Daphne, and northern Santa Cruz. This is an interesting example of speciation, as it appears to have developed from *B. graveolens* on Baltra and North Seymour, and then spread back to Santa Cruz.

(n) Matazarno *Piscidia carthagenensis*

The tallest tree in the Transitional Zone, growing to over 15 m, recognisable by its large alternate, pinnate leaves, its sprays of pink to purplish flowers and when present, by its seeds which look a little like an old butter paddle with four 'wings'. It often has leaves in the dry season and so can be clearly seen from afar. The wood of this tree has long been used locally as it is very hard, virtually indestructible, and impervious to marine borers which makes it valuable for boats, mooring docks and piers. Most of the National Park marker posts are made of this wood.
Best viewed: Santa Cruz between Puerto Ayora and Bellavista and on the trail to Tortuga Bay, San Cristóbal.

(e) Pega Pega *Pisonia floribunda*

A large many-branched Transitional Zone tree growing to 10–15 m in height, and frequently festooned with mosses and lichens. The flowers are in small inconspicuous clusters. They produce sticky fruit which helps their dispersal by birds. Hence the Spanish name *pega pega* which translates as 'sticky sticky'. It is a much broader tree than most in the zone and is recognisable by its shape as well as its fairly dense foliage.
Best viewed: Santa Cruz – between Puerto Ayora and Bellavista.

ⓔ Guayabillo *Psidium galapageium* var. *galapageium*

Also known as Galápagos Guava. An easily identifiable Transition Zone tree growing to 8–10 m with smooth reddish-grey bark. The branches are often quite crooked and covered in long hair-like lichen, especially higher up near the moist zones. It has thin elliptical, pale-green leaves, large white flowers 10–15 cm in diameter, which produce small apple-like fruit. Found also in the Scalesia Zone, the wood is used locally for fencing and buildings, but is not as hard or enduring as Matazarno *Piscidia carthagenensis*.
Best viewed: Santa Cruz, on Airport Road from Puerto Ayora to Baltra; Isabela – V. Sierra Negra; Santiago.

Psidium galapageium var. *howellii*
This rare variety is found only on San Cristóbal and Santa Cruz. It has slightly smaller flowers, up to 1-cm across, smaller petals, 4–9-mm long and flower buds that have five lobes at their tips.

ⓝ Poison Apple *Hippomane mancinella*

Also known as Manchineel. Large evergreen tree growing up to 10 m in height with small very shiny elliptical leaves. Not widespread in the islands, but locally common.The greenish-white flowers appear on a long (up to 10 cm) spike at the end of the branch. They produce small, highly alkaline, green apple-like fruit about 5 cm in diameter. The tree gets its English name from the milky sap which is poisonous and can burn the skin. Avoid contact with the tree or its fruit, and do not sit underneath it. The antidote to the sap, if you should get any on your skin, is lemon juice.
Best viewed: Santa Cruz – Puerto Ayora, Academy Bay; Santiago – Espumilla Beach.

ⓝ Flame Tree *Erythrina velutina*

Large spiny tree found throughout the islands. Spikes of large, flaming red flowers which appear before the leaves and following rain. The flowers are a favoured food of the finches. The seeds are red with a black line and are produced in a pod. *Erythrina* is found mainly in the Arid Zone and provides a welcome flash of colour in the often sombre vegetation.
Best viewed: Santa Cruz – Puerto Ayora.

ⓘ Rose Apple *Syzygium jambos*

A tall tree up to 15 m with opposite, dark green, pointedly elliptical leaves. The flowers are greenish white and have four petals, but these are almost entirely obscured by the mass of long delicate stamens. The apple shaped fruit can be eaten raw or cooked.
Best viewed: in the inhabited and cultivated areas. .

ⓘ Lead Tree *Leucaena leucocephala*

A small (to 3m) tree with the same delicate bipinnately compound leaves as the mimosa and acacia families, but with no spines. The flowers are a delicate white ball and the seeds are produced in long pods. Found mainly on rocky areas on San Cristóbal.
Best viewed: San Cristóbal – Puerto Baquerizo Moreno.

ⓝ Muyuyu *Cordia lutea*

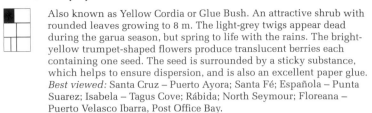

Also known as Yellow Cordia or Glue Bush. An attractive shrub with rounded leaves growing to 8 m. The light-grey twigs appear dead during the garua season, but spring to life with the rains. The bright-yellow trumpet-shaped flowers produce translucent berries each containing one seed. The seed is surrounded by a sticky substance, which helps to ensure dispersion, and is also an excellent paper glue.
Best viewed: Santa Cruz – Puerto Ayora; Santa Fé; Española – Punta Suarez; Isabela – Tagus Cove; Rábida; North Seymour; Floreana – Puerto Velasco Ibarra, Post Office Bay.

ⓝ Parkinsonia *Parkinsonia aculeata*

Also known as Jerusalem Thorn. A graceful spreading tree to 10 m. Leaves are long narrow spikes (17–45 cm) with 20 to 30 pairs of small oval leaflets along their length. Attractive yellow flowers on a spike, which produce seedpods up to 20-cm long. Branches have many strong, hooked spines. The sap of the tree is food for small scale-insects (Coccidae) which are tended or farmed by ants who feed off their sugary liquid.
Best viewed: Baltra; Santa Cruz – Puerto Ayora; Floreana – Post Office Bay, Punta Cormoran; Española – Gardner Bay; Isabela – Puerto Villamil; San Cristóbal – Puerto Baquerizo Moreno; North Seymour.

ⓝ Acacia *Acacia* spp.

Also known as Thorn Tree. Large spreading tree with small yellow or orange ball-like flowers which produce long seedpods. The leaves are compound with small pairs of leaflets giving them a very delicate appearance. The branches are armed with fierce straight thorns up to 4 cm long.

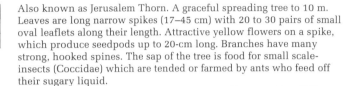

A. rorudiana
5–30 pairs of leaflets. Each leaflet has 14–24 pairs of secondary leaflets, each less than 1-mm long.
A. macracantha
Slightly bigger secondary leaflets 1–3-mm long, sometimes viewed as variant of *A. rorudiana*.
A. insulae-iajobi
1–5 pairs of leaflets, 5–10 pairs of secondary leaflets, each 3–15-mm long.
A. nilotica (Nile Acacia)
3–16 pairs of leaflets, 10–30 pairs of secondary leaflets, each 3–15-mm long.
Best viewed: Santa Cruz – Puerto Ayora, Floreana; Santiago, – Espumilla Beach, Post Office Bay.

ⓝ Mesquite *Prosopis juliflora*

A large tree very similar to the Acacia, but with a long yellow flower-spike instead of a ball. The spines are shorter (1–2 cm) and are found at the base of the leaves. Similar seedpod and leaves to *A. insulae-iacobi* but with one or two pairs of leaflets with six to 20 secondary leaflets.
Best viewed: Floreana – Punta Cormoran, Post Office Bay; Española – Gardner Bay, Punta Suarez; Isabela – Elizabeth Bay; Santa Cruz – Tortuga Bay.

Arid and Transitional Zone Shrubs

(e) Galápagos Croton *Croton scouleri*

Slender shrub or tree to 6 m. Four varieties distinguishable largely by location. Bark grey, leaves grey-green varying in size according to location. Fruit round and divided into three segments. Flowers small, cream-coloured on spikes up to 10-cm long. The sap of the Croton is well known to stain clothes a dark brown.
Best viewed: Santa Fé; Santa Cruz; Genovesa; Isabela–Tagus Cove; Santiago – Puerto Egas.

(e) Lance-leaved Cordia *Cordia leucophylactis*

Shrub to 2.5 m. Leaves alternate, lance-shaped and rough, slightly serrated. Flowers small and white in clusters. Fruit bright red, ovoid 4–6-mm long. Often nearly leafless in dry season. Two similar species are *C. anderssonii* and *C. scouleri*.
Best viewed: Santa Cruz – Puerto Ayora; Santa Fé; Isabela – Villamil.

(e) Lantana *Lantana peduncularis*

Small shrub up to 2 m. Branches four-sided, leaves pointed with serrated edges. White flowers have yellow centres, forming compact dome-shaped heads. Var. *peduncularis* is widespread, and var. *macrophylla* which has smaller leaves is found only on Genovesa and Gardner by Española.
Best viewed: Santa Cruz – Puerto Ayora; Santa Fé; Española – Punta Suarez; Isabela – Tagus Cove; Floreana – Post Office Bay, Punta Cormoran.

(n) Glorybower *Clerodendrum molle*

Deciduous shrub to 5 m, dark-green elliptical leaves. Long (to 3 cm), trumpet-shaped, white flowers with stamens extending 2 cm beyond petals. Fruits ball-shaped, less than 1 cm in diameter.
Best viewed: Santa Cruz – Puerto Ayora, Airport Road.

(n) Black Stick *Tourefortia psilostachya*

Spreading, vine-like shrub, leaves alternate, sage green, broad but pointed. Flowers brown and in scorpoid spikes. Seeds round and green. Older stems black, hence its common name.
Best viewed: Santa Cruz – Puerto Ayora.

(e) White-haired Tournefortia *Tournefortia pubescens*

Shrub up to 4 m in height. Young branches covered in white hairs. Leaves alternate, elliptical and pointed. White flowers in scorpoid sprays. Fruit is a white berry.
Best viewed: Santa Cruz – Airport Road.

(e) Red-haired Tournefortia *Tournefortia rufo-sericea*

Shrub to 5 m with reddish-brown bark, young branches having reddish hairs. Leaves alternate and have a corrugated appearance. White flowers in scorpoid sprays. Fruit is a white berry.
Best viewed: Santa Cruz – Airport Road.

(e) Spiny Bush *Scutia spicata* var. *pauciflora*

Also known as Thorn Shrub. Dark green, wonderfully spiny bush up to 2.5 m. It appears to have few leaves, being elliptical and about 1-cm long. The spines are numerous and up to 6-cm long. The small greenish flowers produce bright-red berries, edible but sour, eaten by finches and Land Iguanas. Common near the shore but found inland also.
Best viewed: Widespread; present at most visiting sites.

(e) Bitterbush *Castela galapageia*

Spiny, many-branched, normally erect shrub to 2 m. Alternate leaves are small, dark green, waxy and oval. Plants either male or female; both produce small red or yellow flowers. The fruits are bright red.
Best viewed: Santiago – Puerto Egas; Española – Punta Suarez, South Plaza; Santa Cruz – Puerto Ayora; Floreana – Punta Cormoran.

(e) Desert Thorn *Lycium minimum*

Dense spiny shrub to 3 m. All twigs and branches end in a spine but no other spines. Leaves club-shaped in groups up to five. Flowers are numerous and white. The fruit is small (5–6 mm), egg-shaped and red-orange. Found mainly close to the coast.
Best viewed: Española – Punta Suarez.

(n) Spiny-headed Chaff Flower *Altenanthera echinocephala*

A low compact shrub with narrow pointed opposite leaves. The flowers are clearly identifiable with their white spiky tuft-like flowers, which are found either at the base of the leaves, or at the ends of the branches.
Best viewed: Santa Cruz – Puerto Ayora, Airport Road.

(n) Thread-leafed Chaff Flower *Altenanthera filifolia*

Low compact shrub, often dome-shaped, with a dense mass of thin green branches which turn brown during dry periods. Leaves are opposite, very narrow and relatively few in number. Flowers are like small green-white pincushions, petals may be yellowish.
Best viewed: Santa Cruz – Puerto Ayora, Airport Road.

(e) Pearl Berry *Vallesia glabra*

Shrub or small tree growing to 6 m. Leaves alternate, long and pointed, and droop down from the branch. Flowers white with five petals in small clusters, and grow upwards from the branch. Fruit, a white translucent elongated berry. Var. *pubescens* is endemic and has the leaves, stems and flowers covered in fine hairs. Var. *glabra* is native and lacks these hairs.
Best viewed: Floreana, Post Office Bay; Isabela – Villamil; San Cristóbal – Puerto Baquerizo; Santiago – Espumilla; Santa Cruz – Airport Road.

(e) Lance-leafed Darwin Bush *Darwiniothamnus tenuifolius*

Thickly foliaged shrub growing to 3 m. The leaves are alternate, narrow, pointed and grow very close together. Flowers in small clusters at the branch tips are daisy-like with white petals and yellow stamens.
Best viewed: Isabela – Volcan Sierra Negra.

ⓔ Floreana Daisy *Lecocarpus pinnatifidus*

Also known as Cutleaf Daisy. A small bushy evergreen shrub (found on bare lava or cinder) up to 2 m, but more commonly 1 m with a single stem and a bushy head of leaves and flowers. The flowers are yellow and daisy-like. One species of *Lecocarpus* found on each of San Cristóbal, Española and Floreana.
Best viewed: Floreana – Punta Cormoran.
   Darwin's Daisy, *Lecocarpus darwinii,* is similar to *L. pinnatifidus*, but found only on San Cristóbal.
   Fitzroy's Daisy, *Lecocarpus lecocarpoides*, again very similar to *L. pinnatifidus* but found only on Española.

ⓝ Galápagos Cotton *Gossypium barbadense* var. *darwinii*

A rather open shrub growing up to 3-m high. The leaves are large (15–20 cm) and three- to five-lobed. Easily identified by its spectacular large yellow (up to 16 cm) flower with a purple centre. The seeds are oval, up to 3-cm long, and break open to produce a white lint or cotton, which is commonly used by finches and other smaller birds for nest lining. Normally flowers only after heavy rains. Largest flower on any native or endemic plant in Galápagos.
Best viewed: Floreana – Post Office Bay; Isabela – Tagus Cove; San Cristóbal – Frigatebird Hill, Puerto Baquerizo Moreno; Santa Cruz – Airport Road.

ⓝ Waltheria *Waltheria ovata*

A small many-branched shrub with the twigs changing from reddish-brown to dark grey with age. As its name suggests, the leaves are 'ovate', which means egg-shaped, but with a broad rather flat base and slightly pointed tip. They are also slightly serrated along the edge. The small yellow flowers occur in small clusters at the branch ends.
Best viewed: Santa Cruz.

ⓔ Needle-leafed Daisy *Macraea laricifolia*

A bushy shrub growing up to 2.5 m in height. The leaves are short, very narrow with the edges down-turned and in clusters especially towards the ends of the branches. The flowers are composite, yellow and on stalks 2–3-cm long. The Spanish common name, *Romerillo*, refers to its resemblance to rosemary, although it is in fact a member of the sunflower family.
Best viewed: Floreana; Isabela; Rábida; San Cristóbal; Santa Cruz; Santiago.

(n) Flat-fruited Senna *Senna pistaciifolia*

This low shrub, previously known as *Cassia picta*, is common along roadsides and in quarries. The leaves are alternate and pinnate with rounded tips. The flowers which are on spikes, are yellow and pea-like. The seeds are held in flattened pods. Not to be confused with *S. bicapsularis* and *S. alata*, both recently introduced and found on Santa Cruz.
Best viewed: Santa Cruz – Airport Road, New and Old Quarries.

Arid and Transitional Zone Herbs and Vines

(i) Sticky Caper *Cleome viscosa*

An annual herb growing to 1.6 m. The stems and seed-pods are covered with sticky hairs. The leaves are alternate with three lobes. The flowers are yellow with four petals. The fruit is a long (to 10 cm) pod containing many reddish-brown seeds. The sticky hairs have ensured the rapid spread of this plant, first recorded on Baltra in 1984 to Santa Cruz, Floreana, Seymour, Pinta and Santiago.
Best viewed: Santa Cruz – Airport Road; Seymour; Baltra.

(n) Dwarf Rattlebox *Crotalaria pumila*

An upright perennial herb growing to 1 m in height. The leaves are alternate, pinnate with three leaflets. Flowers are on long spikes, are yellow and pea-like. The seeds are held in short (to 2 cm) long pods. This species is similar to Fuzzy Rattlebox *C. incana*, which is rather larger.
Best viewed: Santa Cruz; San Cristóbal; Santiago.

(i) Poreleaf *Porophyllum ruderale* var. *macrocephalum*

An annual herb growing up to 1 m in height. The stems are purplish. The leaves are sage green, oval with slightly scalloped edges. Both stems and leaves have a waxy covering. The flowers are sunflower-shaped, 6–7-mm across, purplish with yellow flecks. The fruit capsule contains a single seed and is hairy.
Best viewed: Santa Cruz – Airport Road; Española; Floreana; Seymour; San Cristóbal.

(e) Galápagos Passion Flower *Passiflora foetida*

A vine found covering rocks or shrubs. The leaves are large (6 cm) and ivy-shaped. It has long tendrils, which wrap around branches or stems of other plants and easily identifiable white flowers with a purple centre. The fruits are egg-shaped (up to 1.5-cm long), green becoming orange as they ripen, and wrapped in a protective mesh. Found from near sea level up into the Scalesia and Miconia Zones.
Best viewed: Santa Cruz – Puerto Ayora; Floreana; Isabela.

ⓔ Grey Matplant *Tiquilia nesiotica*

Commonest of four species, found only in arid sandy locations. Small, grey-green leaves with very small white flowers hidden amongst them. Flowers are often eaten by the Lava Lizards which also eat flies or other insects visiting them.
Best viewed: Bartolomé; Santiago – Sullivan Bay.

Of the other three species, *T. darwinii* and *T. gusca* form spreading mats up to 1-m across. The third, *T. galapagoa* is a low spreading shrub up to 50 cm in height.
Best viewed: Bartolomé; Isabela; San Cristóbal; Floreana; Rábida; Santa Fé; Española; Plazas; Baltra; Daphne; Santiago – Sullivan Bay.

ⓔ Spurge *Chamaesyce* spp.

The ten Galápagos species of this genus show a considerable degree of adaptive radiation. They are varied, with both annual and perennial herbs, and small shrubs up to 1.5 m in height. All have the characteristic milky white latex-like sap and small white flowers.

C. amplexicaulis (middle left photo) Small shrub with round stemless leaves. Found on Bartolomé, Daphne and Genovesa.
C. punctulata Similar but with narrow pointed leaves. Found on Isabela and Santiago.
C. viminea Shrub to 1.5 m with long (to 4 cm) leaves with parallel edges occurring individually or in clusters. Found widely in the islands including Puerto Ayora, Genovesa, Isabela and Floreana.

ⓔ Galápagos Milkwort *Polygala* spp.

There are three species and four subspecies in Galápagos. *P. anderssonii* and *P. galapageia* are perennial growing to around 1 m in height, found on light sandy or ashy soils at low altitudes. *P. sancti-georgii* is an annual herb growing to 50 cm. Stems of all three are reddish yellow with alternate, pointed, sage-green elliptical leaves on *P. anderssonii* and *P. galapageia* but more rounded on *P. sancti-georgii.* The flowers are small and yellow in clusters at the end of the stems.
Best viewed: Isabela; Santiago; Santa Cruz; Floreana; San Cristóbal; Rábida.

ⓝ Horse Purslane *Trianthema portulacastrum*

Low perennial succulent herb with red stems. Oval leaves are opposite, of differing sizes. Flowers are individual, white and have five petals. The seeds are held in a small dark egg-shaped capsule.
Best viewed: Baltra; Española – Punta Suarez; Floreana; Genovesa; Isabela; Rábida; San Cristóbal; Santa Cruz; Santa Fé; Seymour.

ⓔ Mollugo *Mollugo flavescens*

Perennial herb, normally low growing but occasionally erect. There are five species and seven subspecies of this genus in Galápagos. *M. flavescens* has reddish stems and small baseball bat-shaped leaves. The flowers are white and have five petals. One of the earliest colonisers of fresh lava.
Best viewed: Fernandina; Genovesa; Isabela – Punto Moreno; San Cristóbal – Frigatebird Hill; Santa Cruz; Santiago; Bartolomé.

ⓔ Galápagos Tomato *Lycopersicon cheesmaniae*

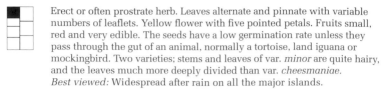

Erect or often prostrate herb. Leaves alternate and pinnate with variable numbers of leaflets. Yellow flower with five pointed petals. Fruits small, red and very edible. The seeds have a low germination rate unless they pass through the gut of an animal, normally a tortoise, land iguana or mockingbird. Two varieties; stems and leaves of var. *minor* are quite hairy, and the leaves much more deeply divided than var. *cheesmaniae*.
Best viewed: Widespread after rain on all the major islands.

ⓝ Goat's Head *Tribulus cistoides*

Also known as Puncture Weed. Low creeping plant has pinnate leaves with six to eight pairs of leaflets. The bright-yellow flowers are simple with five well-separated petals. Seed is enclosed in a fearsome spiked casing which gives it its common name and which can penetrate all but the stoutest shoe soles.
Best viewed: Baltra; Bartolomé; Seymour; Santa Cruz; Daphne; Española – Gardner Bay, Punta Suarez; South Plaza; Santiago – Puerto Egas; Sombrero Chino.

ⓘ *T. terrestris*, an annual pan-tropical weed, is best distinguished by its larger and spikier seed casings, 2-cm across (1.5 cm in *T. cistoides*).
Best viewed: Near inhabited areas.

ⓝ Mormordica *Mormordica charantia*

Vine with five-lobed fig-leaf shaped leaves up to 8-cm across and long tendrils. Flowers large (4–5 cm) and pale yellow with five petals. Fruits are spiny, 5–10-cm long and turn orange red as they ripen, then burst open to reveal 20–30 bright red seeds each about 1-cm long. The seeds stick to the inside of the capsule even after it has burst open.
Best viewed: Isabela – Villamil; Santa Cruz – Puerto Ayora.

ⓝ Stickleaf *Mentzelia aspera*

An annual herb, generally spreading. Stems with barbed hairs. Leaves alternate, pointed with serrated edges. Flowers are yellow with five petals. Seed capsule is cone-shaped, 5–11-mm long and covered in barbed hairs. Extremely successful at sticking to any human or animal and is widespread in the islands.
Best viewed: Baltra; Española; Floreana; Genovesa; Isabela; Rábida; San Cristóbal; Santa Cruz; Santa Fé; Santiago.

ⓔ Galápagos Purslane *Portulaca howellii*

Fleshy-leaved perennial growing on lava close to the shore. In the dry season, it loses its leaves and is reduced to a clump of grey smooth stems. After rain it produces leaves and large yellow flowers up to 4-cm across. Now largely restricted to offshore islets due to goats, but its relative, *Portulaca oleracea* (Native) is found throughout the islands and in the Arid rather than Coastal Zone. It has smaller flowers and less fleshy leaves which used to be valued as a salad vegetable.
Best viewed: Santa Cruz – Puerto Ayora; Genovesa; Daphne; Santa Fé; Sombrero Chino; South Plaza; North Seymour.

ⓔ Arrow-leafed Morning Glory *Ipomoea linearifolia*

A perennial vine that climbs over vegetation or across bare lava. The leaves are alternate and distinctly arrow-shaped. The flowers are large white, occasionally pink, trumpets with a well-defined pink throat. The seeds are dark brown and held in an oval capsule.
Best viewed: Fernandina; Genovesa; Isabela; Rábida; Santa Cruz; Seymour.

ⓝ Hairy Morning Glory *Merremia aegyptica*

An annual vine with hairy stems that covers vegetation after heavy rains. Leaves alternate with five elliptical and slightly ribbed leaflets. Flowers are white and trumpet-shaped. They are only open in the early morning. The brown seeds are held in a brown capsule.
Best viewed: Disturbed sites and roadsides and on: Genovesa; Española; Isabela; Rábida; Santa Cruz; Santa Fé; Santiago; Seymour.

ⓝ Climbing Pea *Rhynchosia minima*

A perennial vine with purplish stems found especially on disturbed sites. The leaves are alternate and have three leaflets. The flowers are yellow and pea-shaped. The seeds are held in a short 1.5-cm long pod.
Best viewed: All major islands, but not on Volcan Sierra Negra, Isabela.

ⓝ Hairy Ground Cherry *Physalis pubescens*

Annual herb up to 1 m. Purplish stems are hairy and slightly sticky. Leaves are oval to elliptical and pointed with clearly visible veins. Flowers are bell-shaped, pale yellow to white. Fruit is a round berry, contained in a lantern-like capsule. Three other related species *P. galapagoensis* (endemic), *P. angulata,* and *P. peruviana* are found in Galápagos. This last is the cultivated Cape Gooseberry.
Best viewed: Baltra; Española; Fernandina; Genovesa; Rábida; Santa Cruz; Santiago; Seymour.

ⓝ Yellow Ground Mallow *Bastardia viscosa*

Annual herb growing to 1 m in height with slightly hairy stems. Leaves are an elongated heart-shape, pointed and with edges slightly serrated. Flowers are yellow with five rounded petals. Fruit has six or seven sections, each with a single seed.
Best viewed: Española; Floreana; Isabela; Rábida; San Cristóbal; Santa Cruz; Santiago; Seymour.

ⓔ Oily Pectis *Pectis tenuifolia*

A low perennial herb often forming a low tussock to 15 cm in height, frequently found on bare rock. The leaves are opposite, needle-like, with oily glands on the underside. They have a distinct purplish tinge, especially during dry periods. The flowers are yellow with five petals and are carried on short stems facing upwards. Two other similar species, *P. subsquarrosa* which is much less compact and lacks the purplish tinge, and *P. linifolia,* are also found in the islands.
Best viewed: Fernandina; Floreana – Post Office Bay; Genovesa; Isabela – Elizabeth Bay; San Cristóbal; Santa Cruz; Santa Fé; Bartolomé.

ⓔ Galápagos Bean *Phaseolus mollis*

Annual vine with stems to 3 m. Young stems are quite hairy. Leaves alternate with three shield-shaped leaflets. Flowers pea-shaped, pink or purplish in colour and on long racemes or sprays. The short (2.5–3 cm) pod holds between two and four seeds.
Best viewed: Fernandina; Isabela; Santa Cruz.

P. adenanthus a similar species found only on Española, has paler flowers, almost white, and a larger seed-pod, (7–12-cm long).
Best viewed: Española.

ⓘ Blue Morning Glory *Ipomoea nil*

A vine with slightly hairy stems up to 5-m long. It may be annual or perennial. The leaves are large, up to 18-cm long and like a three-lobed maple. The large (3–5 cm) flowers are blue to purplish with a white throat. The seeds are held in a small capsule.
Best viewed: Floreana; San Cristóbal; Santa Cruz; Santiago.

ⓝ Boerhaavia *Boerhaavia caribaea*

Annual herb, often prostrate. The stems are hairy and sticky. Leaves are opposite and have a wavy edge. Flowers are in clusters at the base of the leaves and are reddish purple. The seeds are sticky.
Best viewed: Española; Fernandina; Floreana; Genovesa; San Cristóbal; Santa Cruz; Santa Fé; Santiago.

ⓝ Wartclub *Commicarpus tuberosus*

Prostrate herb with green stems. The leaves are opposite and rounded and appear to grow around the stem. Flowers are small, up to 1-cm long, bell-shaped and pinkish purple. Seed has longitudinal grooves and small 'warts' near the top. These are very sticky and adhere to passing animals.
Best viewed: Floreana; Isabela; Rábida; San Cristóbal; Santa Cruz; Santiago.

ⓝ Heliotrope *Heliotropium angiospermum*

Upright perennial with woody lower stems. Leaves are alternate, rather pointed, and very heavily veined, sometimes almost corrugated. White flowers are on a backwards-curving spike which gives it its Spanish name, *Cola de escorpion* (Scorpion tail). Not to be confused with *H. andersonii*, a rare endemic which has pale-yellow flowers, found only on Santa Cruz.
Best viewed: Española; Fernandina; Floreana; Genovesa; Isabela; Rábida; San Cristóbal; Santa Cruz; Santa Fé; Seymour.

ⓘ Maple-leafed Mallow *Anoda acerifolia*

A herb which can grow to 70 cm in height. The alternate leaves are triangular when young, becoming maple-shaped as they develop. The flower is white with five petals and the fruit is an attractive five-pointed star. Found mainly along the roadsides in Santa Cruz.
Best viewed: Santa Cruz – Airport Road.

(e) Scalesia *Scalesia* spp.

Scalesia is a genus endemic to Galápagos and one of the best demonstrations of adaptive radiation to be found in the islands. The 15 species and six subspecies have adapted to different vegetation zones on different islands. They vary in size from under 1 m to over 15 m in height. Most species occur in the Arid and Transitional Zones, though the largest and most easily identified one, *S. pedunculata* is found in the zone that bears its name, where it is the dominant plant. Several species are threatened, thanks mainly to the grazing of feral goats. One species, *S. gordilloi,* was discovered as recently as 1985.

The Scalesias are members of the daisy family, one of the commonest plant families in Galápagos. The flowers are similar in having a flower head made up of a number of small flowers. In some species there are petals around the outside of the main flower disc. These are 'ray flowers' that are similar to the internal flowers but have one large petal on the outside. The following species are the most likely to be seen and identified by the visitor.

(e) Radiate-headed Scalesia *Scalesia affinis*

Found from sea level to around 600 m. A pioneer on barren lava and cinder slopes, a shrub normally growing to no more than 3-m high. The leaves are alternate, pointed with a serrated edge and up to 15-cm long. The single white daisy-like flowers appear at the ends of the branches. Three subspecies have been identified: *S. affinis affinis* on Floreana; *S. affinis brachyloba* on Santa Cruz; and *S. affinis gummifera* on Isabela and Fernandina.
Best viewed: Isabela – Villamil, Punta Moreno, Tagus Cove, Sierra Negra, Punta Albermarle; Santa Cruz.

(e) Heller's Scalesia *Scalesia helleri*

Low shrub growing to 2.5 m. Found mainly on cliffs and near the shore, this species appears to be favoured by feral goats. The leaves are alternate or opposite and, while being generally oval in shape to 10-cm long, are very heavily divided, giving a fuzzy appearance. Flower heads are up 1.7-cm across and are made up of 30–100 individual flowers. There are two subspecies, *S. helleri helleri* found on Santa Cruz and Santa Fé (left photo), and *S. helleri santacruziana* found only on Santa Cruz (right photo).
Best viewed: Santa Cruz – Tortuga Bay; Santa Fé.

(e) Tree Scalesia *Scalesia pedunculata*

By far the largest member of the genus, with trees reaching 15 m or more. This is the dominant species in the Scalesia Zone on Santa Cruz, Santiago, San Cristóbal and Floreana. The tree has a largely unbranched trunk, often covered in a variety of mosses, with a dome of branches on top making it look rather like a calabrese flower head. When the trees grow close together, they provide a dense and uniform canopy. As the Scalesia Zone provides some of the best farming land, much of the zone has been destroyed. The leaves are alternate, elliptical/lanceolate, and slightly hairy. Flowers are white, in bunches at the ends of branches, up to 2-cm across and are made up of 50–150 individual flowers.
Best viewed: Santa Cruz – Los Gemelos, Airport Road; Floreana – highlands.

ⓔ Longhaired Scalesia *Scalesia villosa*

An open, rather untidy shrub up to 3 m with characteristically narrow hairy leaves which are alternate and found at the tip of the stems, often with a bunch of dead leaves beneath them. The flower heads which are large, white and almost thistle-like are up to 2-cm across and made up of 200–300 individual flowers. This species is found only on Floreana and its offshore islets.
Best viewed: Floreana – Punta Cormoran.

ⓔ Crocker's Scalesia *Scalesia crockeri*

left page

A small, Arid Zone shrub to 1 m in height. The leaves are opposite, broadly elliptical, and are found at the end of the branches with a bunch of dead leaves beneath them. The flower heads are up to 2-cm across and are made up of 20–60 individual flowers.
Best viewed: Baltra; Santa Cruz; North East.

ⓔ Stewart's Scalesia *Scalesia stewartii*

left page

A shrub growing to 3 m in height. The leaves are alternate, lanceolate, 6–10-cm long and with white hairs on the undersides. The flower head is around 15 mm in diameter with 35–90 individual flowers on each head.
Best viewed: Santiago – Sullivan Bay; Bartolomé.

ⓔ Heart-leafed Scalesia *Scalesia cordata*

right page

A tree up to 10 m in height. The leaves are alternate, 4–9 cm in length and shaped like an elongated heart. The edges are sometimes serrated. The white flower heads consist of some 15–30 individual flowers.
Best viewed: Isabela – Sierra Negra.

ⓔ Cut-leafed Scalesia *Scalesia incisa*

right page

Found only on San Cristóbal, *S. incisa* grows to some 4 m in height. The leaves are opposite and divided into lobes, the lobes themselves are divided or toothed. The flower head is up to 15-mm across and consists of up to 30–50 flowers, together with the occasional individual ray flowers.
Best viewed: San Cristóbal – Punta Pitt.

Scalesia species and their distribution

Species	Islands and zones	Types
S. affinis affinis	Floreana (W); Arid	Shrub, large flower
S. affinis brachyloba	Santa Cruz (S); Arid, Transitional	Shrub, large flower
S. affinis gummifcra	Fernandina, Isabela; Arid	Shrub, large flower
S. aspera	Santa Cruz (NW); Arid, Transitional	Shrub, large flower
S. atractyloides atractyloides	Santiago; Transitional	Shrub, narrow hairy leaves
S. atractyloides darwinii	Santiago; Transitional	Shrub, narrow hairy leaves
S. baurii baurii	Pinta, Pinzón, Wolf; Arid	Shrub, divided leaves
S. baurii hopkinsii	Pinta, Wolf; Arid, Transitional	Shrub, divided leaves
S. cordata	Isabela; Arid	Tree to 10 m, small flower
S. crockeri	Baltra, Seymour, Santa Cruz (N); Arid	Shrub, large flower
S. divisa	San Cristóbal; Arid	Shrub, divided leaves
S. gordilloi	San Cristóbal; Arid	Shrub
S. helleri helleri	Santa Cruz (S), Santa Fé; Arid	Shrub, divided leaves
S. helleri santacruziana	Santa Cruz (S); Arid	Shrub, divided leaves
S. incisa	San Cristóbal (N); Arid	Shrub, large flower
S. microcephala microcephala	Fernandina, Isabela; Humid	Small tree, small flower
S. microcephala cordifolia	Isabela (N), Wolf; Transitional	Small tree, small flower
S. pedunculata	Floreana, Santa Cruz, Santiago, San Cristóbal; Scalesia	Tree to 15 m, small flower
S. retroflexa	Santa Cruz (SE); Arid	Shrub, large flower
S. stewartii	Bartolomé, Santiago (E); Arid	Shrub, narrow leaves
S. villosa	Floreana and islets; Arid	Shrub, hairy leaves, large flower

Humid Zone Trees and Shrubs

There are up to four clearly defined humid or moist zones:
- The Scalesia Zone, named after the dominant tree.
- The Brown Zone, here the dominant trees and other shrubs are covered with epiphytes, giving the zone its brown colour.
- Miconia Zone, named after the dominant shrub, *Miconia robinsoniana*. This is found only on Santa Cruz and San Cristóbal.
- Pampa or Fern-sedge Zone which is open moorland.

The zones vary from island to island, and on Isabela from volcano to volcano. They are very noticeable on the south side of the islands. Northern slopes of volcanoes are generally in a rain shadow and the transition from the Pampas Zone to the Arid Zone takes place over a short distance.

ⓘⓟ Quinine Tree *Cinchona succirubra*

Trees growing to 12 m. Leaves opposite, large (to 20 cm) and glossy with distinct ribbing. Initially dark green, turning pink and then red with age. Flowers small and pink, fruit winged. Introduced to Galápagos in 1948 in response to a quinine shortage. No longer cultivated. Serious threat to the Miconia Zone as it is taller than Miconia and has dense foliage, cutting out the light. Also a threat to the breeding success of Dark-rumped Petrel.
Best viewed: Santa Cruz – Media Luna.

ⓘ Common Coral Bean *Erythrina corallodendron*

One of several species of *Erithrina* introduced to the farming regions. Used as living fence posts growing to 5–6 m. Flowers bright red and on a long spike. Seeds are small red beans in a pod.
Best viewed: Santa Cruz.

ⓘ Balsa *Ochroma pyramidale*

Very large tree to 30 m. Trunk has buttresses at the base, bark is smooth and grey with white blotches. Leaves alternate, three-lobed and very large (30 cm). Flowers white with five petals. Fruit is a pod to 25 cm.
Best viewed: Farming zones; Isabela; Santa Cruz.

ⓘⓟ Common Guava *Psidium guajava*

Very common shrub or tree to 8 m in height. Leaves are opposite, dark green, elliptical to 15-cm. Flower white with five petals and grows alone or in small axillary clusters with a large brush of stamens. Fruit is round, up to 5 cm and is edible. Forms dense thickets and is a major threat to the natural vegetation of the Humid Zones.
Best viewed: Farming zones on Floreana, Santa Cruz, Isabela and San Cristóbal.

ⓘ Brazilian Tea *Stachytarpheta cayennensis*

Also known as False Vervain. A much-branched shrub to 2.5 m. Leaves have a slightly purplish tinge, are opposite, elliptical, and have coarsely serrated edges. The bluish-purple flowers have a whitish throat, on long (to 35 cm) terminal spike.
Best viewed: Floreana; Isabela; San Cristóbal, Santa Cruz.

ⓝ Soapberry *Sapindus saponaria*

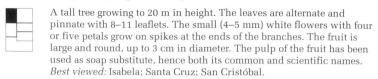

A tall tree growing to 20 m in height. The leaves are alternate and pinnate with 8–11 leaflets. The small (4–5 mm) white flowers with four or five petals grow on spikes at the ends of the branches. The fruit is large and round, up to 3 cm in diameter. The pulp of the fruit has been used as soap substitute, hence both its common and scientific names.
Best viewed: Isabela; Santa Cruz; San Cristóbal.

ⓘ Silky Inga *Inga schimpffii*

A tree growing to 10 m in height. The leaves are alternate, elliptical, dark green, waxy and clearly ribbed. The white flowers grow in axillary clusters and are tube-shaped, with the stamens extending beyond the petals. The fruit are held in a long pod and the white pulp surrounding them is very good to eat.
Best viewed: Farming zones on Isabela and Santa Cruz.

ⓘ Spanish Cedar *Cedrela odorata*

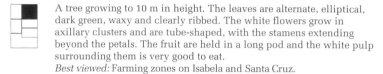

A large tree with smooth brownish bark, growing to over 30 m in height. The leaves are alternate and pinnate with 10–20 leaflets. The pale greenish-yellow flowers are small and hard to see from the ground, even though they grow in clusters. The seeds are numerous and winged. The tree was introduced to provide wood for construction, furniture and shipbuilding. It is fast growing, light and adaptable. Owing to the winged seeds, it is a potential threat to the native vegetation as it now grows outside the farming zones.
Best viewed: Floreana; Isabela; San Cristóbal; Santa Cruz.

ⓔ Miconia *Miconia robinsoniana*

A shiny-leaved shrub up to 5 m in height, growing in dense almost impenetrable stands above the Scalesia Zone. The long (to 25 cm) slender pointed leaves turn reddish in periods of drought giving the whole zone a reddish tinge when seen from afar. The clusters of pink or purple flowers are produced at the end of the branches. The fruit is a small blue-black berry. It provides an excellent nesting habitat for the Dark-rumped or Hawaiian Petrel *Pterodroma phaeopygia*, which nests in this area during the garua season. This species is threatened both by agriculture and by invasive Guava *Psidium guajava* and Quinine *Cinchona succirubra* trees.
Best viewed: Santa Cruz; San Cristóbal.

ⓝ Cat's Claw *Zanthoxylum fagara*

Also known as 'Wait-a-Minute Bush', this shrub or small tree grows to a height of 10 m. It is the dominant plant in the Brown Zone and is frequently encrusted with a dense growth of epiphytic mosses, lichens and liverworts. The branches are armed with sharp hooked spines which give the plant its common name. The leaves are compound with five to eleven leaflets. The inconspicuous greenish-white flowers produce small dark berries.
Best viewed: Santa Cruz by Airport Road.

ⓔ Galápagos Mistletoe *Phoradendron henslowii*

Widespread parasitic shrub, growing on a variety of woody shrubs and trees in all zones. It is not alone in particularly liking attachment to Cat's Claw (*Zanthoxylum fagara*). The leaves are broadly elliptical and rather leathery. The small greenish flowers are on spikes which grow from the base of the leaves. The fruit are small (up to 6 mm) translucent berries.
Best viewed: Santa Cruz – highlands.

ⓘ Multicoloured Lantana *Lantana camara*

A shrub to 3 m in height, the stems are hairy, often prickly. The leaves are opposite and ovoid with a serrated edge. The flowers which grow from the base of the leaves are clustered in bunches. Each flower is small, 3–4 mm, starting off yellow-orange but turning pinkish purple with time. This results in flowers of more than one colour on each head. This is a recent introduction which has spread out of people's gardens.
Best viewed: Santa Cruz – Puerto Ayora, Bellavista; San Cristóbal – Puerto Baquerizo; Floreana – Puerto Velasco Ibarra.

ⓘⓟ Mora *Rubus niveus*

Also known as Hill Raspberry. Climbing shrub or vine very similar to the Blackberry of Northern Hemisphere. Introduced to San Cristóbal; now also found on Santa Cruz in or close to the farming zone. It threatens to be a serious pest species forming dense thickets. Stems are 3 m or more in length and covered with sharp stout prickles. Leaves are alternate, pinnate with prickles on the underside; leaflets are up to 5-cm long. Flowers have five petals, dark pink, found in bunches at the end of the stems. Fruit are raspberry-like, red, turning black and edible.
Best viewed: Farming zones on Santa Cruz and San Cristóbal.

ⓘ Angel's Trumpet *Brugmansia candida*

A readily recognisable shrub growing to 7 m in height. The leaves are alternate, broad and oval with distinct veins. The flowers are large white trumpets, up to 20-cm long and 10–15-cm across. They hang vertically downwards. The seeds are held in a capsule 4–8-cm long. The leaves are poisonous as they contain the alkaloid hyoscine.
Best viewed: Inhabited and cultivated parts of Floreana, Isabela and Santa Cruz.

ⓘ White Valerian *Astrephia chaerophylloides*

Weak-stemmed herb growing with and over other plants. Leaves pinnate and feathery looking pinnae and leaflets heavily indented. Flowers white on long axillary stems, three flowers per stem.
Best viewed: Farming zone, Santa Cruz.

ⓔ Galápagos Dead Nettle *Pilea baurii*

Erect annual, or occasionally perennial herb, reddish stems and leaf stalks. Leaves opposite, oval to 10 cm, pale-green tending to yellow as they age, sometimes pinkish. Leaf edges serrated. Flowers green on axillary sprays. Seeds in tiny (0.4 mm) individual capsules.
Best viewed: Floreana; Isabela; San Cristóbal; Santa Cruz; Santiago.

Humid Zone Herbs and Vines

(e) Galápagos Peperomia *Peperomia galapagensis*

Small upright perennial herb to 20 cm, stems grow closely together. Slightly fleshy leaves in whorls of three or four, often with red edges and spatula shape. Flowers small and green, on short spikes. Two varieties of this plant: var. *galapagensis* is hairless, while var. *ramulosa* is found on Floreana, Isabela, Pinta and Santa Cruz.
Best viewed: Santa Cruz – Los Gemelos.

(e) Galápagos Orchid *Epidendrum spicatum*

Epiphytic perennial herb growing on trees, often hanging downwards. Leaves alternate, slightly fleshy, to 15-cm, encircling the stem at their base. Flowers whitish green on a spray at the end of stem, three petals in typical orchid form. Seeds are like a fine powder, in an elliptical capsule 2.5-cm long.
Best viewed: Santa Cruz – Los Gemelos.

(n) White Leadwort *Plumbago scandens*

Sprawling perennial herb, stems normally green, sometimes dark red, up to 6 m. Leaves are alternate, generally elliptical, often red. White flower has five petals and a long (2.5-cm) tube. Seed capsule, is covered with sticky hairs.
Best viewed: Highlands of Santa Cruz, Floreana, Isabela and San Cristóbal, common on roadside.

(n) Purple Vervain *Lippia strigulosa*

Dense low, perennial herb, the stems purplish towards the base. Leaves opposite, elliptical, surfaces are slightly hairy, edges serrated and often purplish. Flowers form clusters on the end of axillary stalks, white with yellow throat and purple bracts.
Best viewed: Isabela; San Cristóbal; Santa Cruz.

(e) Bromeliad *Tillandsia insularis*

An unmistakable plant, a member of the Pineapple Family. An epiphyte found throughout the humid zones, grows on trees, shrubs and rocks. Long pointed leaves up to 45-cm, green to reddish- green in colour. Flower spike can be 75-cm tall. Flowers themselves are small and whitish. Bromeliads are an important feature of the ecosystem as they collect water in their centres, which becomes a breeding place for mosquitoes and other invertebrates.
Best viewed: Santa Cruz.

(n) Verbena *Verbena litoralis*

An erect perennial herb growing up to 2 m in height. The leaves are opposite, long (to 10 cm) and narrow with serrated edges on the outer two-thirds. The flowers are a pale pinky violet colour and are on spikes at the end of the stems.
Best viewed: Floreana; Isabela; San Cristóbal; Santa Cruz.

(i) Purple Cuphea *Cuphea carthagenensis*

Annual upright herb to 50 cm, stems are reddish and slightly hairy. Leaves are opposite, elliptical and slightly hairy. Purple flowers in small axillary spray, have a long (1 cm) tube which is distinctly wider at the base and longitudinally striped. Six very narrow, well-separated petals.
Best viewed: Farming zones on San Cristóbal and Santa Cruz.

(i) Bush Violet *Browallia americana*

A straggling annual herb to 1 m in height. The leaves are alternate and narrowly egg-shaped. The purple flowers are tubular with a white lip to the throat and a yellow spot in the centre.
Best viewed: Farming zone of Santa Cruz.

(n) Blechum *Blechum pyramidatum*

Low perennial herb. Leaves are opposite, spear-shaped, and hairy, especially when young, at the growing points forming an unusual and distinctive pyramidal shape. Flowers pale purple, occasionally almost white, with five square-ended petals, grow on an upright spike.
Best viewed: Floreana; Isabela; San Cristóbal; Santa Cruz; Santiago.

(e) Galápagos Justicia *Justicia galapagana*

Untidy perennial herb with hairy stems, growing to 1 m height. Leaves opposite, hairy, especially when young, and spear-shaped with a distinct mid-rib. Flowers, pea-shaped with three lower lobes, are a bright purplish pink with a striking white pattern at the entrance to the throat.
Best viewed: Isabela; Santa Cruz; Santiago.

(n) Ageratum *Ageratum conyzoides*

Upright, annual herb with purplish stems growing to 1 m. Leaves opposite, oval with purple veins and edges, which are also serrated. The purplish pink flowers grow in multiple clusters at the ends of the stems. An identifying factor is its rather unpleasant smell.
Best viewed: Floreana; Isabela; San Cristóbal; Santa Cruz; Santiago.

(n) Germander *Teucrium vesicarium*

Upright, square-stemmed perennial herb growing to 1.2 m. Leaves are opposite, elliptical with serrated edges. The flowers, which are a mid-pink to near white, are tubular and grow on a densely packed spike.
Best viewed: Floreana; Isabela; San Cristóbal; Santa Cruz.

(i) False Mallow *Sida rhombifolia*

An upright perennial herb growing to 1.5 m in height. The older stems become woody. The leaves are alternate, elliptical, slightly rhomboid, with serrated edges towards the tip. The flower is yellow with five petals and a brownish-purplish ring around the stamens. The stiff straight woody stems are used to make brooms, hence the Spanish common name of *Escoba*. Eight other species of *Sida* occur in Galápagos. The plant is a favourite food of tortoises.
Best viewed: Floreana; Isabela; San Cristóbal; Santa Cruz.

(e) Galápagos Jaegeria *Jaegeria gracilis*

An annual herb found most frequently in the Humid Zone. The stems are purplish-brown, the leaves are opposite and oval to pointed. The flowers are yellow, daisy-like, and on long stalks at the ends of the shoots.
Best viewed: Fernandina; Floreana; Isabela; San Cristóbal; Santa Cruz; Santiago.

(e) Indefatigable Passion Flower *Passiflora colinvauxii*

Distinguished from *P. foetida* (p. 168) by its leaves which are shaped rather like a boomerang or a crescent moon, and its larger and more brightly coloured flower. A similar species, *P. suberosa,* is also found in the islands but is much less common.
Best viewed: The highlands Santa Cruz – Los Gemelos.

(i) Common or Greater Plantain *Plantago major*

A low, perennial, stemless herb. The leaves are a broad oval shape and all emanate from the central root. The small yellowish-green flowers are on long (to 40 cm) spikes. This common worldwide weed is a recent arrival and found in the towns, where it is sometimes cultivated, as well as highlands.
Best viewed: Floreana; Isabela; San Cristóbal; Santa Cruz; Santiago.

(n) Indian Heliotrope *Heliotropium indicum*

A bushy perennial herb growing to 1 m in height. The leaves are alternate, broadly elliptical and very crinkly, especially when young, with the veins clearly indented. The small purplish to bluish flowers have a white or sometimes yellowish throat and are on just one side of a backwards-curving spike.
Best viewed: Floreana; San Cristóbal; Santa Cruz.

(n) Beggar's Tick *Bidens pilosa*

Also known as Spanish Needle. An annual many-stemmed herb growing to 1 m in height. The leaves are opposite, with serrated edges. Some are simple, others pinnate with three leaflets, the central one being longer than the two lateral ones. The yellow daisy-like flowers are on a stalk, either individually or in a cluster.
Best viewed: Floreana; Isabela; San Cristóbal; Santa Cruz.

ⓘ Smooth Sow Thistle *Sonchus oleraceus*

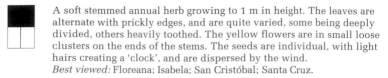

A soft stemmed annual herb growing to 1 m in height. The leaves are alternate with prickly edges, and are quite varied, some being deeply divided, others heavily toothed. The yellow flowers are in small loose clusters on the ends of the stems. The seeds are individual, with light hairs creating a 'clock', and are dispersed by the wind.
Best viewed: Floreana; Isabela; San Cristóbal; Santa Cruz.

ⓝ St John's Wort *Hypericum uliginosum* var. *pratense*

A perennial herb growing to 50 cm in height. The leaves are opposite, narrow and pointed, and turn reddish with age or during dry periods. The yellow flowers have five well-separated petals and are in loose sprays at the end of the stems.
Best viewed: San Cristóbal; Santa Cruz; Santiago.

ⓝ Clubmoss

There are at least six species of clubmoss in Galápagos. They are not mosses, but are related to ferns. The shortness of their yellowish-green leaves (less than 1 cm) gives them a furry look like mosses; the club shape of their seed capsules explains their English name. They are epiphytes, and may have individual branches up to 60-cm long.

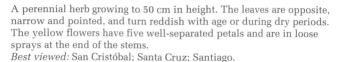

Lycopodium cernuum An upright species looking like a miniature Christmas tree, found mainly in the Miconia Zone.
L. clavatum A terrestrial species growing close to the ground but with the ends of the branches turning upwards and producing candelabra-like flower spikes (bottom right photo).
L. dichotomum Generally found hanging from trees in the humid zones.
L. passerinoides Another species found hanging from trees and shrubs.
L. reflexum A species generally found growing on rocks, either upright or spreading with the tips turned upwards.
L. thyoides An upright terrestrial species found especially in shaded ravines.

Best viewed: Highlands of major islands.

Lichens

A lichen is not a higher plant but a fungus that can only exist by means of a symbiotic relationship with an alga. The alga provides the fungus with carbohydrate and in return gains protection. Some 300 species of lichen are found in Galápagos, mainly in the Arid and Transitional Zones where they are very much in evidence on trees, rocks and even tortoises. The Palo Santo tree, which is characteristic of the Arid Zone, derives its white colour from crustose lichens; the bark is actually a brown-purplish colour. In the Transitional Zone trees can be found that are almost completely hidden beneath festoons of long grey-green lichen. One of these, Dyers' Moss *Rocella babingtonii*, is well known to produce a purple dye. The lichens obtain their moisture from the garua, and also when close to the coast from the moist air off the sea. They come in a wide range of forms and colours and have been little studied. There are likely to be a number of endemic species that have yet to be described.

Grasses and Sedges

(n) Feather Fingergrass *Chloris virgata*

An erect annual herb growing to 80 cm in height. The leaves are alternate and narrow, 3–7-mm wide. The flowers are on short, 5–10 cm, spikelets which have numerous minute flowers and hairs giving the grass a feathery appearance. There are three other species of *Chloris* in Galápagos and opinions differ as to whether any or all of them are native or introduced.

Best viewed: Baltra; Española; Floreana; San Cristóbal; Santa Cruz; Santa Fé; Seymour.

(ip) Elephant Grass *Pennisetum purpureum*

A perennial herb growing to 6 m, more commonly 2–3 m, forming dense clumps. The leaves are alternate, narrow (3–4 mm) and up to 120-cm long. The flowers are brown and produced on a spike 10–30 cm in length. A recent introduction for forage for cattle. *The Flora of the Galápagos* (Wiggins and Porter 1971) says 'There is no previous report of this species from Galápagos.' Now it is widespread in the farming zone and has spread outside it. A potentially very dangerous invasive species due to the denseness of its clumps which excludes all other species.

Best viewed: In and close to the farming zones on Floreana, Isabela, San Cristobál; Santa Cruz.

(e) Galápagos Sedge *Cyperus anderssonii*

A perennial herb with one or more upright triangular stems to 70 cm in height. The leaves are basal and of similar length, 2–6-mm wide. The brown flowers appear in a number of short spikes or sprays at the stem-ends. Found in most of the vegetation zones. There are 18 species of *Cyperus* found in Galápagos. Three of these are endemic.

Best viewed: Baltra; Fernandina; Floreana; Genovesa; Isabela; Rábida; San Cristóbal; Santa Fé; Santiago.

C. ligularis is similar to *C. andersonii* but is generally taller, has wider leaves and is less widely distributed, being found in the coastal zone only, on Fernandina, Isabela, and Santa Cruz.

(i) Bermuda Grass *Cynodon dactylon*

A low creeping grass with alternate leaves and flowering spikes growing to 40 cm in height. The flowering spike divides into five or six spikelets, each with many small greenish flowers. Commonly used for lawns and pasture.

Best viewed: Floreana, Isabela, San Cristóbal, Santa Cruz.

Ferns

Ninety species found in Galápagos, largely in the humid zones. Most are terrestrial, others are epiphytes, most native with a few endemics. Ferns have no flowers but produce spores on the undersides of their leaves.

(e) Galápagos Tree Fern *Cyathea weatherbyana*

An unmistakable fern growing to 6 m. Older plants have a distinct trunk which may be up to 30 cm in diameter, topped by a luxuriant spray of typically fern-like fronds. Found in the Fern-sedge Zone but very often hidden in potholes or gullies or on the inside of small crater walls.
Best viewed: Santa Cruz – Los Gemelos, Mount Crocker.

(n) Bracken *Pteridium aquilinum* var. *arachnoideum*

Large branching fern to 3 m in height. Fronds bipinnately compound and up to 2 m in length The variety of bracken found in Galápagos is virtually indistinguishable from that found elsewhere in the world.
Best viewed: Santa Cruz; San Cristóbal; Isabela.

(n) Maidenhair Fern *Adenostemma coccinium*

Low drooping perennial herb. Fronds up to 15-cm long with ten or more individual pairs of leaflets. Stems and leaves often have a purplish tinge. A similar species, *A. henslovianum*, is also found but has branching rather than simple fronds.
Best viewed: Isabela; Floreana; Santa Cruz.

(n) Hart's-tongue Polypody *Polypodium phyllitidis*

A distinctive fern with broad (3–10-cm wide) shiny, yellow-green fronds. The symmetrically lanceolate fronds are 20–80-cm long. Not to be confused with the Lance-leafed Polypody *Polypodium lanceolatum* which is epiphytic and grows individual lance-shaped fronds from a long rhizome.
Best viewed: Santa Cruz – Los Gemelos.

(n) Hand Fern *Doryopteris pedata* var. *palmata*

Individual stems growing vertically upwards from the rhizome. The leaves lie horizontally and are broad but deeply indented, with three or five lobes, at times hand-shaped.
Best viewed: Floreana; Santa Cruz; San Cristóbal; Isabela.

(n) Golden Polypody *Polypodium aureum var areolata*

A large fern with golden yellow-green, deeply indented, leathery fronds up to 1 m. Underside has a whitish bloom and clearly visible sporangia containing the spores.
Best viewed: Santa Cruz – Los Gemelos.

Bryophytes, Mosses and Liverworts

Over 110 species of liverwort and 90 species of moss have been described in Galápagos. As with ferns identification is very technical. *Frullania aculeata*, a liverwort, can be identified. It is the brown moss-like species that adorns many trees in the Scalesia and Brown Zones.

GEOLOGY AND VULCANOLOGY

The Galápagos lie in the eastern Pacific Ocean 1,000 km west of the mainland of South America and astride the Equator. Geologically they lie at the meeting point of two submarine ridges, the Carnegie Ridge running westward from South America and the Cocos Ridge running south from Central America. The meeting point of these two ridges is known as the Galápagos Hot Spot. The islands lie at the northern edge of the Nazca Plate which is moving eastward at a rate of 2 cm per year. This movement is responsible for the building of the Andes mountain range and for the continuing earthquake and volcanic activity along the western edge of South America. As the plate moves and the hot spot stays stationary, so a series of volcanic islands are formed. This explains why the oldest islands in Galápagos lie to the east and the youngest to the west. Fernandina and Isabela, especially the former, are two very active volcanic islands. In 1968 there was a major event when the floor of the caldera on Fernandina fell over 300 m. This was accompanied by a large ash eruption which covered much of the north-western slope of the volcano. There was a large eruption on the flank of Fernandina in 1997, and another on the southern slopes of Cerro Azul on Isabela in 1998.

Blowhole on the basaltic shore of Española (Hood) Island.

The isthmus of Bartolomé and Pinnacle Rock, the remains of a tuff cone.

fernadina, a large Shield Volcano.

For the most part the islands are the tips of large submarine volcanoes. However, most of the eastern islands, Santa Fé, Plazas, the north-eastern edge of Santa Cruz, Baltra, Seymour and Genovesa, are uplifted submarine lava. It is, however, clear that the sea level has varied considerably over the millennia because, underneath the submarine lava, are volcanic deposits which must have been laid down above water. Fernandina and Isabela are huge shield volcanoes, looking from a distance like upturned soup bowls. These all have large calderas measuring several kilometres across and up to 1,000 m deep.

Another feature which illustrates the continuing volcanic activity in the islands is the volcanic uplift which occurred in 1954 at Urvina Bay on the western coast of Isabela. Here some 5 km of coastline was uplifted by up to 4 m. In 1994, a further uplift of some 90 cm occurred making the landing dock unusable except at high tide.

As a visitor it is interesting to note the different geological features and types of rock or lava, some of which are very clearly in evidence. There are two distinct types of lava. The Aa (pronounced 'Ah Ah') and Pahoehoe (pronounced 'Pahoyhoy'). The former is very rough and hard to walk over. Aa is Hawaiian for 'hurt' and is the result of the lava containing a lot of gas. The latter is smooth and ropy. Pahoehoe is Hawaiian for 'ropy'. You can see excellent Pahoehoe lava on Santiago opposite Isla Bartolomé or on Fernandina at Punta Espinosa. Most other fresh lava you encounter is likely to be Aa!

Sunken volcanic crater, Bartolomé.

Volcanic uplift – the white line is the old sea bed.

Caldera

A caldera develops as the top of a large volcano starts to collapse back into the magma chamber, from whence came the lava that built it in the first place.

Cinder Cones

These are normally found further inland than tuff cones, and on the flanks of the main volcano. They are often termed 'parasitic cones', and are frequently nearly perfect cone shapes. Cinder cones are the result of very explosive eruptions, where there is a lot of gas in the magma, which expands rapidly as the magma comes to the surface. The cinder or scoria is used on the inhabited islands to make roads, which are very dusty when dry.

Collapse or Pit Craters

These form when the roof of a large subterranean lava tube or magma chamber collapses. The best examples of these are Los Gemelos (the twins) on Santa Cruz. The road to the airport goes right between the two craters. Calderas are effectively huge collapse craters.

Driblet Cone or Hornito

A small cone, generally less than 50 cm in height formed by escaping gas or steam. The lava is often shiny and colourful due to the minerals in it. Generally found on Pahoehoe flows.

Fumaroles

Volcanic vents which emit gases, these very often contain sulphur dioxide and result not only in a foul smell, but also in yellow deposits of sulphur. The volcanoes of Alcedo and Sierra Negra on Isabela have accessible fumaroles.

Lava Bomb

A lava rock that has been ejected with explosive force during a volcanic eruption. Generally rounded in shape and often isolated and some distance away from its point of origin.

Lava Tubes

These are formed when a crust forms on a lava flow, insulating the hot core. When the lava stops flowing it leaves behind a tube which is often very nearly circular and up to 10 m or more in diameter running at times for several kilometres.

Lava Tongues or Driblets

Small pieces of lava that have been ejected from a small spatter cone and have solidified independently.

Magma

This is the molten volcanic material while it is still beneath the ground, hence 'magma chamber' where the molten magma is 'stored' before an eruption.

Pumice

This is the result of a very violent eruption involving water. In Galápagos it is found only on Isabela on Volcan Alcedo. However, because pumice floats, you may find it washed up on beaches around the islands, especially after the rainy season.

Spatter Cones

These are small cones formed by rather glutinous lava which is thrown out in dollops, but which solidifies into smooth and often quite colourful cones which look as if they are made of melted toffee.

Tree Shapes

With Pahoehoe lava, it is not uncommon to find the outline shapes of trees that were enveloped by the lava. When the lava cooled the wood burned away leaving a mould of the tree.

Tuff and Tuff Cones

Tuff is formed when water is present during an eruption and is a form of compacted volcanic ash. Tuff cones are generally found near the coast. The famous pinnacle rock on Bartolomé is made of tuff.

Volcanic Dyke

This is the result of molten lava being forced up into a crack in older material, often tuff. If the surrounding material is softer then the dyke is left standing proud as the surrounding material erodes more rapidly.

Volcanic Plug

Very often when a tuff or cinder cone ceases to be active, the magma tube or vent remains filled with magma which has not formed into tuff or cinder. As the cone is eroded away, the plug, which is made of much harder material, is left behind.

Aa Lava

Very rough, normally black, lava formed when there is a lot of gas in the magma which escapes as the lava cools. Often clinker-like. The name, pronounced 'Ah Ah' is Hawaiian for 'hurt'.

Pahoehoe Lava

Smooth or ropy lava, often forming amazing patterns. It is a result of the magma containing very little gas. The name is pronounced 'pahoyhoy', which is the Hawaiian for 'ropy'.

HISTORY

The islands were discovered in 1535 by Fray Tomas de Berlanga, the Bishop of Panama, who drifted there while on a voyage from Panama to Lima, Peru. It is strange to note that no single geographical feature in the islands bears his name. The islands soon became a useful base for pirates who used them when raiding Spanish ports along the coast of South America. They quickly picked up the name *Las Encantadas* or bewitched islands due to the strong currents, which not only made navigating difficult, but when combined with the *garua* and mists, often made it seem as though the islands were moving rather than the ships.

The islands were named by Abraham Ortelier in 1874 after one of their principle attractions, both then and now, the giant tortoises. *Galapago* is a Spanish name for a saddle not unlike the carapace of the saddleback tortoises found on the drier islands. In the days before

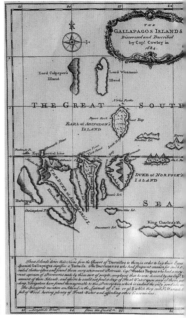

Early map of Galápagos by Ambrose Cowley.

Pirate Cave, Floreana.

refrigeration, an animal that could live for months without food or water was extremely valuable and tens of thousands of tortoises were taken on to ships to provide fresh meat. Charles Darwin who visited the islands in 1835, as the naturalist on board HMS *Beagle*, certainly enjoyed their flesh though the *Beagle* had no hold to store any for the onward voyage. They did though bring a number of small specimens back to England.

Post Office Bay, Floreana.

Puerto Ayora, Santa Cruz.

The first recorded resident of Galápagos was an Irishman named Patrick Watkin who was marooned on Floreana in 1807. By then, Post Office Bay on Floreana had become a regular but infrequent stopping place for whaling ships. Vessels recently arrived from Europe would leave letters there to be collected by those returning home, often after voyages of four or five years. The first post barrel appears to have been erected by Captain James Colnett in 1792. By the time that the islands were annexed by Ecuador in 1832 there was a small settlement on San Cristóbal as well as on Floreana; this latter was soon turned into a penal settlement. The settlement at Villamil on Isabela dates from 1893 and Puerto Ayora on Santa Cruz was started by a group of Norwegians who had come out to set up a fish-processing plant at Post Office Bay in 1926. The plant failed but you can still see the rocks used to mark out their settlement and various large iron vessels that had been a part of the processing plant. Floreana has had more than its fair share of stories and became known world-wide in the mid 1930's due to the antics of 'The Baroness', Eloise Bosquet-Wagner and her two companions, and Dr Friedrich Ritter and his companion Dore Strauch. It is now the quietest of the four inhabited islands.

The first successful commercial venture in the islands was a sugar plantation and mill, built at Progreso in the highlands of San Cristóbal in the 1880's by Manuel Cobos, who rapidly turned the island into a personal fiefdom and was eventually murdered in 1904 by his own slaves.

Cobos grave.

Hoax carving.

From then on a variety of commercial ventures were developed, but nearly all ended in failure and few were really successful. Not until tourism came along in the late 1960's did the islands start to develop commercially.

Ecuador recognised the scientific importance of the islands in 1934, passing legislation to protect the fauna and flora, but was unable to do anything effective to implement the laws. In 1942 following its entry into the Second World War, the United States obtained permission to build a military base on the island of Baltra. Galápagos controlled the approaches to the Panama Canal and had suddenly acquired a strategic importance. Two airstrips and a large number of clapboard houses were built. These were almost all removed after the war, when each family living in the islands was allowed to come and remove a building for their own use. Until the mid '70s, most of the buildings in the islands were made of wood from the base. The one stone building left on Baltra by the Americans was the officers' club and this can still clearly be seen near the centre of the island. The airstrip and dock are still those that were built for the base, though both have been renovated by the Ecuadorian government.

Until 1968, the only way to get to Galápagos was by sea. An occasional flight used the airstrip at Baltra but there was no permanent base there and after one DC3 failed to find the islands and only just made it back to the mainland, flights were suspended. The trip out from Guayaquil by sea took 3–4 days and the return trip was shared with the cattle, coffee and dried fish that were the islands' principle exports. Tourism was possible using the supply vessel, but very few hardy souls made it and there were no vessels available in the islands to enable you to visit the other islands.

In 1968 the first regular tourist flights started on a fortnightly basis, servicing the schooner, Golden Cachalot. This was increased in 1969 to two flights a week with the arrival of the first cruise ship, the 'Lina A'. Now there are two flights a day to Baltra and regular flights to San Cristóbal as well. There is also now an airstrip at Villamil on Isabela, used for internal flights. The population was about 2,500 in 1968 but had increased to over 16,000 by 1999. The first 'master plan' for the development of tourism within the National Park called for a maximum of 12,000 visitors each year. There are now more than 60,000 visitors each year and the boats and hotels have a capacity for well over 100,000.

Charles Darwin and Evolution

Charles Darwin aged 40, painted by TH Maguire.

Charles Darwin would have been an important scientist even if he had never visited the Galápagos Islands. His visit there in September and October 1835 was the catalyst that ensured that he would be remembered, not only as the pre-eminent scientist of his time, but as one of the truly great scientists of all time. The idea of evolution was not a new one. Lucretius, writing in the first century BC in his *De Rerum Natura* put forward the first suggestion of a form of evolutionary theory. Darwin's grandfather, Erasmus, put forward his own theory of evolution in 1794–96 in his work entitled *Zoonomia*. At the time of Darwin's visit to Galápagos, the most accepted theory was Lamarckism, named after the French scientist Jean Baptiste Lamarck. This proposed that animals inherited acquired characteristics, but it lacked any real examples and was not widely accepted. The example most widely quoted is that of how the giraffe has a long neck. Individuals which stretch their necks to feed from tall trees inherited this acquired characteristic. The theory is now discredited. What none of these earlier theories could provide was a realistic and credible mechanism for the process of evolution.

Darwin was born in Shrewsbury in England in 1809. In 1825 he went to Edinburgh to study medicine but in 1827 he left there in order to study divinity at Cambridge. He was destined for the life of a country parson, when in 1831 he was invited by Captain Robert Fitzroy to be the naturalist on board *HMS Beagle* which was soon to depart on a five-year voyage, surveying the waters around the southern tip of South America. The voyage was without doubt the turning point in Darwin's life, and the visit to the Galápagos was the most significant single episode on that voyage.

On his return in to England, he published his book on the voyage of the *Beagle*. This in itself is a classic and established Darwin as an important figure in the scientific community of his day. His powers of observation were acute and he is credited with developing two new sciences, quite apart from his work on evolution. He was the first person to develop the study of both ethology (the study of animal behaviour in natural surroundings) and ecology (the study of the relationship between animals and their environment). If you read his *Voyage of the Beagle* you will appreciate the detail that he put into this, and the amount of time that he spent observing animal behaviour, in a detailed and disciplined manner.

In 1859, after much hesitation, he finally published *On the Origin of Species*, a book that was to have a revolutionary impact on the way man viewed himself. The mechanism that Darwin had discovered, due in large part to his observations and collecting activity in the Galápagos, was natural selection. Put simply, this says that those species that changed and adapted to their environment through a series of random genetic mutations would be the ones that were best able to survive. Darwin was initially reluctant to publish his theory as he was aware of its implications, and was only persuaded to do so because Alfred Russell Wallace had come up with the same theory.

Before arriving in Galápagos, Darwin was chiefly interested in their geology, but it is quite clear from his diary that after a few days he started to realise that their zoology was most unusual, and by the time he left he was already starting to suspect their true significance.

> When I see these islands in sight of each other, and possessed of but a scanty stock of animals, tenanted by these birds, but slightly differing in structure and filling the same place in nature, I must suspect they are only varieties. ... If there is the slightest foundation for these remarks, the zoology of Archipelagoes will be well worth examining; for such facts would undermine the stability of species.

Giant Galápagos Tortoise.
(Right) *Saddleback tortoise.*
(Below) *Large Ground Finch.*
(Below right) *Small Ground Finch.*

It was Darwin's genius that he not only noted the differences between species on the various islands, but that he was able to develop his theory of evolution using that visit in 1835, followed by years of painstaking research into barnacles, pigeons and other animals. These later studies gave him the necessary grounding to develop his theory and to be able to defend it. Over 140 years later, it is still the accepted backbone of our understanding of the natural world and of our own origins. Since Darwin's visit in 1835, scientific research and investigation has only reinforced his conclusions that the Galápagos really are a laboratory of evolution. The small birds, Darwin's finches, that were one of the key groups to alert him to the significance of the islands, have been the subject of frequent investigation. A 30-year study on Daphne, that is still ongoing, is the longest and most detailed.

Scalesia crockerii.   Scalesia pedunculata.

Evidence for evolution in Galápagos is shown not only in the finches and tortoises but everywhere you look. There are impressive examples of adaptive radiation, the result of evolution on isolated archipelagos. There were at one time 66 species of land snails of the genus *Bulimulus* all descended from one original species. There are seven, largely island-specific, species of cricket of the genus *Gryllus*. In the plant world there are several examples. The best known of these is *Scalesia*, a member of the daisy family. There are some 21 species and subspecies of this genus found in all vegetation zones.

So why did Galápagos become such a remarkable showcase for evolutionary development? It was not just that the islands were over 1,000 km west of South America, nor even that the individual islands are often isolated from each other by 20 or 30 km. It is not just that the prevailing winds and currents come from the continent, nor the remarkable variation in the vegetation and climatic conditions. It is a combination of all of these factors. Additionally, it is due to the fact that the islands were, until recently, not attractive to human habitation. Herman Melville of *Moby Dick* fame 'doubted whether any other spot on earth can in desolateness furnish a parallel to this group'. This isolation has meant that in this small group of islands we have been able to study and observe the processes by which life has evolved everywhere on earth.

OCEAN CURRENTS AND CLIMATE – EL NIÑO

One of the factors that helps to make Galápagos the 'laboratory of evolution' is its location and its very distinct climate. It is remarkably cool and dry for an equatorial oceanic group of islands. The reasons for this are complex and due to a number of different influences.

Ocean Currents

The chief influences on the climate of the Galápagos are the ocean currents. Galápagos lie on the equator at the confluence of several major ocean currents. The three currents which influence the climate are the Humboldt, which turns into the South Equatorial current, the Cromwell or Equatorial Undercurrent and El Niño. The major influence is the Humboldt or Peru Coastal current, which brings cool, nutrient-rich water up from the southern oceans. This heads out westwards from the coast of Peru, becoming the South Equatorial current in the process. This current extends some 300 m below the surface. The deeper water is cooler and more saline sub-antarctic water, which tends to upwell when it hits the Galápagos. The overall impact of this current, which flows through the

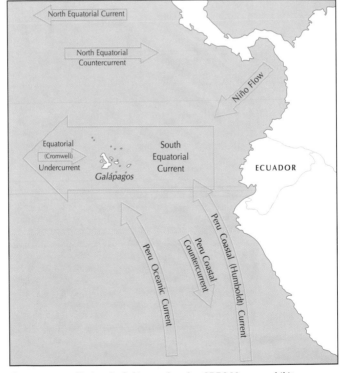

Ocean currents affecting the Galápagos, based on CDRS Museum exhibit.

islands for some eight to nine months of the year, is to produce relatively cool air temperatures and a lower humidity than might be expected for islands that straddle the equator.

The current is driven in part, especially on the surface, by the southeast trade winds, which blow towards the equator from May to December. When they retreat southwards, then so does the surface current. This then allows an influx of much warmer water from the north, ostensibly out of the Gulf of Panama, which brings high humidity and heavy tropical rains to the islands. This warmer water is known as El Niño. It is generally a much shallower current extending to less than 100 m in depth.

The third current, the Cromwell or Equatorial Undercurrent, is a submarine current which flows eastward from the central Pacific. It is cool and saline and creates very cool water conditions around the islands of Fernandina and the western side of Isabela. This is a favoured area for whales and dolphins, as well as yellow fin tuna which are fished illegally by commercial fishermen from outside the islands.

The Climate

The climate of Galápagos can be divided into two seasons, the garua or cool season lasting from June to November, and the warm season which runs from January to April. The months of May and December are changeover periods when the weather can vary considerably from year to year. On the coast the garua season is very dry, rainfall records in Academy Bay on the south side of Santa Cruz show the average monthly rainfall in the months of August, September and October to be less than 10 mm while February to April the average is 50–70 mm. In the highlands it is much wetter during the garua season. The warm season may or may not include a rainy period, El Niño, which is normally of four to six weeks, exceptionally longer. Here again there is generally more rainfall in the humid zones than on the coast.

During the garua season, the cool water around the islands results in a temperature inversion, where the air close to the sea is cooler than that which is higher up. This means that when moisture evaporates and rises due to the warmth of the sun, it forms clouds, but as it cannot rise far because of the temperature inversion, it is trapped at between 500 and 1,000 m and forms flat strato-cumulus clouds. These clouds produce very light rain or drizzle, know locally as 'garua', whereas the tall cumulo-nimbus clouds which appear in the rainy season, when the water is warmer and there is no temperature in version, produce heavy rain.

The strato-cumulus cloud is the predominant cloud in Galápagos during the garua season. They accumulate around the tops of the higher volcanoes and sit there, sometimes for weeks on end. This produces a lush and in parts fertile, humid zone, though the higher reaches tend to be so wet and fog enshrouded that they have become bogs and moorlands. This is a far cry from the arid lowlands which only receive any appreciable rain during the El Niño periods. Additionally, because the prevailing wind is from the south-east, the south sides of the major islands are much moister than the north sides, which are in a rain shadow. Here the arid zone stretches well up beyond the 500 m contour, and the humid vegetation zones which are so evident on the south sides are compressed. The exception to this is on Cerro Azul in southern Isabela where, due to the height and steepness of the volcano, the moist zone extends almost to the coast while the rim is normally above the clouds which results in an arid zone on the rim.

El Niño

El Niño occurs every year along the coast of Ecuador and Peru. Its name in Spanish means 'The Child', after the Christ Child, because along the coast of Ecuador and Peru the warm water and the rains come in December. In Galápagos the rains come between January and March, though in some years they do not come at all. In some years, this phenomenon is far larger and affects the whole Pacific Ocean, when the Pacific weather system is disrupted and the rains can last for six to nine months. When this happens species that depend upon the sea for their food, such as sea lions, boobies and Marine Iguanas, suffer dramatically and large numbers of

El Niño, Santiago vegetation.

Urvina Bay in an El Niño year.

Urvina Bay: the contrast with an El Niño year.

El Niño, Floreana

them die. In contrast, land species such as birds, butterflies and Land Iguanas flourish.

The variations in rainfall can be dramatic. During the El Niño event of 1982–83, over an eight-month period, well over 3 m of rain was recorded in Academy Bay on the south side of Santa Cruz, and over 5.5 m was recorded at Santo Thomas in the highlands of Isabela. In contrast, the average annual rainfall in Academy Bay for the years 1965–70 was only 200 mm. Variations in rainfall of this magnitude must exert considerable evolutionary pressures of their own, and yet the ecosystem as a whole appears to recover quite rapidly from such violent changes.

Galápagos Sea Lion, a casualty of El Niño.

The cause of these major El Niño events is unknown. There have been two in the last 20 years, in 1982–83 and 1997–98. Over the past hundred years the normal pattern has been to have a strong El Niño every three or four years. However, no events of the magnitude of 1982–83 or 1997–98 have previously been recorded. There is naturally a suspicion that global warming may be involved. It is though too early to entirely attribute this to human activities.

The isolated equatorial oceanic situation, allied with the influences of the climate, has resulted in a most

El Niño, Santiago.

unusual biodiversity in Galápagos. It explains why species that arrived in Galápagos, by whatever means, successfully adapted to survive. It also helps us to appreciate the importance of preserving the islands to continue studying the evolution of the animals and plants.

215

ONSERVATION

anic islands, by their very nature, tend to have a much smaller num-
r of species than continental land masses. It follows that as a rule there
e fewer predators, and that the individual species, while well adapted to
their own ecological niches, do not have to fight particularly hard to retain
those niches. On a continental land mass, species have many competitors
and need to fight hard to survive. In Galápagos this is not the case and
many species of both animal and plant are very susceptible to competition
from species introduced from South America, or elsewhere in the world.

Charles Darwin was the first to draw attention to the remarkable biodiversity of the Galápagos and in his subsequent writings attracted the attention of other scientists. In 1935, on the centenary of Darwin's visit to the
islands, the Ecuadorian government passed the first legislation to protect
the animals and plants of the Galápagos. No actual steps were taken and
the proposed research station was not established. War broke out soon
after and the idea was shelved until the centenary, in 1959, of the publication of Darwin's *On the Origin of Species*. In 1959, the Ecuadorian government passed new legislation, declaring the islands a National Park. In
the same year a committee was set up under the auspices of UNESCO,
which eventually became the Charles Darwin Foundation for the Galápagos Islands. This was an international body which in 1960 established a
research station at Academy Bay, on the edge of the village of Puerto
Ayora, on Santa Cruz Island. Since its establishment, the Charles Darwin
Research Station has gone from strength to strength. In its early years it
was the only agent of conservation in the islands, developing a strong and
coherent conservation strategy, albeit on a very slim budget. This programme was taken over by the Ecuadorian National Park (PNG) which
was set up in 1968. The two organisations have always worked closely,
with the CDRS providing the information and the scientific basis for the
conservation programme, which is carried out by the National Park.

Park signs.

Park warden ringing a Dark-rumped
Petrel.

In the early years of the CDRS and the National Park, the emphasis was
on pure conservation. Resources were modest, and programmes such as
the eradication of goats from Santa Fé, Española and Pinta were priori-
ties, as was the attempt to rid Pinzón of rats. Alongside this was the very
successful captive breeding programme, initially of tortoises from
Pinzón and Española, and later of other threatened populations. This has
been expanded to include Land Iguanas. While captive breeding will

always be a temporary measure, it is an essential step in helping to ensure the survival of some species in the face of alien invasion.

More recently, the conservation programmes have taken into account the needs of the inhabitants of Galápagos. The population has grown rapidly, largely due to the success of tourism, from a level of 2,000 inhabitants in the early 1960s to around 18,000 in 2000 – a 900 per cent increase in 40 years. While attempts to reduce immigration may help to slow the rate of increase, by 2020, at a population growth rate of only 5 per cent per annum, the population of Galápagos will exceed 50,000 people. It is hence essential, if the measures to protect the biodiversity of the islands are to succeed, that the people who live there are brought into the process, and that they help provide the answers to the problems, rather than being part of them. This can only be achieved by means of education and carefully crafted programmes to make full and sustainable use of the islands' economic resources.

Tourism is a classic example of a renewable resource. When the first 'Plan Maestro' was published in 1970, it envisaged that the maximum number of visitors the islands

Goat damage, Alcedo Rim, Isabéla.

Cinder Quarry, Santa Cruz.

Visitor Interpretation Centre, San Cristóbal.

could handle without seriously impacting on the environment was 12,000. Today there are in excess of 60,000 visitors a year and the immediate impact is minimal. The problems that the success of the industry has brought with it are twofold. Firstly the influx of people looking for jobs, as Galápagos has the highest level of income per capita of any province in Ecuador. Secondly, it is the importation of consumables, especially food and building supplies, both of which are prime sources of alien and invasive species. While there is clearly a strong need for an effective quarantine programme to reduce the danger, the real answer lies with the reduction of the importation of these supplies. There is here an excellent opportunity to resolve several problems at once, through better usage of agricultural land, resulting in less importation of foodstuffs and other supplies with their attendant alien species. This in turn will help to strengthen the local economy.

Invasion of Quinine Tree, El Puntudo, Santa Cruz.

Aliens

Probably the biggest single threat to the stability of the Galápagos ecosystem and to its biodiversity comes from alien species. These have, without exception, been introduced by man, either deliberately or accidentally. The most obviously destructive aliens in Galápagos are goats, which were probably introduced in the nineteenth century by whalers, looking for an alternative source of meat. Goats are exceptionally well adapted to survive in Galápagos, either in the arid lowlands, or the moist highlands. They are very hardy, can climb trees, drink seawater, and if left to their own devices will, in time, turn a low-lying island into a desert. Miguel Castro, conservation officer of the CDRS started the first systematic eradication programme in 1965, to rid the island of Santa Fé of goats. Santa Fé is a low island with no transitional or humid zones and it was know for the wide open plains studded with large opuntia cacti *Opuntia echios barringtonensis* and Palo Santo trees *Bursera graveolens*. Ten years later, the last goat was culled and the vegetation is now so dense that it is really quite difficult to walk anywhere off the trail. The native rice rat is thriving, as are the Land Iguanas. The recovery of the island is impressive.

Volcan Alcedo on Isabela is another story. In 1969, goats were either introduced there, or managed to cross the Perry Isthmus which separates it from Volcan Sierra Negra to the south. Now there are estimated to be in excess of 100,000 goats on Alcedo and the two volcanoes to the north, Darwin and Wolf, in spite of some 35,000 háving been shot since 1996. Alcedo is largely covered in pumice and ash and the vegetation is particularly vulnerable to herbivores. In 1975 the rim of the caldera was densely covered in thorny scrub, largely Cats Claw *Zanthoxylum fagara*. It is now a large open plain with hardly a bush in site except where the endemic tree ferns *Cyathea wetherbyana*, have been fenced off to protect them.

There is now a major campaign to eradicate the goats on northern Isabela. The cost will be over $40 million and will probably take at least five years to complete, involving helicopters, specially trained dogs, 'judas goats' and an enormous amount of manpower. Once northern Isabela is cleared there will still be goats on Santiago, Santa Cruz, San Cristóbal and southern Isabela.

Feral goats.

While goats are the most obvious of the alien species currently threatening the delicate Galápagos ecosystem, they are relatively easy to eradicate as they are large and visible. There are many other invaders that are much harder to eradicate and which, while they are much less obvious, may be equally damaging to the ecosystem. The following is a list of some of the worst offenders.

MAMMALS

Pigs	Santiago (nearly eradicated after a thirty-year campaign), Isabela, Santa Cruz, Floreana, San Cristóbal
Dogs	Isabela, Santa Cruz, San Cristóbal, Floreana
Cattle	Isabela, Santa Cruz, San Cristóbal, Floreana
Donkeys	Isabela, Santiago, Santa Cruz, San Cristóbal, Floreana,
Horses	Isabela, Santa Cruz, San Cristóbal, Floreana
Cats	Isabela, Santa Cruz, San Cristóbal, Floreana
Rats	Isabela, Santiago, Santa Cruz, San Cristóbal, Floreana, Pinzón
Mice	Isabela, Santa Cruz, San Cristóbal, Floreana

Feral donkeys (top) *and feral cat* (bottom).

Some of these, such as cattle and horses, do relatively little damage. They are few in numbers and are susceptible to rigorous eradication programmes. More serious are the invertebrates and plants which have arrived uninvited, and whose eradication is far more problematic. In virtually all cases, control is the best that can be hoped for, as eradication is simply not practicable.

INVERTEBRATES

Little Red Fire Ant	*Wasmannia auropunctata*
Tropical Fire Ant	*Solenopsis geminata*
Destructive Ant	*Monomorium destructor*

Blackfly	*Simulium bipunctatum*	
Cottony Cushion Scale	*Icerya purchasi*	
Yellow Paper Wasp	*Polistes versicolor*	
Dark Paper Wasp	*Brachygastra lecheguana*	
Cockroaches	At least 11 introduced species	

Cottony Cushion Scale Icerya purchasi

PLANTS

Quinine Tree	*Cinchona succirubra*
Guayava	*Psidium guajava*
Elephant Grass	*Pennisetum purpureum*

These are only the most visible and possibly the most threatening invaders. There are over 300 species of introduced plants and unknown numbers of invertebrates. The Galápagos National Park is becoming a world leader in the development of processes to control invasive plant species. Some of this is simply physical destruction of the plants such as the Quinine Tree and the Guayava, but the use of chemical agents is essential if the plants are to be removed permanently. Simply controlling these species will require enormous financial and human resources, but if we want Galápagos to remain the amazing place that it is, then funds will have to be found and the work done.

Quinine Tree Cinchona succirubra.

Marine Conservation

In many ways just as important as the conservation of the terrestrial ecosystem, is the protection of the marine environment. Many of the most visible species in Galápagos depend upon the sea for their survival, most obviously the Marine Iguana, Galápagos Penguin, the three boobies, the sea lion and the fur seal. Without these species, the islands would be infinitely poorer and far less able to attract the thousands of tourists, who must in one way or another help to fund the preservation of these islands. In 1986 the Galá-

pagos Marine Reserve was established, but little was done until 1998 when the 'Ley de Galápagos' was passed, by the Ecuadorian Congress after much pressure and politicking. It is still not fully accepted by the fishermen from mainland Ecuador, but it establishes a marine reserve 40 miles out from the outer points of the island. Only by enforcing this law, will there be any real hope of preserving the Galápagos as we know them, and would want future generations to know them too.

Fish hook in sea lion.

NOTES FOR THE VISITOR

This is not a general guide for the visitor, but these notes may be helpful when planning your trip to Galápagos.

Galápagos are a province of Ecuador. All visitors, except those arriving by private yacht, must travel via mainland Ecuador. Only a few nationalities are required to obtain visas before arriving in Ecuador. Check with your travel agent or the local Ecuadorian Consul.

There are daily flights to the island of Baltra, and most days to San Cristóbal also. If you arrive in Baltra and do not board your boat there, then you must travel by bus and ferry to Puerto Ayora on the island of Santa Cruz. Both Puerto Baquerizo on San Cristóbal and Puerto Ayora have hotels and guesthouses. Reservations are recommended especially during peak seasons, December through March and June through August.

To visit most of the visitor sites you need to travel by boat. The majority of the boats offer cruises around the islands lasting from 3 to 15 or more days. It takes about 15 days to see most of the best sites, but much depends on the size and speed of the boat you are on. Some boats are available for private charter, or you can just join as an individual. There are many tour operators offering group trips, sometimes with special interests such as scuba

Tourists enjoying the Galápagos wildlife.

diving, photography, botany or ornithology. You should certainly aim for at least a one-week cruise, more if you are able to. It is possible to arrange a number of day trips out of both San Cristóbal and Santa Cruz. These are generally less satisfactory than overnight trips as you tend to be visiting the sites during the middle of the day. Wildlife is best viewed early and late, when it is also cooler and preferable for most people. Generally, a boat will visit two visiting sites a day, morning and afternoon, possibly with swimming, snorkelling or scuba diving in between. Remember that you are close to the equator and the sun rises around 0600 and sets at about 1800 every day, all year round, so an early start is always recommended.

There is no 'best time to visit', but it is warmer and may be wet from December through April and cooler from June through November. The one endemic species that is absent for a period of the year is the Waved Albatross *Diomedea irrorata*. If you specifically want to see this bird, come between May and December. If you are worried about seasickness, consider a larger boat and remember that the sea is generally calmer in the warm season than in the garua season.

Darwin's first thoughts on the islands were not complimentary: 'The country was compared to what we might imagine the cultivated parts of the Infernal regions to be.' He was I think you will agree, being singularly ungenerous. The Galápagos islands are a very special place and will have a very special impact on you.

VISITOR SITES

WATCH OUT FOR:

MARINE IGUANA
SALLY LIGHTFOOT CRAB
BROWN PELICAN
BLUE-FOOTED BOOBY
MAGNIFICENT FRIGATE BIRD
LAVA GULL
GREAT BLUE HERON
LAVA HERON
STRIATED HERON
GROUND FINCHES
CACTUS FINCH

CANDELABRA CACTUS
PRICKLY PEAR CACTUS
RED MANGROVE
BUTTON MANGROVE
BLACK MANGROVE
GALÁPAGOS ACACIA
MUYUYU
SPINY BUSH
PALO SANTO
LEATHERLEAF
VELVET SHRUB
SEA GRASS
GLORYBOWER

SANTA CRUZ – ACADEMY BAY AND PUERTO AYORA

Situated at the head of Academy Bay, Puerto Ayora is the largest town in Galápagos and is the centre of the tourism industry. The main airport in the islands is on Baltra, just to the north. This was linked to Puerto Ayora by a road in 1975. It is also the home of the Charles Darwin Research Station and the Galápagos National Park. As a result, it is on the itinerary of virtually all visitors. The town has a number of hotels, bars and restaurants as well as numerous small shops. There is a bank, hospital, several dentists, a 'supermarket' and other delights of civilisation that are entirely absent elsewhere in the islands.

The public dock is a good place to observe pelicans, frigatebirds and Blue-footed Boobies fishing in 'Las Ninfas' the inner anchorage and in Pelican Bay especially when the fishermen are cleaning their catches. To the west of the town towards Punta Estrada is Bud's Bay and Las Grilletas (The Cracks). A dinghy trip to this area is well worthwhile. Here you may see Common Noddies, herons, and migrant waders. Marine Iguanas and Sally Lightfoot Crabs are also easily seen on the rocks on Angermeyer Point. They often bask on the roofs on the houses here.

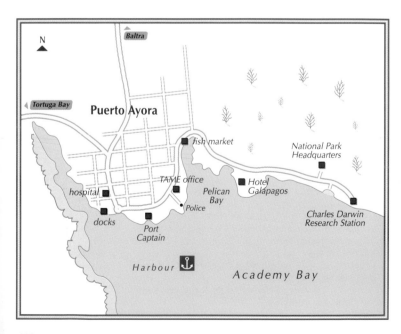

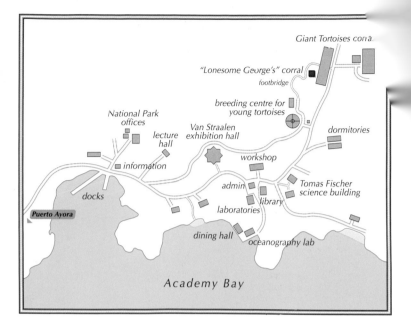

Santa Cruz – National Park and Charles Darwin Research Station

The Charles Darwin Research Station (CDRS) is situated at the eastern end of Academy Bay. The Galápagos National Park (GNP) offices are next to the CDRS. You can get there by sea or by road from the town of Puerto Ayora. The sea approach can be difficult at low tide. To walk there takes some 15 to 20 minutes from the public dock. The road is paved all the way.

The walk to or from the CDRS is strongly recommended with a good selection of coastal and arid zone plants as well as the possibility to view the elusive Dark-billed Cuckoo. The main interest is the Tortoise Breeding Centre where you can also see Lonesome George, the last remaining Pinta tortoise. This is the only place where you have the opportunity to compare the different shapes of carapace of the various Galápagos Tortoise. CDRS also has a breeding programme for Land Iguanas.

The Van Straelen exhibition hall is named after Victor Van Straelen, the first President of the Charles Darwin Foundation, the parent body of the CDRS.

Here you can see displays illustrating different aspects of the Galápagos ecosystem, the conservation problems and the programmes that the CDRS and the National Park have in place to combat them.

WATCH OUT FOR:

Tortoises
Marine Iguana
Land Iguana
Darwin's Finches
Yellow warbler
Dark billed Cuckoo
Galápagos Mockingbird

Saltbush
Prickly Pear Cactus
Candelabra Cactus
Parkinsonia
Red Mangrove
Button Mangrove
Black Mangrove
White Mangrove
Leatherleaf
Poison Apple
Muyuyu
Red-haired Tournefortia
Spiny Bush
Palo Santo
Thread-leafed Chaff Flower

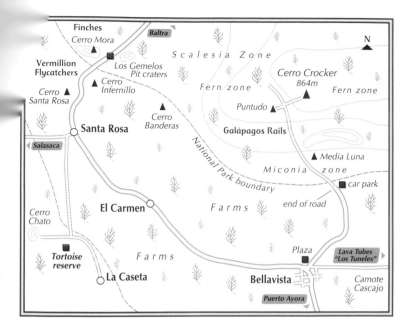

WATCH OUT FOR:

SANTA CRUZ GIANT TORTOISE
GALÁPAGOS RAIL
SHORT-EARED OWL
VERMILION FLYCATCHER
LARGE-BILLED FLYCATCHER
YELLOW WARBLER
SMALL TREE FINCH
LARGE TREE FINCH
WOODPECKER FINCH
VEGETARIAN FINCH
CATTLE EGRET
SMOOTH-BILLED ANI

MICONIA
TREE SCALESIA
QUININE TREE
BALSA
SILKY INGA
SPANISH CEDAR
COMMON CORAL BEAN
SOAPBERRY
CAT'S CLAW
GALÁPAGOS MISTLETOE
PRICKLY POINCIANA
ANGEL'S TRUMPET
COMMON GUAVA
GALÁPAGOS PEPEROMIA
GALÁPAGOS ORCHID
WHITE LEADWORTT

Los Gemelos are a pair of collapse or pit craters, one on either side of the road in the Scalesia Zone. Here you get an excellent opportunity to see *Scalesia pedunculata*. There are also many mosses, ferns and other epiphytes on the trees. Watch out for the Small and Large Tree Finches. From Los Gemelos the road descends in a straight line to South Channel, which separates Santa Cruz from Baltra. Almost immediately it turns into the Transitional Zone and then, in marked contrast to the south side, there is a very long Dry Zone.

From the village of Santa Rosa you can hike down through the Guayabillo forest *Psideum galapageum* to the Tortoise Reserve, though it is easier to view them on one of the farms where they share the fields with cattle. Watch out for the only 'Tortoise Crossing' signs in the world!

From Bellavista there is a trail up to Media Luna, an eroded and overgrown crater, and eventually on to Cerro Crocker, the highest point on the island. This takes you through the last remnants of the Brown Zone, into the Miconia Zone, and finally to the Pampa or Fern Sedge Zone. In the Miconia Zone you can see clearly the threat posed by the introduced Quinine tree. The Miconia, which is key to the breeding of the Dark-rumped Petrel, will only survive if the National Park continues its programme to eradicate the Quinine tree. Watch out for El Puntudo, a very pointed volcanic cone. On a clear day, the views alone are worth the effort.

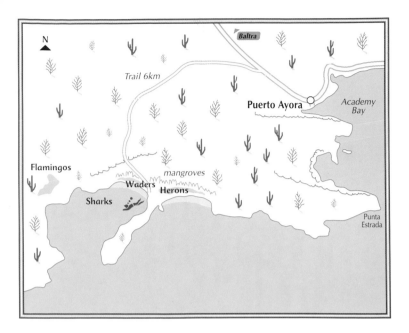

SANTA CRUZ - TORTUGA BAY

Tortuga Bay is a beautiful white sand beach with a mangrove lagoon behind situated some 5 km west of Academy Bay. There is an excellent trail which starts from the main street of Puerto Ayora. You take the second street on your left after the hospital. Once you have climbed the steps up the cliff the trail is on the level and trainers are suitable. From the top of the cliff you will get a superb view over Academy Bay. The walk will give you an excellent opportunity to view the Coastal and Arid Zones vegetation. You should also see Darwin's finches, mockingbirds and yellow warblers and if you are very lucky, a Santa Cruz Giant Tortoise.

The beach is backed by sand dunes which offer further examples of coastal vegetation and beyond the beach is a lagoon backed by mangroves. This is a good swimming area. Do not swim off the beach as the undertow can be very strong. You may swim in the lagoon where you can often see the White-tipped Reef Shark *Triaenodon obesus* which is clearly identifiable by the white tip on the dorsal fin. These shark are not aggressive. There is a salt lagoon behind the mangroves, this is an excellent bird-watching site where you should see flamingos and other waders.

It is best to leave early in the morning to visit this site.

WATCH OUT FOR:

WHITE-TIPPED REEF SHARK
MUSTARD RAY
(PACIFIC COWNOSE)
GALÁPAGOS GREEN TURTLE
LAVA HERON
HORSEFLY
BROWN PELICAN
GREATER FLAMINGO
WHIMBREL
BLACK-NECKED STILT
VARIOUS MIGRANT WADERS

BLACK MANGROVE
WHITE MANGROVE
RED MANGROVE
POISON APPLE
PRICKLY PEAR CACTUS
HELLER'S SCALESIA
MESQUITE
SPINY BUSH
SALTWORT
SALTBUSH
HELIOTROPE
SCORPION WEED
BEACH MORNING GLORY
INKBERRY
COMMON CARPETWEED

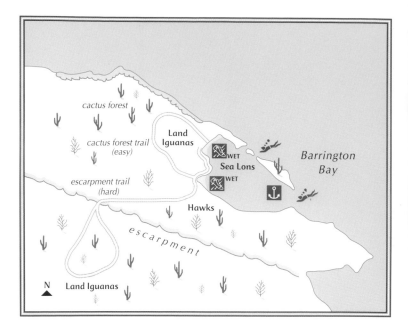

WATCH OUT FOR:

GALÁPAGOS SEA LION
SAND DOLLAR
GHOST CRAB
GALÁPAGOS RICE RAT
CENTRAL GALÁPAGOS RACER
SANTA FÉ LAND IGUANA
GALÁPAGOS HAWK
GROUND FINCHES
CACTUS FINCH

PALO SANTO
MUYUYU
GALÁPAGOS LANTANA
LEATHERLEAF
PRICKLY PEAR CACTUS
HELLER'S SCALESIA
SALTBUSH
SPINY BUSH
GALÁPAGOS CROTON
VELVET SHRUB
FEATHER FINGERGRASS

SANTA FÉ – BARRINGTON BAY

Barrington Bay, the visiting site on Santa Fé, is on the northeastern corner of the island. The anchorage is very sheltered, being protected by a small cactus-covered islet, 'Islote Black', named after the late Juan Black, one of the first Directors of the Galápagos National Park. The bay is quite shallow and you can often see sting rays and green turtles in the clear water. There is good snorkelling around Islote Black.

Santa Fé is noted for its large colony of sea lions that live on the two white sand beaches at the head of the bay. Visitors often have to find their way around groups of sleeping cows and pups. Be careful of the bull sea lion or beachmaster. He is normally not very aggressive, but can be during the breeding season.

On shore there are two trails. Both should give you the opportunity to view the Santa Fé Land Iguana, found only on this island, and the delightful endemic rice rat, which is particularly in evidence towards sunset. The vegetation on Santa Fé is notable for the very large Prickly Pear Cacti found here. Not quite as tall as some on Santa Cruz, it is larger and more heavily trunked than any other in the islands.

The longer trail to the top of the cliff gives an excellent view over the bay. You should also see the Galápagos Hawk and the rare Heller's Scalesia. Watch out for the dark stains on your clothes caused by the sap of the Croton bushes. This is indelible.

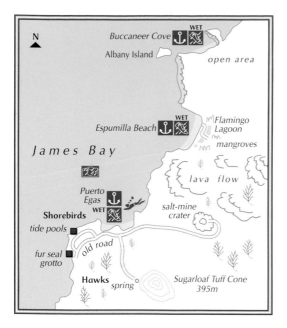

WATCH OUT FOR:

Puerto Egas

GALÁPAGOS FUR SEAL
FERAL GOAT
FERAL DONKEY
MARINE IGUANA
SALLY LIGHTFOOT CRAB
GREATER FLAMINGO
GALÁPAGOS HAWK
AMERICAN OYSTERCATCHER
GROUND FINCHES
YELLOW-CROWNED
NIGHT HERON
LAVA HERON
STRIATED HERON
GALÁPAGOS DOVE
GALÁPAGOS SNAKE
PAINTED LOCUST

PALO SANTO
GALÁPAGOS CROTON
BITTERBUSH
MUYUYU
PRICKLY PEAR CACTUS
PUNCTURE WEED
SPINY BUSH
SCORPION WEED

■ ■ ■

Espumilla Beach

BROWN PELICAN
VERMILION FLYCATCHER
LARGE-BILLED FLYCATCHER
BLACK-NECKED STILT
WHIMBREL
WHITE-CHEEKED PINTAIL
DARWIN'S FINCHES
GHOST CRAB

BUTTON MANGROVE
BLACK MANGROVE
GALÁPAGOS ACACIA
PALO SANTO
GLORYBOWER
POISON APPLE
LEATHERLEAF
PEGA PEGA
PEARL BERRY
SALTBUSH
FLAME TREE
WHITE MORNING GLORY

SANTIAGO – JAMES BAY, PUERTO EGAS AND ESPUMILLA BEACH

Puerto Egas

The most prominent physical feature here is the large tuff cone to the south, Pan de Azucar (Sugarloaf), climbed by Darwin in 1835. At the base of this, there is a trail leading up to Hawk Spring. A longer trail leads to the Mina de Sal or Salt Mine Crater. The bottom of this crater is below sea level and has a salt-water lake. The salt deposits here were mined commercially until 1970.

A third trail takes you to the Fur Seal Grotto where there is a colony of fur seals which live in a series of caves and grotto-like formations formed when the lava flowed into the sea. There is also a good opportunity to visit the tide-pools along the coast here where you can see Marine Iguanas, crabs and a variety of sea-weeds and molluscs as well as coastal birds.

Espumilla Beach

The sand on Espumilla is dark golden colour with a backdrop of mangroves. Green Turtles nest here but until recently feral pigs have dug up virtually all of the nests. Behind the beach are a series of lagoons, once the favoured haunt of flamingos. They are now occasional visitors, but you should see duck and waders here. This is a good location to see many of the ten species of finch found on Santiago. There is a 2-km trail up behind the beach into the Transitional Zone.

227

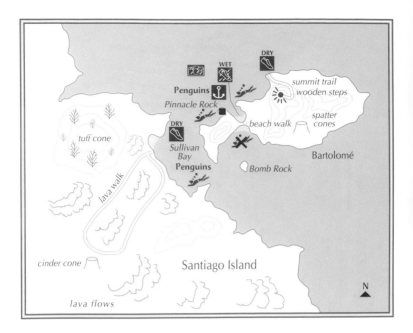

In the map:

DRY

WET

Penguins

Pinnacle Rock

summit trail
wooden steps

spatter
cones

beach walk

tuff cone

DRY

Sullivan
Bay

Penguins

Bartolomé

lava walk

Bomb Rock

cinder cone

Santiago Island

lava flows

N

SANTIAGO – SULLIVAN BAY AND ISLA BARTOLOMÉ

Sullivan Bay

The chief attraction at this site is the large black lava flow, thought to be about 200 years old. The trail takes you from the small sandy beach, across the lava, with dramatic examples of pahoehoe or ropy lava, to a series of small cinder cones. The shapes and formations of the lava are remarkable and it looks so fresh that it might have been formed last week. Moulds formed by Leatherleaf trees are visible in the lava. This is an excellent site to see the very first plant colonisers of bare lava, particularly *Mollugo flavescens* and Lava Cactus *Brachycereus nesioticus*.

Isla Bartolomé

This is the classic beauty spot of the Galápagos. The view from the top of the island of the volcanic landscape is spectacular. It is reached by a series of flights of wooden steps, and is the most photographed in all Galápagos. Pinnacle Rock is the eroded remains of a tuff cone, a small submerged crater, which can be seen just offshore. To the east you can see a series of small spatter cones. You may swim from the beach on the north side of the island and the snorkelling is excellent close to Pinnacle Rock. A trail leads across a sandy isthmus to a sand beach on the south side. Swimming is not allowed here but you may see a small school of Black-tipped Sharks *Cacharhinus limbatus* close to the beach. Turtles nest here from January to March. There are many interesting Coastal and Arid Zone plants.

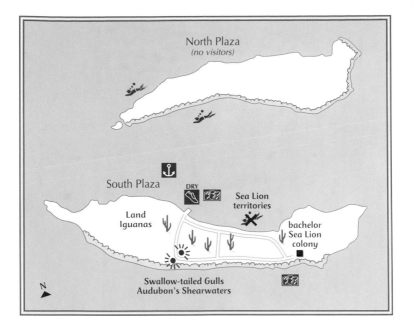

SOUTH PLAZA

The two Plaza islands lie just off the eastern tip of Santa Cruz. They are formed from uplifted marine lava. Only the southern of the two islands is open to visitors, but this is one of the most concentrated wildlife sites in the islands.

The trail takes you up from the small dock, frequently occupied by sea lions, past the rather droopy Prickly Pear Cacti with their yellow flowers, and up to the cliff from where you can often see a shoal of the endemic Yellow-tailed Mullet. *Mugil cephalus rammelsbergii*. The cliff is an excellent place to view the Swallow-tailed Gull and the Red-billed Tropic Bird which, along with boobies and frigates, use the updraft for soaring. At the eastern end of the islands is an area where the bachelor bull sea lions congregate. There is a colony of Land Iguanas here as well as Marine Iguanas, and you may also see a hybrid of the two species.

At certain times of the year, the Galápagos Carpetweed which covers much of the eastern end of the islands turns a brilliant red-orange, adding a welcome touch of colour.

WATCH OUT FOR:

GALÁPAGOS SEA LION
MARINE IGUANA
LAND IGUANA
LAVA LIZARD
YELLOWTAIL MULLET
SALLY LIGHTFOOT CRAB
AUDUBON'S SHEARWATER
RED-BILLED TROPIC BIRD
MAGNIFICENT FRIGATEBIRD
BLUE-FOOTED BOOBY
MASKED BOOBY
COMMON NODDY
BROWN PELICAN
SHORT-EARED OWL
CACTUS FINCH
GROUND FINCHES
BITTERBUSH
DESERT PLUM
LEATHERLEAF
PRICKLY PEAR CACTUS
GALÁPAGOS PURSLANE
SPINY BUSH
GALÁPAGOS CARPETWEED
PUNCTURE WEED

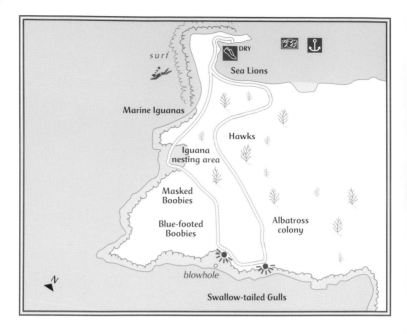

ESPAÑOLA – PUNTA SUÁREZ

Española is the southernmost island in the archipelago. It is one of the oldest islands in the group and has very few obviously volcanic features. The whole of its south coast is a low cliff which makes it an ideal nesting site for the endemic Waved Albatross. This is the only location where you can see these birds that are so ungainly on land but so elegant once they take to the air. Boobies, tropic birds and Swallow-tailed Gulls also breed here. The trail takes you from a sheltered beach on the north side of the point, through low scrubby vegetation, past a pebble beach where Marine Iguanas nest, through a mixed colony of Masked and Blue-footed Boobies and up to the cliff where the main albatross colony is located. The cliff is an excellent spot to watch albatross and other seabirds soaring. There is also a blowhole that can be spectacular with the right tide and sea conditions. The Marine Iguana, Mockingbird and Lava Lizard are specific to Española. It is also one of only two sites that you are likely to see the Large Cactus Finch.

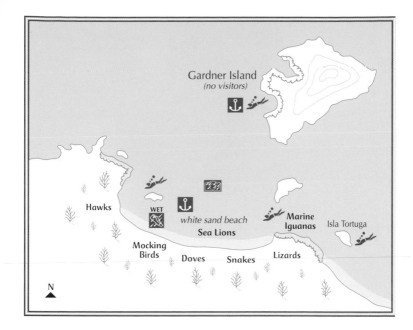

Española – Gardner Bay

Gardner Bay has two brilliant white sand beaches separated by a rocky outcrop. The beaches are backed by a dense thicket of Parkinsonia and Mesquite. There is no trail. The beach is an open area where you will see an interesting variety of wildlife and some typical Coastal Zone plants. Watch out for the Puncture Weed whose seeds can penetrate even quite stout soles. This is a turtle-nesting beach and their tank-like tracks can often be seen during the nesting season, January to April. If you are ashore early, then you may find a female, exhausted from her exertions. Take your time here and you will see and experience more of the wonders of the Galápagos. The wildlife will approach you, especially the inquisitive Hood Mockingbird and the Galápagos Hawk. There is also a good chance of seeing a snake, the Hood Racer, here. There is good snorkelling around the two small islets close to the beach.

WATCH OUT FOR:

GALÁPAGOS SEA LION
GREEN TURTLE
MARINE IGUANA
HOOD RACER
SALLY LIGHTFOOT CRAB
GHOST CRAB
GALÁPAGOS HAWK
AMERICAN OYSTERCATCHER
WANDERING TATTLER
HOOD MOCKINGBIRD
LARGE CACTUS FINCH
SMALL GROUND FINCH
WARBLER FINCH

SALTBUSH
PARKINSONIA
MESQUITE
BEACH DROPSEED
PUNCTURE WEED
BEACH MORNING GLORY

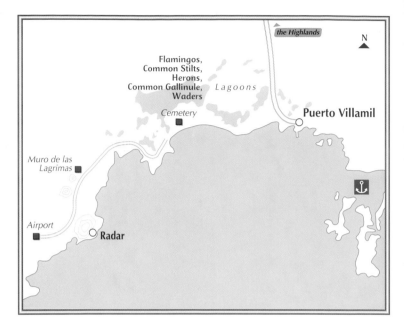

On the map: *the Highlands*, N, Flamingos, Common Stilts, Herons, Common Gallinule, Waders, *Lagoons*, Cemetery, Puerto Villamil, *Muro de las Lagrimas*, *Airport*, Radar

ISABELA – PUERTO VILLAMIL

This is the main settlement on Isabela, situated on the south side of Volcan Sierra Negra. The small settlement, which was originally a penal settlement in the nineteenth century, has grown over recent years and now has an airstrip. There is also a Tortoise Breeding Centre run by the National Park.

The main wildlife interest here are the various salt and brackish lagoons close to the town which harbour a wide range of coastal and sea birds including many migrant waders. The lagoon at Quinta Playa has the largest concentration of flamingos in the islands.. This is probably the best 'birding' place in the islands. It is also the landing point for visiting Sierra Negra. On the road to the airport you pass the Muro de las Lagrimas (The Wall of Tears) built by convicts from the penal colony.

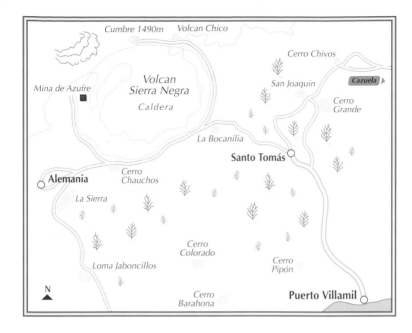

Cumbre 1490m   Volcan Chico

Mina de Azufre

Volcan Sierra Negra

Caldera

Cerro Chivos

San Joaquin

Cazuela ▶

Cerro Grande

La Bocanilia

Santo Tomás

Alemania

Cerro Chauchos

La Sierra

Cerro Colorado

Loma Jaboncillos

Cerro Pipón

N

Puerto Villamil

Cerro Barahona

Isabela – Volcan Sierra Negra

This volcano in the southeastern corner of Isabela has the largest caldera in diameter of any in Galápagos, measuring 10 km by 9 km. It is well worth a visit for the scenery, the volcanic activity and the vegetation. You may also be fortunate to come across a Giant Tortoise. Volcan Chico on the northeast side of the caldera is an area of fumarolic activity and to the west there is the 'Mina de Azufre' or sulphur mine, where there is more fumarolic activity and sulphur deposits. There are excellent opportunities to view the Humid Zone vegetation and up to seven species of Darwin's finch. The view from the caldera rim is one of the best in the islands, in all directions!

WATCH OUT FOR:

Galápagos Giant Tortoise
Feral Donkey
Galápagos Hawk
Short-eared Owl
Small Ground Finch
Medium Ground Finch
Vegetarian Finch
Small Tree Finch
Large Tree Finch
Woodpecker Finch
Warbler Finch

Soapberry
Heart-leafed Scalesia
Radiate-headed Scalesia
Guayabillo
Pega Pega
Galápagos Acacia
Galápagos Croton
Lance-leafed Darwin's Bush
White-haired Tournefortia
Red-haired Tournefortia

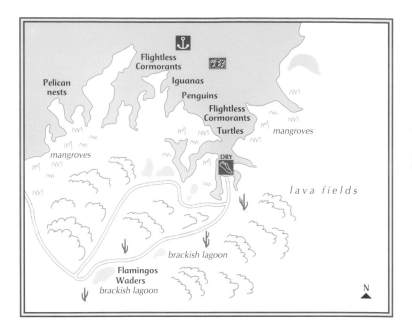

ISABELA – PUNTA MORENO

One of Galápagos' many surprises, what looks at first sight to be a barren lava field, turns out to be dotted with oases – brackish water ponds where the plate lava surface has collapsed into the lava tubes beneath. There is a wealth of animal and plant life, including flamingos, duck and waders. Invertebrates are here in strength also, with dragonflies and damselflies being the most obvious. Watch out also for a large eel-like fish. It is rarely seen and has not yet been identified. On the coast there are mangroves where Brown Pelicans nest and you may also see the Flightless Cormorant, penguins and herons.

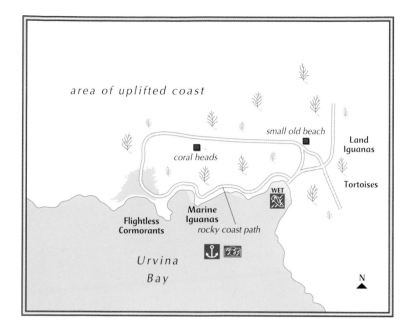

ISABELA – URVINA BAY

Urvina is another rather special site. Situated at the foot of Volcan Alcedo you can see tortoises, Land and Marine Iguanas, hermit crabs and a variety of Coastal and Arid Zone vegetation. You can also find coral heads several hundred metres inland.

In 1954 the whole area was raised, by up to 10 m in places. A further uplift of some 90 cm took place in 1994, which has resulted in the landing dock being unusable except at high tide. All the vegetation has grown up since then. You can still find many signs of the underwater origin of the land – shells, pebbles and sea urchin segments – and the trail leads to a raised beach. The Marine Iguanas found here are some of the largest in the islands.

WATCH OUT FOR:

FERAL DONKEY
GALÁPAGOS GIANT TORTOISE
MARINE IGUANA
LAND IGUANA
SEMI-TERRESTRIAL HERMIT CRAB
GALÁPAGOS PENGUIN
FLIGHTLESS CORMORANT
BROWN PELICAN
YELLOW WARBLER
GROUND FINCHES

POISON APPLE
PALO SANTO
PRICKLY PEAR CACTUS
SALTBUSH
LANCE-LEAFED DARWIN'S BUSH
GALÁPAGOS SHORE PETUNIA
SPINY BUSH
GALÁPAGOS ACACIA
GALÁPAGOS COTTON
RED-HAIRED TOURNEFORTIA

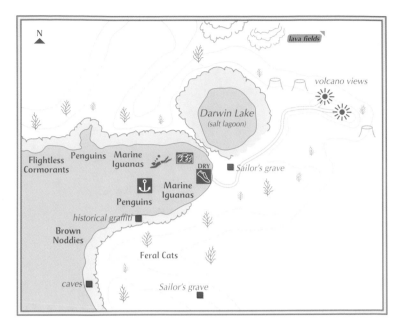

WATCH OUT FOR:

FERAL GOAT
FERAL CAT
GALÁPAGOS SEA LION
MARINE IGUANA
GALÁPAGOS PENGUIN
FLIGHTLESS CORMORANT
BROWN PELICAN
GALÁPAGOS HAWK
SALLY LIGHTFOOT CRAB
WHITE SEA URCHIN

PALO SANTO
MUYUYU
PRICKLY PEAR CACTUS
BITTERBUSH
GALÁPAGOS CROTON
DARWIN'S COTTON
GALÁPAGOS LANTANA
NEEDLE-LEAFED DAISY
DARWIN'S DAISY
HAIRY GALÁPAGOS TOMATO
RADIATE-HEADED SCALESIA
GALÁPAGOS ACACIA
PUNCTURE WEED
VELVET SHRUB

ISABELA – TAGUS COVE

An anchorage long used by pirates, whalers and other early visitors, Tagus Cove is a flooded valley between two large tuff cones, with the flooded crater of a third at the head of the anchorage. An historic location which still bears the inscriptions from visitors in the nineteenth century, the area has a good selection of Arid Zone plants as well as some interesting volcanic features. This is an excellent site for a dinghy ride along the coast as it is deep close to, so that a lot of marine life is easily observed.

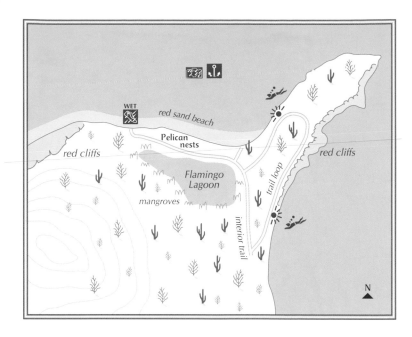

RÁBIDA – RED BEACH

A small island just south of Santiago. The source of the red sand beach is easily explained. The cinder cone to the west is the same colour, showing that it contains a high proportion of iron. It

is a good site to become acquainted with the spines of the Prickly Pear Cactus as they are soft here. Behind the beach is a lagoon with flamingos and other wading birds as well as duck. The trail from the beach up onto the red cinder cone gives an excellent selection of Arid and Coastal Zone plants. There are nine species of Darwin's finch on Rábida. There is good snorkelling at the foot of the red cliff.

WATCH OUT FOR:

GALÁPAGOS SEA LION
GALÁPAGOS PENGUIN
BLUE-FOOTED BOOBY
BROWN NODDY
GREATER FLAMINGO
WHITE-CHEEKED PINTAIL
GALÁPAGOS HAWK
DARWIN'S FINCHES

BLACK MANGROVE
SALTBUSH
LEATHERLEAF
PRICKLY PEAR CACTUS
PALO SANTO
MUYUYU
GALÁPAGOS CROTON
HAIRY GALÁPAGOS TOMATO
GALÁPAGOS MILKWORT

Rábida.

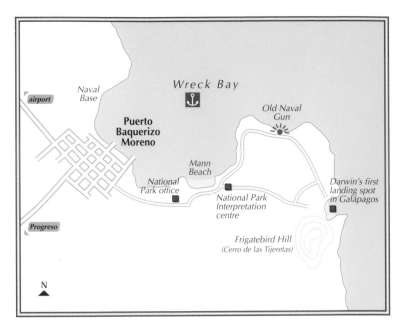

WATCH OUT FOR:

Galápagos Sea Lion
Lava Lizard
Great Frigatebird
Magnificent Frigatebird
Blackfly

Palo Santo
Matazarno
Pega Pega
Mesquite
Muyuyu
Gordillo's Scalesia
Galápagos Croton
Spiny Bush
Saltbush
Darwin's Cotton
Pearlberry
Mollugo
Sida

San Cristóbal – Puerto Baquerizo Moreno

The second largest town and provincial capital, Puerto Baquerizo lies at the head of Wreck Bay at the northeastern end of San Cristóbal. The island's second airport is here, with regular flights from the mainland. There are also hotels, shops, bars and restaurants. The National Park has offices and a Visitor Interpretation Centre here.

There is an interesting trail from the town, to the Visitor Centre and then on to Frigatebird Hill where you can see both species of frigatebird, and also start to identify some of the Arid Zone plants. At the foot of the hill is a small beach, thought to be the site of Darwin's first landing in Galápagos.

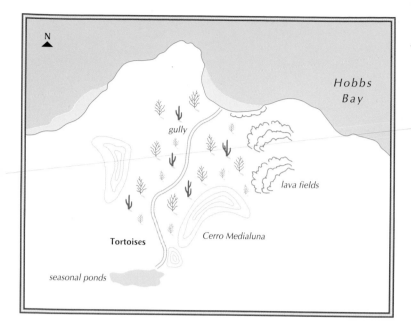

San Cristóbal – La Galapaguera

Just south of Hobbs Bay on the north coast of San Cristóbal, is La Galapaguera, so named as the trail leads through an area of volcanic activity with Arid Zone vegetation to an eroded tuff cone called Media Luna where there is a small population of the Galápagos Giant Tortoise.

You need to allow a whole day for this hike, taking plenty of water and wearing boots. It is though well worthwhile and provides an excellent opportunity to see and identify Arid Zone plants. The beach is long and the swimming and snorkelling excellent. Green Turtles nest here in the warm season, January to April. There is a good chance of seeing the Eastern Galápagos Racer snake. This species is found only on San Cristóbal and Floreana.

WATCH OUT FOR:

FERAL GOAT
GALÁPAGOS GIANT TORTOISE
GREEN TURTLE
LAVA LIZARD
EASTERN GALÁPAGOS RACER
CHATHAM MOCKINGBIRD
BROWN PELICAN
BLUE-FOOTED BOOBY
VERMILION FLYCATCHER
LARGE-BILLED FLYCATCHER

SALTBUSH
DARWIN'S COTTON
MATAZARNO
GALÁPAGOS LANTANA
SCORPION WEED
GALÁPAGOS CARPETWEED
SEA PURSLANE
STICKLEAF
GALÁPAGOS ACACIA
DARWIN'S DAISY
VELVET SHRUB
HAIRY MORNING GLORY
THREAD-LEAFED CHAFF
FLOWER
SPINY BUSH
PALO SANTO
MUYUYU
GALÁPAGOS CROTON

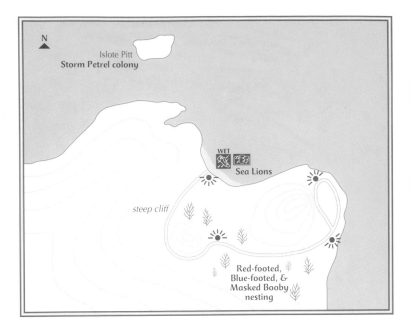

N
Islote Pitt
Storm Petrel colony

WET

Sea Lions

steep cliff

**Red-footed,
Blue-footed, &
Masked Booby
nesting**

SAN CRISTÓBAL – PUNTA PITT

A very beautiful site on the northeastern tip of San
Cristóbal, this is the only place in the islands that you can
see all three species of booby nesting. The landing is on
a green sand beach, the colour coming from its high con-
tent of olivine crystals. The trail climbs an eroded tuff
cliff around to the far side of the large eroded tuff cone
that forms the point. On the way you pass the Great
Frigatebird and Red-footed Boobies nesting in the trees
with the Blue-footed and Masked Boobies on the ground.
The vegetation is typical of the Arid Zone and the volcanic scenery is spectacular.

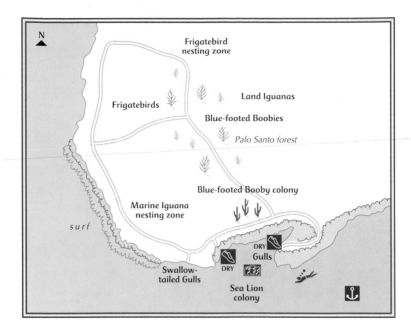

Seymour

Lying just to the north of Baltra, Seymour is a low island consisting of uplifted submarine lava. It is covered with a forest of Dwarf Palo Santo trees and is the breeding site of both frigatebirds and two of the boobies. The trail leads from the small dock, along the coast, past an area where Marine Iguanas nest and then loops into the Palo Santo forest past nesting frigatebirds and both Masked and Blue-footed Boobies. You may also see a Red-footed Booby here though this species does not nest on Seymour.

The Land Iguanas here are actually from Baltra from where they were brought in the 1930s. Some have recently been returned to Baltra as the original population was wiped out during the period that Baltra was a US military base. You can often see young sea lions surfing in the large waves off the rocky beach.

WATCH OUT FOR:

Galápagos Sea Lion
Marine and Land Iguana
Lava Lizard
Striped Galápagos Snake
Great Frigatebird
Magnificent Frigatebird
Blue-footed Booby
Masked Booby
Red-footed Booby
Brown Pelican
Swallow-tailed Gull
Lava Gull
Common Noddy
Waders
Ground Finches

Dwarf Palo Santo
Parkinsonia
Prickly Pear Cactus
Muyuyu
Leatherleaf
Saltbush
Spiny Bush
Galápagos Carpetweed
Sea Purslane
Galápagos Croton
Hairy Morning Glory
Hairy Ground Cherry
Puncture Weed

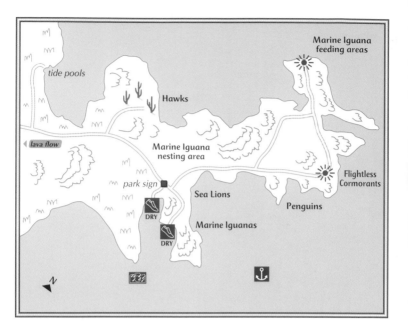

WATCH OUT FOR:

GALÁPAGOS SEA LION
MARINE IGUANA
GREEN TURTLE
LAVA LIZARD
GALÁPAGOS BANDED SNAKE
WESTERN GALÁPAGOS RACER
SALLY LIGHTFOOT CRAB
GALÁPAGOS PENGUIN
FLIGHTLESS CORMORANT
AMERICAN OYSTERCATCHER
BLUE-FOOTED BOOBY
GALÁPAGOS HAWK
YELLOW WARBLER

RED MANGROVE
BLACK MANGROVE
WHITE MANGROVE
LAVA CACTUS
SALTBUSH
GALÁPAGOS SHORE PETUNIA

FERNANDINA – PUNTA ESPINOSA

One of the most impressive and varied visiting sites in the islands, surrounded on all sides by the huge shield volcanoes of Fernandina and Isabela. It is a low point jutting out into the Canal de Bolivar. You can often see whales and dolphins offshore as well as large flocks of Blue-footed Boobies fishing.

For observing the marine environment of Galápagos it is unrivalled, with large colonies of Marine Iguanas, often basking impassively in the sun. There are penguins and Flightless Cormorants here as well as the ubiquitous sea lion and an excellent opportunity to observe the intertidal life with lots of tidepools and gently shelving foreshore. There is a good area of mangroves, which provides a habitat for herons, yellow warblers and just possibly the Mangrove Finch. Watch out for the Marine Iguana nesting area, snakes, lava cacti and both pahoehoe and the very rough aa lava.

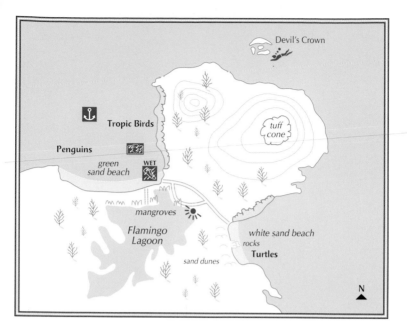

FLOREANA – PUNTA CORMORÁN

Located between two tuff cones, this is an excellent site for waders and Arid Zone plants. The green sand of the landing beach is due to the presence of olivine. Behind the beach are mangroves and a large salt lagoon. Flamingos nest here – their mud pie-shaped nests are often visible on the far side. Watch out for other waders and also the White-cheeked Pintail. The trail leads to a white sand beach known as 'Flour Sand Beach', due to the fineness of the sand. Turtles nest here and stingrays can be seen in the shallows. The plant life is of particular interest as several species are found only on Floreana. You should also see the semi-terrestrial hermit crab *Coenobita compressus* here. There is excellent snorkelling at Corona del Diablo (Devil's Crown), an eroded volcanic crater, just off the point.

WATCH OUT FOR:

GREEN TURTLE
GREATER FLAMINGO
WHITE-CHEEKED PINTAIL
WHIMBREL
RUDDY TURNSTONE
BLACK-NECKED STILT
WILLET
SEMI-TERRESTRIAL HERMIT CRAB

BLACK AND BUTTON MANGROVE
LEATHERLEAF
PARKINSONIA
MESQUITE
LONG-HAIRED SCALESIA
GALÁPAGOS CROTON
PALO SANTO
BITTERBUSH
SPINYBUSH
PEARL BERRY
VELVET SHRUB
SALTBUSH
FLOREANA DAISY
GALÁPAGOS CLUBLEAF
GALÁPAGOS LANTANA
BEACH MORNING GLORY
ST GEORGE'S MILKWORT
STICKLEAF
PASSION FLOWER
INKBERRY

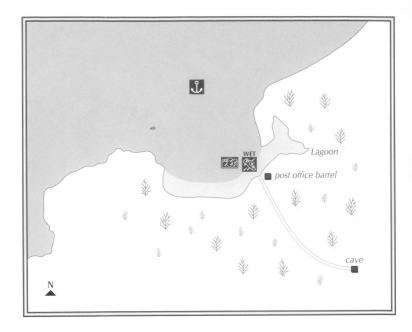

GALÁPAGOS SEA LION
BLUE-FOOTED BOOBY
BROWN PELICAN
GREATER FLAMINGO
WHIMBREL
COMMON NODDY
YELLOW WARBLER
GROUND FINCHES

PALO SANTO
PARKINSONIA
MESQUITE
GALÁPAGOS LANTANA
DARWIN'S COTTON
SPINYBUSH
SALTBUSH
PUNCTURE VINE

FLOREANA – POST OFFICE BAY

One of the earliest visiting sites in Galápagos, due largely to its ease of access by sailing ships. In 1792 a barrel was erected by whalers and served as a primitive post office for whaling ships which often spent up to five years away from home. More recently, visiting yachts have used it and it has become an historical curiosity. This was also the site of the ill-fated Norwegian fish-canning factory in 1926. Several of the people involved here later moved to Santa Cruz. The trail leads through Palo Santo and Parkinsonia trees to a cave. This is in fact a lava tube which runs down into the sea. Watch out for the spiny seeds of the puncture vine here. The lagoon at the back of the beach sometimes has migrant waders and an occasional flamingo.

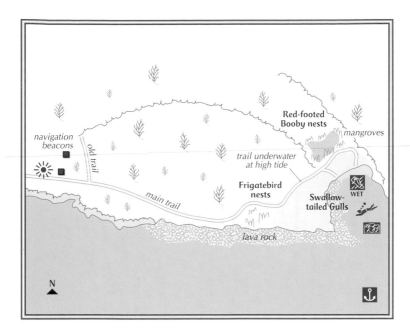

Genovesa – Darwin Bay, Beach

Genovesa is a low flat island, the most isolated of the main islands. It has a limited flora and fauna but makes up for this with quantity. In particular it has large numbers of seabirds. The landing is on the white sand and coral beach where you are likely to be greeted by Lava and Swallow-tailed Gulls and Yellow-crowned Night Herons. Be careful if the gulls are nesting, not to disturb them. Behind the beach there is a small lagoon with White-cheeked Pintails and occasional waders. The trail takes you through mixed vegetation of Palo Santo, Prickly Pear Cactus and Saltbush where you will see nesting frigatebirds and Red-footed Boobies. The Marine Iguana here are very small and black. There are no Lava Lizards and only three species of finch.

WATCH OUT FOR:

GALÁPAGOS SEA LION
MARINE IGUANA
GREAT FRIGATEBIRD
RED-FOOTED BOOBY
MASKED BOOBY
YELLOW-CROWNED NIGHT HERON
LAVA GULL
SWALLOW-TAILED GULL
WHITE-CHEEKED PINTAIL
GALÁPAGOS DOVE
LARGE GROUND FINCH
SHARP-BEAKED GROUND FINCH
WARBLER FINCH

RED MANGROVE
PALO SANTO
PRICKLY PEAR CACTUS
MUYUYU
GALÁPAGOS CROTON
SALTBUSH
GALÁPAGOS SHORE PETUNIA
GALÁPAGOS SPURGE
HELIOTROPE
SCORPION WEED

245

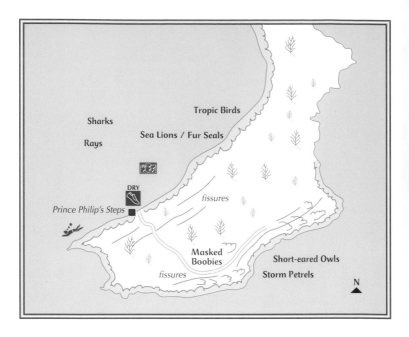

Tropic Birds

Sharks

Sea Lions / Fur Seals

Rays

DRY

Prince Philip's Steps

fissures

Masked
Boobies

Short-eared Owls

Storm Petrels

fissures

N

GALÁPAGOS FUR SEAL
MASKED BOOBY
RED-FOOTED BOOBY
SHORT-EARED OWL
GALÁPAGOS STORM PETREL

LAVA CACTUS
PALO SANTO
MUYUYU
GALÁPAGOS CROTON
GALÁPAGOS SPURGE
VELVET SHRUB

GENOVESA – PRINCE PHILIP'S STEPS

The naming of this site stems from a visit by Prince Philip on the RY *Britannia* in 1965. The dinghy ride to the landing on the rocks at the foot of the cliff gives you an excellent chance to view the Galápagos Fur Seal. After climbing the cliff, the trail takes you past nesting Masked Boobies, through a forest of low Palo Santo with nesting Red-footed Boobies, to the cliff top. This is bare rather hollow sounding lava, and you will find yourself surrounded by a cloud of Galápagos Storm Petrels which nest here in large numbers in the crevices and lava tubes. The same colony is occupied at night by the Madeiran Storm Petrel. Keep an eye open for the Galápagos Short-eared Owls which live here and prey on the petrels. They are not uncommon but are quite well camouflaged.

Key to Maps

Lava	○ Blowhole
	WET Wet landing site
Dense vegetation	DRY Dry landing site
Cacti	Camera protection needed
Mangrove	Snorkelling

Cinder cones

Viewpoint

Point of interest

Anchorage

BIBLIOGRAPHY

Many books and papers have been written on and about the Galápagos Islands. This bibliography makes no attempt to be comprehensive. It will provide you with some further fascinating reading on these very special islands.

Angermeyer, J. *My Father's Island*. Nelson, Walton-on-Thames, 1998.

Anhalzer, JJ. *National Parks of Ecuador*. Imprenta Mariscal, Quito.

Beebe, W. *Galápagos – World's End*. Putman, London, New York, 1924.

Berry, RJ. *Evolution in the Galápagos Islands*. Linnean Society & Academic Press, 1984.

Black, J. *Galápagos, Archipiélago del Ecuador*. Imprenta Europa Quito, 1973.

Bowman, RI. (ed.) *The Galápagos. Proceedings of the Symposia of the Galápagos International Scientific Project*. University of California Press, Berkeley, 1966.

Carlquist, SJ. *Island Biology*. Columbia University Press, New York, 1974.

Castro, I, and Phillips, AA. *Guide to the Birds of the Galápagos*. Christopher Helm/A&C Black, 1996.

Constant, P. *Marine Life of the Galápagos: A Guide to the Fishes, Whales, Dolphins and other Marine Mammals*. Constant, 1992.

Constant, PC. *The Galápagos Islands*. Odyssey Publications, 1995.

Conway, A, and Conway, F. *The Enchanted Islands*, Geoffrey Bles, 1948

Darwin, C. *On the Origin of Species*. John Murray, London, 1859.

Darwin, C. *The Voyage of the Beagle. Journal of researches into the Natural History and Geology of the Countries visited during the Voyage round the World of HMS 'Beagle' under command of Captain Fitzroy, RN*. John Murray, London, 1845.

De Roy, T, and Jones, M. *Portraits of Galápagos*. Imprenta Mariscal, Quito, 1990.

De Roy, T. *Galápagos Islands Born of Fire*. Airlife, 1998.

Epler, D, White, A, and Gilbert, C. *Galápagos Guide*. Imprenta Europa, Quito,1972.

Fritts, TH, and Fritts, PR. *Race with Extinction, Herpetological Field Notes of J.R. Slevin's Journey to Galápagos 1905–06*. Herpetologists' League, 1982.

Grant, PR. *Ecology and Evolution of Darwin's Finches*. Princeton University Press, New Jersey, 1986.

Grove, JS, Garcia, S, and Massey, S. *Lista de los Peces de Galápagos. Boletin Cientifico y Technico*. Instituto Nacional de Pesca, Guayaquil, Ecuador, 1984.

Grove, JS, and Lavenberg, RJ. *The Fishes of the Galápagos Islands*. Stanford University Press, Stanford, California, 1997.

Harris, MP. *A Field Guide to the Birds of the Galápagos*. Collins, London, 1974.

Harrison, P. *Seabirds: an Identification Guide*. Christopher Helm, London, 1993.

Hickin, N. *Animal Life of the Galápagos. An Illustrated Guide*. Ferrendune Books, 1979.

Hickman, CP. Jr. *Crustaceans of the Galápagos*. Sugar Spring Press, 1999.

Hickman, CP Jr, and Finet, AY. *Field Guide to the Marine Molluscs of Galápagos*. Sugar Spring Press, 1999.

Hickman, J. *The Enchanted Islands: The Galápagos Discovered*. Anthony Nelson, 1985.

Horwell, D, and Oxford, P. *Galápagos Wildlife. A Visitor's Guide*. Bradt, 1999.

Humann, P. *Reef Fish Identification: Galápagos*. Libri Mundi, Ecuador, 1993.

Jackson, MH. *Galápagos: A Natural History*. University of Calgary Press, Calgary, 1993.

Lack, D. *Darwin's Finches*. Cambridge University Press, London, 1947.

McBirney, AR, and Williams, H. Geology and Petrology of the Galápagos Islands. *Geological Society of America Memoirs*, 118, 1969.

McMullen, CK. *Flowering Plants of the Galápagos Islands*. Cornell University Press, 1999.

Merlen, G. *A Field Guide to the Fishes of Galápagos*. Wilmot Books, London, 1998.

Moore, A, Moore, T, and Cifuentes, M. *Guide to the Visitor Sites of Parque Nacional Galápagos*. Servicio Parque Nacional, Galápagos, Ecuador, 1996.

Moore, T. *Galápagos, Islands Lost in Time*. Viking Press, New York, 1980.

Moorhead, A. *Darwin and the Beagle*. Penguin, Harmondsworth,1971.

Nelson, B. *Galápagos: Islands of Birds*. Longmans Green, 1968.

Nelson, JB. *The Sulidae*. Oxford University Press, London, 1978.

Perry, R (ed.). *Galápagos (Key Environments)*. Pergamon, Oxford, 1984.

Pritchard, PCH. *The Galápagos Tortoises Nomenclature & Survival Status*. Chelonian Research Foundation, 1996.

Robinson, G, and del Pino, EM (eds). *El Niño in the Galápagos Islands – The 1982–1983 Event*. Charles Darwin Foundation, Quito 1985

Ryan, PR. *Oceanus. The International Magazine of Marine Science and Policy*. Vol. 30, No. 2. Woods Hole Oceanographic Institute, 1987.

Schofield, EK. *Field Guide to Some Common Galápagos Plants*. Ohio State University Research Foundation, Columbus, 1970.

Schofield, EK. *Plants of the Galápagos Islands*. Universe Books, 1984.

Swingland, IR, and Klemens, MW. *The Conservation Biology of Tortoises*. IUCN Species Survival Commission, 1989.

Thomas, RA. Galápagos Terrestrial Snakes: Biogeography and Systematics. *Herpetological Natural History* **5** (1). 1997.

Thornton, I. *Darwin's Islands: A Natural History of the Galápagos Islands*. Natural History Press, Garden City, New York, 1971.

Treherne, JE. *The Galápagos Affair*. Jonathan Cape, London, 1983.

Vonnegut, K. *Galápagos, A Novel*. Dell, New York, 1985.

Weiner, J. *The Beak of the Finch: A Story of Evolution in Our Time*. Jonathan Cape, London, 1996.

Wellington, GM. *The Galápagos Coastal Marine Environment*. Unpublished report to Department of National Parks & Wildlife, Quito, 1975.

Wiggins, IL, and Porter, DM. *Flora of the Galápagos Islands*. Stanford University Press, Stanford, California, 1971.

Wittmer, M. *Floreana*. Anthony Nelson, 1989.

GLOSSARY

annual	a plant that lives only one growing season
axillary	growing out of the upper angle between leaf or branch, and the stem or trunk
bipinnate	doubly compound leaves with leaflets, results in a feather-like leaf
bivalve	type of mollusc with two similar or identical halves to its shell
calyx	all the sepals – the outside of a flower bud
coccid	aphids and other scale insects
endemic	particular to a geographic region, and found nowhere else
epiphyte	a plant that grows on another plant, but takes no nutrients from it
feral	domestic animal that has 'gone wild'
garua	light drizzle; scotch mist
genus	group of two or more similar species
gravid	pregnant; with eggs
introduced	brought from another region by people, intentionally or accidentally
lanceolate	lance-shaped, much longer than wide, and tapering
lepidoptera	order of insects, comprising butterflies and moths
lore	head of bird between eyes and base of bill – also same area on fish or snake
native	occurring naturally in a region
olivino	olive-green, translucent volcanic mineral, magnesium iron silicate
parasite	plant growing on, and taking nutrients from, another plant
perennial	lasting year after year
pinnate	compound leaf, with leaflets growing opposite each other
plastron	bony undershell of tortoise or turtle
primaries	main outer flight feathers of bird's wing
raceme	spike of flowers
rhizome	horizontal underground stem, with buds and aerial shoots
rhomboid, rhombic	more or less diamond shaped
rotational symmetry	symmetrical about a radius, like a clock
scapular	small shoulder feathers
scientific name	means of identifying all identifiable life forms using Latin
scientific order	framework for describing all living life forms, see diagram
scorpoid	curved backwards like a scorpion's tail
scute	individual plates on tortoise or turtle shell
skyhop	term used to describe a whale jumping out of the water
sporangia	spore or seed cases
spp.	abbreviation for species
tramp	homeless or nomadic ant
var.	variety of a species
whorl	leaves arranged in a circular pattern

INDEX

HOW _YOU_ CAN HELP THE GALÁPAGOS

If you visit the Galápagos, you will be in no doubt that it is a place worth preserving and at the same time that it desperately needs help if it is to survive. If you would like to help, then the most effective, but not the only, way in which you can is by supporting the Charles Darwin Foundation for the Galápagos Islands. The CDF is an international non-profit-making organisation based in Quito, and is supported by a growing network of Friends of Galápagos organisations in Europe and the USA.

To obtain further information on how you can help, please complete the form below and send it to the appropriate organisation as indicated:

Name . . . .

Address . . . .

. . . .

Country . . . . Postal or Zip code . . . .

Tel No. . . . . Email . . . .

I enclose a donation of . . . .

In _Ecuador_, please send to: **_Fundacion Charles Darwin_**
                                   Casilla 17-01-3891
                                   Quito
                                   email: fcdarwi2@ecnet.ec

In _Europe_ , please send to: **_Galápagos Conservation Trust_**
                                   5 Derby Street
                                   London W1Y 7HD
                                   email. gct@gct.org
                                        www.gct.org

From anywhere else in the world: **_Charles Darwin Foundation Inc._**
                                   100 North Washington Street
                                   Suite 232, Falls Church
                                   Va. 22046 USA
                                   email. darwin@galapagos.org

You can also obtain information on the CDF and its work on: **www.galapagos.org**